THE COMPLETE BOOK OF TRUSTS

Third Edition

THE COMPLETE BOOK OF TRUSTS

Third Edition

Martin M. Shenkman

John Wiley & Sons, Inc.

ISBN 0-471-21458-2

Printed in the United States of America.

10 9 8 7 6

To P.K.

In memory of Rabbi Y. M. Kagan.
The greatest legacy is not financial wealth,
but spiritual wealth, the transmission of values
of kindness, compassion, humility, and more.
Few have left a greater legacy to so many.

PREFACE

This book, my 30th, along with the Web site www.laweasy.com, have all pursued the same goal—making sophisticated yet practical and realistic legal, tax, and financial planning information available to the general public at a nominal cost (or in case of the Web site, no cost). It is an unfortunate reality that most legal advice is available only to the wealthy who can afford to hire attorneys with substantial expertise. Much of the legal advice in "self-help" books seems to have been written by those looking to help themselves to your pocket more than to help you help yourself. Send us an e-mail at www.laweasy.com and let us know how we're doing and how we can be of further help.

Our goal is, through this and other books in combination with the extensive forms and audio clips on our Web site, to help you work with your legal and other advisers in the most cost-efficient manner while addressing the important personal, religious, and human aspects of planning. If you've lived your life according to a particular religious creed, your estate plan should incorporate the dictates of that creed and reflect its values. Your plan should transmit value to your heirs, not just wealth.

Effort was made to assure that examples and text in this book reflect a broad array of people and lifestyles with many different religious and personal preferences. For additional information on the implications of different religious customs on estate planning, see our Web site. Our objective was to try to convey complex information in an understandable manner. To keep the text and examples simple, the explanations and examples were not designed to reflect every situation. The focus, instead, was on simplicity and clarity. In any example, where the feminine form is used, masculine could be used and vice versa. If, in the estate-planning examples, you would like the wife to predecease the husband, you can read the examples accordingly. Wherever the term "child" is used, you can substitute "nephew," "friend," or any other type of person. There are only two important situations for which you cannot substitute. If the text or an example refers to "spouse" (or "husband" or "wife") and the person is not a U.S. citizen, you cannot readily substitute a non-U.S. citizen spouse for a "spouse." Special rules apply in the case of a non-U.S. citizen spouse. Second, if the person is not legally a "spouse," but is a partner, unmarried companion, or a gay or lesbian partner, you cannot substitute that person or relationship for a spouse since the laws are dramatically different. Each of these exceptions, the noncitizen spouse, and the nonmarried partner, are addressed in separate chapters. Other than these two exceptions, please read the text and examples as they would fit your circumstances.

Good luck planning and protecting yourself, your family, and loved ones.

MARTIN M. SHENKMAN

New York City, New York

ACKNOWLEDGMENTS

A number of people were of considerable assistance in the preparation of this book, especially Michael Hamilton of John Wiley & Sons, whose support and encouragement were outstanding, as usual, and Nancy Marcus Land and Publications Development Company, who provided their great production job (as usual!).

I'd also like to thank Gary Goldberg host of *Money Matters,* a syndicated weekly radio show.

CONTENTS

TRUST FINDING TABLE

NOTE: The chapters of this book have been organized by topic. Thus, trusts for various types of people or assets can easily be identified. However, you may read about a trust and wish to find where the book discusses a particular type of trust. The following chart will help. You can look up many types of trusts by name and quickly find the chapter or chapters that discuss them. In addition, alternate names for the trust are provided, and a brief comment to help you understand the particular trust.

CAUTION: Many estate planners, insurance agents, and financial planners create their own names for trusts in order to appear to have some unique or proprietary type of planning others don't. These names could not be included. However, when reading the brochures these planners give you, identify the trust by topic (e.g., does the brochure encourage you to buy insurance?) and look the topic up in this chart, the table of contents or the index. Also, be suspicious. Calling an insurance trust by a fancy name doesn't make it do anything an insurance trust won't do. But it does make your job of analyzing and comparing to determine if it is a trust you need more difficult and confusing.

Name of Trust	Other Names	Brief Description/Comment	Chapter
2503(c) Trust	Children's Trust, Under 21 Trust	Protects your minor children while qualifying for maximum gift tax benefits from the annual $11,000 exclusion. It can assure that monies left for young children are used for educational and other important purposes.	16
Five and Five Trust	Invasion Trust	This is a provision which permits a beneficiary, such as your spouse, to demand a distribution, in addition to any other rights to income and principal granted by the trust, the greater of $5,000 or 5% of the trust assets each year, without the entire trust being taxable in his or her estate. This provision can be added to many types of trusts. It can be used in a by pass (exclusion) or QTIP (marital) trust.	5, 8
Accumulation Trust	Complex Trust Discretionary Trust	This trust can accumulate income if the trustee doesn't believe it appropriate or advisable to distribute income in any particular year. This can protect assets for a child who is involved in risky or questionable endeavors, or where a lawsuit or divorce is pending. This is contrasted with a trust which is required to distribute all income currently (simple trust).	6, 8

(continued)

Name of Trust	Other Names	Brief Description/Comment	Chapter
Alaska Trust	Dynasty Trust; Perpetual Trust; Domestic Asset Protection Trust "DAPT"	A trust formed in Alaska (or Delaware and a few other states), which has enacted special rules to enable you to give assets to the trust, have a measure of protection from creditors and claimants, have the assets removed from your taxable estate, yet remain a beneficiary.	8, 9
Alimony Trust	Divorce Trust	A trust used to pay alimony to your ex-spouse. A special tax rule has your spouse, and not you as the person forming the trust, taxed on trust income.	14
Asset Protection Trust	Domestic Asset Protection Trust "APT"	A trust formed with the intent and planning to make it difficult for creditors, malpractice claimants, and others to reach the assets.	18
Bypass Trust	Credit Shelter Trust; Applicable Exclusion Trust; Family Trust; "A" Trust	A trust to which assets are transferred on the first spouse's death to protect and provide for the surviving spouse, while using the exclusion available to estate of the first spouse to die. This trust prevents doubling up assets in the estate of second spouse to die. With increases in the exclusion after the 2001 Tax Act you must address who the beneficiaries should be (spouse alone?) and if the amount to be placed in the trust (funding) should be less than the maximum exclusion.	18
Charitable Lead Trust (CLT)	Front Trust; Charitable Front Trust	Give money or property to a trust. One or more charities will receive an annual (or more frequent) annuity payment (or unitrust payment in the case of a CLUT). Your designated heirs will receive the principal of the trust when it ends. This can help you achieve substantial gift or estate tax benefits on transferring assets to heirs. If you do not face an estate tax a CLT can still be used to inculcate philanthropic values and defer an heir's receipt of some assets.	17
Charitable Remainder Annuity Trust (CRAT)	Charitable Remainder Trust	A charitable remainder trust makes annuity payments to the charity based on a fixed percentage of the initial value of the assets contributed. Often used to minimize capital gains tax on highly appreciated assets. Contrast with CRUT.	17
Charitable Remainder Trust (CRT)		You can donate appreciated property to a charitable trust. The trust can sell the property without paying capital gains tax and invest in a diversified portfolio. You receive periodic distributions and on your death (or the death of you and your spouse) the charity receives the principal of the trust. You obtain a current income tax charitable contribution deduction (based on the present value of the charity's future interest). The gift to the charity won't become effective until your death or some fixed number of years. Often combined with a life insurance trust.	17
Charitable Remainder Unitrust (CRUT)	Charitable Remainder Trust	A charitable remainder trust which makes payments to the charity based a fixed percentage of the value of the assets owned by the trust each year. This is easier when assets are easily valued, such as publicly traded stocks, not for interests in real estate or closely held business which would require a formal appraisal. Contrast with CRAT. GST consequences of the two types of trusts (CRAT versus CRUT) differ.	17

Name of Trust	Other Names	Brief Description/Comment	Chapter
Children's Trust	Minor's Trust	Trust for a child, grandchild or other minor. Designed to qualify for the $11,000 gift tax annual exclusion and to protect the child from the money. It can be structured as a 2503(c) trust described above, or a crummey power trust. Compare the pros and cons of a gift to a child's trust to the use of a Code Section 529 college savings plan.	16
Complex Trust	Accumulation Trust; Discretionary Trust	Any trust which is not required to distribute all income currently. Note: When a total return trust approach is used, the concept differs.	1
Credit Shelter Trust (CST)	A Trust; Bypass Trust; Unified Credit Trust; Exclusion Trust	The most valuable tax saving trust which enables both you and your spouse to use your $1 million exclusion (2002, but scheduled to increase in later years). Proper use of this technique can enable most families with less than $2 million in assets to avoid estate taxes entirely.	14
Crummey Trust	Annual Demand Power Trust	This provision, when included in a trust, permits you to make gifts to trusts for children (or others) and qualify for the valuable gift tax benefits of having the gift protected from gift tax by the annual gift tax exclusion. This power is necessary so that a gift to a trust will be considered a gift of a present interest.	16, 20
Defective Trust	Grantor Trust; Intentionally Defective Trust "IDIT"; "IDIG"	A trust set up so that the assets are removed from your estate (i.e., the gift of assets to the trust is complete), yet for income tax purposes the trust income remains taxable to you.	6
Delaware Trust	Dynasty Trust; Domestic Asset Protection Trust; Perpetual Trust	A trust formed in Delaware, which has enacted special rules to enable you to give assets to the trust, have a measure of protection from creditors and claimants, have the assets removed from your taxable estate, yet remain a beneficiary.	5, 8
Domestic Asset Protection Trust	Asset Protection Trust	A trust formed in the United States with the intent to protect assets from claimants, creditors, and others. The trust is formed in a state that has enacted laws helpful to achieving this goal, like Alaska or Delaware.	8, 9
Dynasty Trust	Perpetual Trust	A trust formed in a state that has eliminated laws that restrict the time period for which a trust can last. Dynasty trusts are often formed to last forever, unless they run out of money or they cease to serve their intended purpose.	9
Electing Small Business Trust (ESBT)		A trust designed to meet the special requirements to own stock in an S corporation by paying tax at a maximum rate. Compare "QSST."	
Exclusion Trust	Bypass Trust; Family Trust; Applicable Exclusion Trust; "A" Trust	A trust typically formed under your will for the purpose of protecting the amount which you can bequeath estate tax-free on death. The trust often had been used to benefit the entire family. On the death of the surviving spouse the assets pass free of estate tax to your designated heirs. After the 2001 Tax Act, the amount of the exclusion has increased substantially so that you may wish to restrict the amount bequeathed to this trust or limit the beneficiary to solely the surviving spouse.	8, 14
Generation Skipping Transfer Tax Trust (GST Tax Trust)	Dynasty Trust; Perpetual Trust	A trust that wealthy persons can use to minimize the impact of the extremely costly generation skipping transfer (GST) tax on gifts or other transfers to their grandchildren or later generations. Frequently GST Trusts are planned to use the $1 million GST tax exemption which each taxpayer has. See also grandchildren's trust.	11

(continued)

Name of Trust	Other Names	Brief Description/Comment	Chapter
Grandchildren's Trust		A trust a grandparent establishes to provide for the education or other benefits to a grandchild, or to many grandchildren (where a pot trust is used). This type of trust must be planned to avoid unexpected GST tax consequences. See GST Tax trust. Compare a Code Section 529 plan.	11
Grantor Retained Interest Trust (GRIT)		A type of trust where you retain an interest (e.g., the right to income) for some period of time. After that time period the principal of the trust is transferred to the beneficiaries you designated. The time the beneficiaries must wait to receive the actual gift results in a reduction, to reflect the present value of money, in gift tax costs. GRITs may be structured as QPRTs, PRTs, GRATs, or GRUTs. See those entries.	20
Grantor Retained Annuity Trust (GRAT)		You make a gift to a trust and receive a fixed annuity payment each year, for any number of years you choose. This technique enables wealthy individuals to give away substantial assets at a reduced gift tax cost.	20
Grantor Retained Unitrust (GRUT)		You make a gift to a trust and receive a percentage of the fair market value of the property each year, for any number of years you choose. This technique enables wealthy individuals to give away substantial assets at a reduced gift tax cost. Contrast with GRAT.	20
GST Trust	Grandchildren's Trust	Generally, a trust intended to transfer wealth to grandchildren and later descendants. The term has technical meaning in the context of rules which automatically allocate GST exemption.	11, 16
Incentive Trust		A trust with the distributions keyed to certain achievements of the beneficiaries to motivate them to perform or behave in a certain intended manner. For example, a distribution can be made each year while a child beneficiary achieves a certain grade point or better in school, earns income (e.g., $1 trust distribution for every $1 earned), or achieves some other milestone.	5
Intentionally Defective Irrevocable Trust	Defective Trust	A trust formed in a manner that transfers of assets to the trust are completed for gift and estate tax purposes, but the income from the trust remains taxed to the grantor. This technique is sometimes combined with a sale of assets by you to the trust on an installment basis as an alternative to a GRAT for removing appreciation and value from the grantor's estate in a tax advantaged manner.	1, 10, 15, 18, 21
Irrevocable Trust	Insurance Trust; Children's Trust; Grandchildren's Trust; Inter-vivos QTIP Trust; and others	A trust that cannot be changed after it is set up. Compare to *re*vocable trust, which you can change at any time. An irrevocable trust can offer substantial tax benefits and protection from creditors.	14–23
Insurance Trust		Protect your family and heirs and achieve estate tax savings by keeping insurance proceeds out of your taxable estate (and your spouse's taxable estate, if applicable). Protect valuable insurance proceeds from creditors to assure your family's security after your death.	19
Inter-Vivos Trust	Living Trust	See Revocable Living Trust, QTIP Trust (Inter-vivos), CRT, and other trusts.	13

Name of Trust	Other Names	Brief Description/Comment	Chapter
Inter-Vivos Credit Shelter Trust		Permits you to fund a credit shelter trust to use your exclusion while you are alive to remove post-gift appreciation from your estate.	23
Inter-Vivos QTIP Trust		Permits you to use pension or IRA assets to fund a QTIP (marital) trust.	23
Loving Trust	Living Trust	See "Revocable Trust."	13
Marital Trust	QTIP Trust	Trust for spouse usually structured to qualify for the unlimited gift or estate tax marital deduction. See "QDOT."	14
Massachusetts Realty Trust		A special form of trust offering valuable benefits to anyone owning real estate in Massachusetts.	22
Medicaid Trust	Medicaid Avoidance Trust; Nursing Home Trust	Keeps your assets safe from nursing home/Medicaid claims so that Medicaid will pay for your nursing home care rather than your heirs. This trust is intended to give you access to, and benefit from, the trust assets that the law will permit without making those assets subject to the risks of being attached to pay medical bills. Subject to look-back and other limitations.	16, 18
Multiple Children's Trust		Sets up a separate trust for each child so that each child receives exactly the amount you intend (whether equal or not). This keeps each child's assets safe from the demand, needs, and creditors of your other children. This is contrasted with the use of a single trust for many children, called a single trust or pot trust.	16
Perpetual Trust	Dynasty Trust	A trust formed under the laws of a state that permits the trust to last forever.	2, 5, 9
Personal Residence Trust (PRT)		A trust used to remove your home or vacation home from your estate at a reduced gift tax cost. Compare QPRT.	23
Pooled Income Trust	Charitable Remainder Trust	Contribute property to a charitable remainder trust, and receive in exchange the right to participate in an investment pool managed by the charity for the term of the trust (or your life). This provides valuable tax benefits and professional management of your money and diversification of your assets.	17
Pot Trust	Discretionary Trust	Set up a single trust for various beneficiaries so that all of your assets are available to distribute to the beneficiary based on the need of each. This can be used to minimize trustee fees and administrative costs as compared to setting up a separate trust for each beneficiary.	16
Probate Avoidance Trust	Revocable Living Trust	Almost any trust can avoid probate; a revocable living trust is but one. When title to assets are transferred to a trust, those assets will usually pass to the beneficiaries of the trust without the requirement for probate.	13
Qualified Personal Residence Trust (QPRT)		A trust used to remove the value of your home or vacation home from your estate at a discounted gift tax cost.	23
Qualified Subchapter S Trust (QSST)		A special trust to hold stock in an S corporation, the most popular legal form for small businesses, without jeopardizing the valuable S corporation tax benefits. See also, "ESBT."	23

(continued)

Name of Trust	Other Names	Brief Description/Comment	Chapter
Qualified Domestic Trust	QDOT	Obtains maximum gift or estate tax savings by qualifying a gift or bequest to your spouse for the unlimited gift or estate tax marital deduction when your spouse is not a citizen of the United States.	14
QTIP Trust	Qualified Terminable Interest Property Trust	A marital trust which qualifies for the unlimited gift or estate tax marital deduction. It can enable you to preserve assets for future beneficiaries while benefiting your surviving spouse during his or her lifetime and deferring estate tax.	14
Qualified Terminable Interest Property Trust (QTIP)	Marital Trust; B Trust	A trust which qualifies for the unlimited estate tax marital deduction (no tax on bequests or gifts to your spouse), but preserve your right to name the ultimate beneficiaries of your assets. Commonly used for second marriages so that your current spouse can be protected, but your children from your first marriage can be assured of an inheritance.	14
Revocable Trust	Living Trust	Any trust which can be changed, as contrasted to irrevocable trusts which you cannot change once signed and set up. Most common is the Living Trust. Assets given to a revocable trust may not be removed from your estate for tax purposes nor may they be protected from the reach of your creditors.	13
Right of Election Trust		Provides your spouse with the least amount of assets permitted by state property law, and retains (if state law permits) the maximum control over where those assets will ultimately be distributed. Used when you desire to limit your spouse's rights to your estate to the minimum the law requires.	14
Single Children's Trust	Pot Trust	A trust which holds assets for all of your children as compared to separate trusts for each child.	16
Special Needs Trust (SNT)		Protect and provide for a child or other heir with special needs without losing the valuable state or other benefits to which the beneficiary may otherwise be entitled. Often limits the distributions to items not provided by state programs.	16
Spendthrift Trust		A provision added to many types of irrevocable trusts which can help protect trust assets from the reach of creditors of the beneficiary. Almost any type of trust you establish could be a spendthrift trust. Commonly used when a trust is set up and divorce or future lawsuits are a worry.	16
Sprinkle Trust	Spray Trust; Discretionary Trust; Pot Trust	The distribution provisions of your trust give the trustee the flexibility to distribute income and/or assets to the persons from the list of beneficiaries which the trustee chooses most in need (e.g., your spouse, or one of your children). This enables you to defer the decision as to which child or other beneficiary needs the most money or assistance until the time for the payments occurs. This can be done in many different types of trusts.	16

Name of Trust	Other Names	Brief Description/Comment	Chapter
Standby Trust	Unfunded Trust	This is a trust which is formed now (i.e., your lawyer drafts a trust document and the trustee and grantor sign it), but the primary assets which it is to receive (e.g., under a pour-over will, or insurance proceeds) are not intended to be transferred to the trust until a later date. Often a nominal amount of money, say $100 is transferred to the trust when formed to assure that the trust meets the legal requirement of having some assets.	1
Total Return Trust	Unitrust	A trust whose marketable securities are invested in a manner to maximize the aggregate investment return of the portfolio, including income and capital appreciation. Typically, such trusts reconcile the objectives of current (income) beneficiaries and the remainder beneficiaries (who receive the trust asset after the current beneficiaries die or otherwise cease to receive distributions) by mandating payments to the current beneficiaries based on a percentage of the value of the trust each year, rather than paying out income to the current beneficiaries as has been more common historically.	4, 21
Uni-Trust	Charitable Lead Uni-Trust; Grantor Retained Unitrust	A type of grantor retained trust or charitable remainder or charitable lead trust where payments are based on a percentage of the value of the assets in trust each year, rather than as a fixed dollar payment.	15, 23
Voting Trust		Control stock in a closely held or family business to assure management and operations as you determine best.	24

Part One

UNDERSTANDING THE BUILDING BLOCKS OF A TYPICAL TRUST

1 OVERVIEW OF TRUSTS

THE BENEFITS OF USING TRUSTS

Trusts are powerful and useful estate, tax, investment, and financial planning tools. You don't have to be rich to need one. In fact, the less wealthy you are, the less you can afford to risk losing money, so trusts may even be more important for you. With or without, an estate tax trust remains a critical planning tool. But what you do need, in all cases, is a realistic understanding of what these complex tools can, and cannot, do for you. Within limits, trusts can help you achieve several important goals: management of your assets if you are disabled, management of assets for your children or family in the event of your death, avoidance of probate, avoidance of creditors, minimization or elimination of estate and other transfer taxes (even if the estate tax is eliminated, the gift tax will not be), protection for your loved ones, ownership of your insurance policies, and control over your businesses. Trusts can even address religious goals. See www.laweasy.com for details. The first step, however, is to assess your financial position, goals, and objectives.

TRUSTS AND YOUR COMPREHENSIVE PERSONAL PLAN

Only within the context of a total estate and financial plan can you properly use trusts. A basic plan requires the following steps:

- *Identify the people you want to benefit.* This includes preparing a family tree and list of other important people. This will help you identify the people you hope to benefit and protect with your trusts (which may include you).
- *Identify the assets you will have to plan for.* This will generally require developing a detailed balance sheet identifying the various types of assets (special trusts and planning are required for certain assets) and your estimated net worth (for determining insurance needs, tax planning concerns, asset protection steps, etc.).
- *Clarify your goals.* Even two people with identical assets and family structures may choose very different investment, financial, and estate plans because their goals and their tolerances for risk differ.

- *Determine what documents are necessary to achieve your goals in light of the assets and people involved.* For everyone, this will include at minimum a durable power of attorney to handle financial matters in the event of disability, a living will and health care proxy to address medical decisions, a will to distribute assets and name fiduciaries (guardian for minor children, etc.).

With your basic plan in place, the *Complete Book of Trusts* can help you select the right trust arrangements for you and your needs and help you work with the lawyer preparing the trust document. This book provides informed guidance in making decisions about what assets you should transfer to your trusts and what legal provisions you should include in your trusts. It explains the limitations of trusts, and the income, gift, estate, and generation-skipping transfer tax implications of different trust arrangements. Even if you won't face an estate tax because of the increase in the exclusion by the 2001 Tax Act, income tax and nontax aspects of trust planning will remain important.

To properly develop and implement an overall personal plan, you need an estate-planning team. You don't have to be super-rich to achieve this. Although the super-rich may have a family office, staffed with professionals, you can achieve a similar result for a modest cost, with a little creativity and effort. An estate-planning team should, at minimum, consist of the following experts:

- Lawyer (drafting of documents).
- Broker, money manager, or financial planner (investment matters).
- Insurance agent, broker, or adviser (life, disability, health, property, casualty, and other insurance needs).
- Accountant (income tax planning, tax returns).
- Pension or retirement consultant.

In many situations, the financial person can also assist you with insurance, or the insurance person can help you with retirement plans. If you work for a large corporation, the human resources department can often provide tremendous help without any additional cost. The ideal approach is to have all your advisers at a single meeting to formulate your plan. There can be no substitute to having all your advisers seated around a single table to make sure you are taking the optimal planning steps, including trusts. If such a meeting is too costly, try scheduling a conference call with your accountant when you meet with your lawyer. Your insurance and investment professionals may not charge for time and may be willing to attend the meeting with you and your attorney simply to enhance their own networking efforts. Thus, you can achieve the similar result of a personal estate-planning team for the incremental cost of a telephone call to your accountant. The value of this team approach cannot be overestimated. It is always helpful for the professionals to know you have other experts involved. This will encourage coordination between the professionals, which will assure you of a higher level of service and lower costs. It also keeps all the professionals on their toes to know that you have others looking over their work. Finally, be sure to direct each professional to copy the other members of your team on important correspondence.

WORKING WITH THE PROFESSIONALS

The proper use of trusts will often be a key to the financial security of you and your loved ones. Trusts are complex. It is not only the trust document that must be properly addressed. While a document from a form book, typed with the right names inserted, may appear to suffice, this is only a small part of the process. The key is having an experienced and knowledgeable estate-planning specialist who can make sure the trust you are using is the correct approach for your goals and circumstances. You cannot read a book (or two, or three) and obtain the knowledge and judgment that an estate-planning specialist has from years of experience and from formulating hundreds, if not thousands, of estate plans. Similarly, a lawyer with a general practice, who has occasionally completed estate plans or trusts in between house closings, personal injury cases, and other legal work, cannot be expected to bring to the table the knowledge and experience of an estate-planning specialist. Even if you are unlikely to pay an estate tax, planning remains complex. Interpersonal issues, investment clauses, fiduciary powers, and many other factors are far from routine and require a specialist.

How do you find the appropriate specialist? Ask. Obtain references from your insurance agents, financial planner, broker, banker, and others. Inquire of the attorney: "What percentage of your practice is estate planning or ancillary work?" (If it is less than 50 to 75 percent, is that really an estate specialist?) "What types and size estates do you handle?" (Do your circumstances fit the experience level of the attorney?) "Have you published or lectured on estate planning?" "To whom, when, and on what topics?" Most specialists (in any technical area of law, and in many other professions as well) speak and write to stay abreast of current developments in their field. Also, specialists need the exposure of speaking and writing to generate business because the work they handle is so focused. Ask to see copies—or ask where you can obtain copies—of their speeches, articles, and the like. Review them before you make a decision.

Most consumer books on working with lawyers suggest that you get a price quote up front. No competent lawyer can possibly give you a price quote for a trust without knowing your goals, background information, net worth, tax status, and circumstances of your family and loved ones. It is impossible to estimate the cost of a revocable living trust without first ascertaining whether you really need one and, if you could benefit from such a trust, what type of tax and other planning should be incorporated into it. The more complex the planning, the greater the cost.

NOTE: You've attended a seminar on revocable living trusts and determine that this would be the right trust for you to avoid probate and publicity. You call several lawyers and obtain a cost estimate of $1,000 from one lawyer, and $2,500 from a second lawyer, to prepare the trust. The final lawyer refuses to give a price quote, saying that without an initial meeting to obtain more information he cannot determine what you need done. Which lawyer do you use? Consider the following:

Between the $1,000 and $2,500 lawyer, can you tell who will give you a better quality document? Which lawyer will be spending more time customizing the trust document to suit your particular needs? The length of the document is no indication of quality. It might just be a long, but poor quality form. Cost is not necessarily an indication of quality or how much the forms will be customized for you. If you have real estate to transfer to the trust, which, if either, of the two lawyers is including the cost of transferring the real estate? If not, what is the extra charge? What does the fee include? If you have questions after the work is done, is that included? Will the lawyer help you transfer assets to the trust? Are the fees quoted fixed fees or merely estimates based on certain work? If the work exceeds the estimate (and how can you tell), how will you be charged?

It may very well be that the best choice is the third lawyer who refused to quote you a fee. The example in the next box illustrates why.

EXAMPLE: The third lawyer, who would not give you a quote, is an experienced estate and trusts lawyer. He knows from experience that few consumers/nonestate specialists can determine what type of trust they need. To quote an estimate for a trust you may not need is not professional or appropriate. Look at a simple example of why the living trust may not be the best answer for you. Assume you live in New Jersey and have a rental property in New York. You believe that the living trust will avoid publicity and probate for the New York property. You're right about probate. The publicity is a question. The court may, depending on the circumstances, require that the trust be made public. Also, why are you concerned about publicity? For the vast majority of Americans, this is really not an issue. If you truly have a publicity problem, there are more sophisticated techniques that may be appropriate.

Why was the third lawyer hesitant to quote a fee for a living trust? If the preceding facts were your situation, a living trust would not be the best answer (and the only way an estate planner can determine what you need, and hence what it should cost, is to first find out the facts). A living trust will not facilitate making gifts of interests in that property to reduce your estate tax cost. What will?

A limited liability company may be the best choice. If you transfer the New York rental property to a limited liability company, you (1) avoid probate in New York (just as with the revocable living trust); (2) avoid New York estate tax (which the revocable living trust could not accomplish); (3) obtain protection from any lawsuits since a tenant or visitor can only sue the limited liability company that owns the property, but should not be able to reach any of your personal assets; and (4) use the limited liability company to make gifts of noncontrolling interests and claim discounts for lack of marketability and lack of control in valuing the gifts for gift tax purposes. These discounts can range between 20 percent and 50 percent or more. The gift tax savings can be huge. The benefits of using a limited liability company clearly far outweigh the nominal benefits of using a revocable living trust in your situation. Does this mean you don't need a revocable living trust? Hardly. The answer, like all estate-planning answers, depends on your situation. It may be appropriate to have your living trust hold the membership interests in your limited liability company. The key point is: Don't self-diagnose. If you want the work done right, price should not be the sole determining factor. Finally, no truly competent estate planner can quote you a fee without having some reasonable amount of information about you, your circumstances, and your goals.

What is the bottom line? Hire an experienced estate planner, who will not "yes" you, but rather guide you by giving you the pros, cons, and estimated costs of different options. Select a specialist who is published or who speaks professionally, and thus demonstrates an ability to keep up with current laws and planning. Select an expert whom other experts recommend. If you have a lot at stake (either financially or personally) in assuring that you establish the right trusts, consider paying for an initial consultation with several estate planners so that you can make an informed decision after getting a taste of what each can do for you.

OBTAINING MORE INFORMATION AND SAMPLE TRUST FORMS

If you want to obtain free sample forms and other planning tips, including audio clips, see the Web site www.laweasy.com for further information.

TRUSTS OF ALL STRIPES AND COLORS

There are scores of different types of trusts. There are almost certainly a few trusts that could benefit you (which ones depend on your personal goals and life circumstances). For you to identify and then implement appropriate trusts, you need to acquire a basic understanding of trusts. You need this basic background to make sure that the trusts you select are implemented properly and with the least cost. Also, a solid overview of trusts will help you separate the puffing and sales pitches you will undoubtedly hear from the useful information you really need.

Trusts can accomplish a tremendous number of personal, tax, estate, asset protection, legal, and other goals. They can help you accomplish the following:

- Provide for you and your loved ones, in the event of sickness and disability.
- Bridge the gap between life and death by continuing to care for your family after your death.
- Assure management expertise and continuity for your business or investments in the event of your illness or disability.
- Achieve significant income, gift, estate, and generation-skipping transfer (GST) tax savings.
- Protect assets from creditors, malpractice claimants, and divorce actions.
- Manage business or other assets.
- Protect children or other heirs while managing assets for their benefit.
- Minimize or avoid probate.

In accomplishing all of these important goals, trusts can often remain confidential and thus protect your privacy.

Trusts are not only tools for the very wealthy. When properly used, trusts can benefit everyone. There is a lot of misunderstanding about trusts, and much of the information presented to consumers is inaccurate or incomplete. Too often, the information available to consumers is self-serving, coming from a source selling a product, a computer program, or investment. To address these misunderstandings, and to clarify the true advantages and benefits that trusts can offer you, the first step is to understand what a trust is.

DEFINITION OF A TRUST

A trust, like a corporation, limited liability company, or limited partnership, is a creature or fiction of your state's laws. You establish a trust by following the procedures outlined in the laws (statutes) of your state. The simplest way to explain a trust is with an illustration.

NOTE: Greta Grandmother has her lawyer prepare a trust. This is a legal contract that, in Greta's case, is about 22 pages long. Greta obtains a tax identification number from the IRS for the trust. Greta then transfers $10,000 to her daughter Debby as trustee of the trust. This is done by Greta transferring the $10,000 to a bank account opened by Debby using the trust's name and tax identification number. Debby is required to invest the $10,000 in a certificate of deposit and use all the interest each year to pay for dance and music lessons for Debby's two children, Greta's grandchildren. When the youngest of Debby's two daughters reaches age 21, Debby is instructed to divide the money in the trust equally and distribute it to each of her two daughters.

This example also highlights the important time periods in a trust's existence. First the trust is formed by having a legal document prepared and signed. This trust document is a contract between the grantor, who sets up the trust, and the trustee, who administers the trust. Next, assets are transferred to the trust. This completes the establishment of the trust. The trust is then administered for its duration. This is the most important aspect of the trust because during this period the trust fulfills the purpose for which it was primarily formed. Finally, when the trust has fulfilled its primary or initial purposes, the money and assets it holds are distributed, and the trust is terminated. Some trusts have as their purpose to invest and distribute assets to all of the grantor's descendants, so that they may continue in perpetuity with no termination.

SEPARATING THE LEGAL AND BENEFICIAL OWNERSHIP OF AN ASSET

A basic principle of trusts is that a trust separates the legal ownership of an asset from the benefit of that asset.

EXAMPLE: If you own a brokerage account, you can spend the money in your account freely as you wish. You could use the money to pay for a vacation for your child Jane, or your niece Robin's birthday party. You own the account, you are in charge of the account, and you or anyone you choose can benefit from the account. In the case of paying for your child's vacation and your niece's birthday, they both benefit. You can spend your money in any manner. This contrasts with being a trustee of a trust. In a trust, you as trustee do in fact own legal title to the trust assets. However, you cannot benefit yourself from the trust assets (unless, as in a grantor trust or domestic asset protection trust, you are both a trustee and a beneficiary). Assume, for example, that your local bank, Bigbank, is the trustee of the trust for your daughter and niece. What is the difference between the two situations? In the first scenario, you have more flexibility. You retain control over the brokerage account. If you want to benefit from the funds, you can do so. If you want to benefit your niece, you can do so. In a common type of trust, a trust for minors, you would give as a gift assets (e.g., part or all of the particular brokerage account) to Bigbank, as trustee of Jane's and Robin's Trust. Bigbank would then own the assets as a trustee and use the assets to benefit your niece Robin or daughter Jane.

As is apparent, you had a price to pay by setting up a trust with Bigbank as trustee for your niece Robin and daughter Jane. You no longer control the assets, Bigbank does, subject to the requirements of state law and all the detailed instructions you included in the trust document. But the benefits that you can obtain, using the trust rather than retaining the brokerage account in your name, are also valuable. By having given the brokerage account to the trust, the account and all future appreciation should be excluded from your estate for tax purposes and will be unreachable by your creditors. Bigbank can allocate income between Robin and Jane depending on their respective income tax brackets. Thus, you could save substantial income and estate taxes. If you are sued years later, the assets that have been transferred to the trust for Jane and Robin should not be reached by your creditors.

The person holding the legal title, the trustee, has a fiduciary duty to the persons entitled to the benefits of the trust property. A fiduciary duty is a responsibility of care. The trustee is charged with exercising certain care in carrying out the requirements and intent of the trust document governing the relationship of the trustee to the property and to the beneficiary. This duty of care is imposed on the trustee by the provisions of the trust document. In addition, state law and the court cases of your state also create certain obligations and duties on the trustee.

Many of the benefits of a trust arrangement come from this separation of ownership and benefit. This is what enables you to designate a responsible person to manage assets for the benefit of another, such as a minor child.

When the IRS respects the separation of ownership and benefit, important tax benefits can be available. As you read on, you will see that this is generally for irrevocable trusts. These are trusts that cannot be changed once they are formed.

Where the persons to benefit cannot, or should not, be in control of the assets, a trust provides an ideal vehicle to provide for management. Trusts can permit a bank or financially astute family member to manage money for the benefit of a special child who is a minor or otherwise not mature enough to handle large assets, or an incapacitated family member who cannot manage the funds for her own benefit.

EXAMPLE: In the previous example, your niece may not have been of sufficient age to handle her own assets, she may suffer from a disability (e.g., a special child), or you may be concerned about the stability and influence of her husband or partner. A trust addresses any of these concerns by assuring that Bigbank manages the assets and protects those assets from creditors or other claimants. If you did not wish to name a bank or trust company, you could name friends, family members, or longtime family advisers, or any combination of these and an institutional trustee.

Where the separation of the ownership and benefit is recognized by the courts, assets can be used for the benefit of the beneficiaries, but may escape the creditors of the beneficiaries (asset protection trusts).

FIVE KEY ELEMENTS OF EVERY TRUST

A trust must include the following five elements: A *grantor* transfers *trust property* to a *trustee* to hold for the benefit of the *beneficiary* in accordance with the purpose or *intent* of the trust.

Grantor

This is the person who transfers the trust property to the trust. The grantor is also commonly called the trustor, settlor, or donor. The grantor must generally be the owner of the property that he transfers to the trust. This is not always a requirement, however. Many trusts, including several illustrated in this book, permit the trustee to accept contributions of assets from people other than the grantor (e.g., Aunt Nellie may wish to make a gift to the trust your mom established for your son's education to help celebrate your son's graduation from high school).

PLANNING TIP: In light of the favorable changes made by the 2001 Tax Act to Section 529 savings plans, Education IRAs, and so on, you should carefully evaluate all the education savings options before opting to use a trust.

The grantor must also have the proper legal capacity to sign the trust agreement and to transfer assets to the trust. This means that the grantor must be of sound mind and have the intent to form a trust. This intent of the grantor to form a trust must be manifested, generally in the form of a written and signed trust agreement.

CAUTION: The level of competence that you must have to sign a trust is greater than that level which the courts will require to sign a will. As a result, an older person or someone who is ill may have the competence to sign a will but not to sign a trust. This is a technical legal decision that should only be made with the guidance of your attorney, and in consultation with the attending physician of the person involved.

Trust Property

This is the principal or subject matter of the trust. It is also called the *trust res*. Property is usually transferred to the trust. This is called a *funded* trust. An insurance trust is an example of a trust that is almost always funded immediately, with the insurance policy and money to pay annual premiums. In other cases, you may establish a trust to receive property at some future date, but none presently. This is called an *unfunded* or *standby* trust. When you set up a standby trust, you form the trust now, but it may not have the intended assets transferred to it until some future date, such as your death (e.g., a pension plan to which the trust is named beneficiary). In some cases of using a standby trust, your attorney may advise you to open a trust bank account by transferring a nominal amount of money (e.g., $100) to the trust. This may be done to assure that the trust meets a legal requirement of having assets, and perhaps so that a bank or brokerage account is opened to facilitate receipt of assets in the future.

A trust formed under your will does not need to be funded now. It will instead be funded by your executor transferring assets from your estate to the trust following your death, by the payment of insurance proceeds or pension assets to the trust if the trust was named beneficiary, or by a trustee of another trust distributing assets to the designated trust on death.

CAUTION: If you believe an unfunded trust is appropriate, review this with an estate planner in your state. It may be advisable to transfer some nominal asset, say $100, to the trust to fund it so that the trust exists. Apart from legal requirements, it will often be useful to fund a trust to assure everything will run smoothly when you need it. For example, you may wish to establish a revocable living trust to manage assets in the event of your disability. If you decide to sign the trust, but do not fund it now, your agent will have to address all the administrative matters of obtaining a tax identification number, opening accounts, and so forth, in the event of your disability. Funding the trust today may save time and difficulties when the trust is needed.

Assets can be transferred to a trust during life, after death through your will, by gift, or by *beneficiary designation* (e.g., a designation of who inherits your IRA).

EXAMPLE: Because the 2001 Tax Act increased the exclusion (amount you can bequeath free of estate tax), your estate planner may advise you to name the bypass trust under your will as beneficiary of the insurance policy instead of forming a separate trust while you are alive to purchase and own the insurance.

A trust may also be funded by the exercise of a *power of appointment*. A power of appointment can be illustrated by a simple example.

EXAMPLE: Your mother bequeaths under her will assets to a trust for your benefit. On your death, the assets in this trust are to be distributed to your children in any proportions you designate in your will. This is done because your mother has decided she wants your children to receive the assets on your death rather than someone else. However, she may not know the relative economic needs of the children when writing her will. Therefore, she gives you the power to determine what portion of the assets go to each child. This is called a *power of appointment*.

The property of a trust can be cash you contribute, a life insurance policy, stock in a corporation (special rules affect the types of trusts that can hold stock in an S corporation), or any other asset that serves your purposes for establishing the trust and can be owned in a trust. In most trusts, a formal legal description of the trust property is attached to the end of the trust as a schedule. Merely listing the asset in a schedule attached to a trust may not be enough to properly transfer ownership of that asset to the trust. For real estate, a deed must be filed transferring ownership (title) of the property to the trust. For personal property, a bill of sale may be required (see Chapter 3).

Trustee

The trustee is the person responsible for managing and administering your trust. The trustee should make a declaration, often by signing the trust agreement, that he accepts the trust property as trustee. The trustee may be you, a trusted friend, a family member, a bank trust department, or any combination of these and other persons.

CAUTION: Selection of a trustee is one of the most important, and often one of the most difficult, decisions in setting up a trust. With the passage of variations of the Prudent Investor Act in many states (and the likelihood of additional states passing it), consideration of using an institution or bank at least as a cotrustee, is becoming more important. This act requires that trust assets be invested with consideration to all of the facts and circumstances, trust provisions, with an intent to maximize income and to minimize risk. This will generally require a reasonably diversified portfolio invested according to an appropriate plan that considers the purpose of the trust, tax issues, and investment planning. Most individuals, such as friends and family members, who would serve as trustees may not have the investment acumen to handle this. Even if they do, they may not want the liability exposure if investments are not handled properly. The solution will increasingly be to name an institution or other professional trustee to serve as cotrustee with a friend or family member. Where the friend or family member (or more than one) serves without an institution, reliance on a plan by a qualified financial professional will be essential.

An important legal requirement to serve as trustee is that the trustee have the legal capacity to accept title (ownership) of the trust property. A minor or incompetent person should not be a trustee. The grantor will generally specify the trustee, and successor trustees in the event the first-named trustee is no longer willing or able to serve as a trustee. Where the grantor fails to do this, a court may have to name a trustee. It is always advisable to name several successor trustees. Where the trust could be in existence for many years, you should name even more trustees, and persons young enough to serve into future years, or an institution.

The trustee will generally hold legal title to the assets in the trust, but not beneficial title. Legal title means the trust assets are owned in the name of the trustee. The trustee generally has specific duties and responsibilities for the trust property, or has certain powers concerning the disposition of the trust property. Beneficial title to the trust property is held by the beneficiaries of the trust.

EXAMPLE: Tom Taxpayer establishes a trust for the benefit of his children. Tina Taxpayer is named trustee. The stock that Tom transfers is owned by Tina, as trustee of the trust. Thus, Tina holds legal title to the stock "in trust" for the beneficiaries. Beneficial title, however, is held by the children because only the children, as the named beneficiaries of the trust, have the right to benefit from the dividends and principal value of the stock.

Beneficiary

The beneficiary is the person or persons who are to receive the benefits and advantages of the property transferred to the trust. For example, you set up a trust by transferring stock to a trustee to hold and use the dividends to pay for educational expenses of your children. The trust is for the benefit of your children, who are the beneficiaries. It is important that the persons who are beneficiaries can be determined. The description should be clear and certain. If you name "my descendants" as beneficiaries, there must be a time for making the determination of who your descendants are. Otherwise, it is impossible to know when to make the decision. What about children or grandchildren born after you set up the trust? Are they to be included or not? Beneficiaries can be charities as well (Chapter 17). Beneficiaries can receive benefit immediately (e.g., a current or income beneficiary), they can receive benefit in the future after current beneficiaries' interests end (remainder beneficiaries), or only if other beneficiaries die or otherwise cease to qualify for benefits (*contingent* beneficiaries).

Intent of Trust

Every trust has a purpose, or intent, that motivates the grantor to set up the trust in the first place. Apart from the obvious requirement that the intent must be legal, there are few restrictions on the grantor's intent. It can relate to:

- Benefiting a particular beneficiary (yourself, your spouse or partner, your child, a cousin, your favorite charity, or some combination of these).

- Providing for the management of certain assets (real estate, mutual funds, stock in a closely held corporation).
- Achieving certain tax benefits (charitable remainder trust to minimize capital gains and estate taxes, or a marital trust to qualify for the gift or estate tax unlimited marital deduction).

Your intent for a particular trust can include several objectives, and even objectives that change over time or on the occurrence of certain events. The intent of a trust can be spelled out in detail in the trust document, indicated in general terms, or perhaps permitted under the terms of the trust but not referenced specifically at all.

EXAMPLE: You may want the trustee to make distributions to the beneficiary only if the beneficiary is in school or working or otherwise acting responsibly. The trust may simply authorize the trustee to make distributions at his discretion. The trust agreement might remain silent as to your more specific intent.

Where the trust document is silent, state laws and court cases may fill in some of the blanks. Sometimes a letter of instruction may be given to the trustee. Even banks will accept these as a clarification of the trustee's intent. In most cases, the people you name as trustees understand your objectives from their relationship and personal knowledge of you.

HOW TRUSTS COMPARE WITH OTHER LEGAL ARRANGEMENTS

Comparing trust arrangements with other common legal documents and arrangements can help you understand the functions of trusts.

Power of Attorney

A common legal arrangement is called an agency relationship. The most frequently used agency relationship is a power of attorney. A power of attorney is a legal document through which you authorize another person to handle your financial matters. Powers of attorney, however, automatically terminate when you, the grantor, become disabled. The solution is to use what is called a durable power of attorney. When the appropriate language required under your state's laws is included in the power of attorney, it will remain effective even if you become disabled. No power of attorney, however, will remain effective after your death. A trust can remain valid after your death. Therefore, where you wish to provide for the management of your assets even after death, a trust, in addition to a power of attorney (which almost everyone should have), may be the preferred document.

Even during your life, there are several advantages in using a trust compared with a power of attorney. With a trust, the trustee has legal ownership of the assets. In a power of attorney relationship, a person is designated as your agent to act on your behalf. The trustee's relationship to the assets is clearer, and the trustee's powers over the assets are likely to be greater. In a trust (such as a revocable living trust), you can include details as to how you should be cared for, the type of nursing home you should be in (or that you should be in your home as long as feasible), and so forth. This level of detail is rarely included in a power of attorney. Frequently, a bank or institution is named as a co-trustee (but banks or institutions will generally not serve as agents under a power of attorney). Using an institutional co-trustee can help assure that your assets are used as you direct for your care. This situation can compare favorably with having only a family member as agent under a power of attorney to provide for your care if you are disabled. What if the family member serving as agent under the power of attorney decided to conserve your assets instead of spending them on your care, so that the same family member, as a beneficiary of your estate after your death, could inherit them? Thus, in planning for potential future disability, a trust arrangement is often preferable to merely using a durable power of attorney. The costs of using the trust approach, however, make the durable power of attorney the more practical solution in many situations where assets are limited and you can name sufficient trusted people to assist you.

Custodial Accounts (UGMA/UTMA)

Another common arrangement is a transfer under your state's uniform gifts to minors act (UGMA) or under your state's uniform transfers to minors act (UTMA) (see Chapter 16). In the most common type of UGMA transfer, you open a bank account as custodian for your child under your state's uniform gifts or transfers to minors act. There are important differences between such an account and a trust. If you set up the account, are the custodian, and die before the child who is beneficiary, the entire amount in the account can be taxed in your estate. This is not true for a trust. In the preceding example, the beneficiary (your child) owns the property, not the custodian (you). When the beneficiary attains the age specified in your state's UGMA or UTMA law, the child will receive control of the assets. This is typically age 18 to 21. In some instances, you can specify a slightly older age. Trusts can offer substantially more flexibility because you can tailor the trust document to address any concerns that you may have. In particular, the trust can hold assets until the child attains an older age and is more mature. Trusts, however, require legal fees to set up and may require annual tax returns. Assets can be placed in an UGMA or UTMA account at no cost.

Section 529 Savings Plan

You can contribute up to $11,000 per year, and up to $55,000 in advance in one year, to a college savings plan, to benefit a beneficiary you want.

Although these plans are not as flexible as trusts, they offer substantial tax benefits and require no legal fees, making them a better option for many, if not most, people when the primary goal is saving for college.

Partnerships and Limited Liability Companies

Partnerships and limited liability companies can be used in lieu of or in combination with, trusts. These entities can be used to control and manage assets, including their investment and distribution. The general partner of the partnership, or the manager of the limited liability company, can be given powers similar to those of a trustee (although distributions will generally be made in proportion to ownership interests in the partnership or the limited liability company). A key advantage that a partnership and a limited liability company have over a trust is that you can change the governing document (the partnership agreement for a partnership, the operating agreement for a limited liability company) at any time. You cannot change an irrevocable trust agreement after it is established.

PRIVACY AND ANONYMITY OF TRUSTS

Trusts, unlike wills and many other documents, do not always have to be filed in the public record. This can offer the opportunity to retain anonymity and privacy for many trusts. This is often touted as an important advantage of establishing certain trusts, particularly where most assets are placed in trust to avoid the probate process. Privacy, however, can be breached where the court orders that the trust be made part of the public probate record, or where the parties sue each other, forcing the trust into the court records.

NOTE: If you have a pour-over will (a will that requires that assets be poured into, or transferred to, a trust), some probate courts (or surrogate's courts as they are called in some parts of the country) require that the trust be added to their file. Also, if there is a will contest (someone sues to receive more of your assets following your death, by claiming that your will was defective, or that you were not competent when you signed it), the court may require that the trust be made part of the public record.

The privacy aspects of trusts can also be breached by the legal steps necessary to transfer assets into the trust. For example, where real estate is transferred to a trust, a deed will have to be filed. Deeds are recorded in the public record. So even if the trust document itself remains private, the fact that the real estate was transferred to the trust will be public knowledge. In some counties, the county clerk (where deeds are filed) may require that the trust, or a summary of the trust (called a *Memorandum of Trust*), be recorded. Recording makes the document part of the public record, which means anyone can look up the trust (or the summary if that is all that is required to be filed) in the county records. When certain other property is transferred to the trust, a public filing requirement such as the provisions of the Uniform Commercial Code could be triggered. Thus, the privacy factor, although available in many situations, is not as foolproof as many people like to believe. Do you need to be concerned?

NOTE: The typical will, or the comparable provisions of a typical living trust addressing distribution of your assets, may provide for the distribution of property to your spouse, and on your spouse's death, equally to your children. In most cases, neither a will nor living trust includes any personal information, or financial details, so why be concerned about disclosure?

DIFFERENT TYPES OF TRUST

Trusts can be as varied as the people who set them up. It is, however, useful to categorize trusts to help you better understand how to pick the right trust (or trusts) for you. Just remember that the trust (or trusts—you may need several) that meets your goals is likely to overlap many categories. Further, the way many trusts are labeled and offered is misleading because a hybrid or combination of approaches is generally best. With these caveats, trusts can be categorized by the following factors.

When the Trust Is Formed

During Your Life

You can set up a trust during your lifetime (inter vivos or living trust). Common living trusts include a revocable living trust (sometimes called a loving trust) (Chapter 13), a charitable remainder trust (Chapter 17), an insurance trust (Chapter 19), a children's trust (Chapter 16), or a charitable lead trust (Chapter 17). Be careful, the categories aren't rigid. For example, a charitable lead trust can also be set up on death under your will.

At Your Death

A trust can also become effective upon your death (testamentary trust). Testamentary trusts are frequently contained in your will. Common testamentary trusts include a marital trust for your spouse (Chapter 14) and trusts for minor children (Chapter 16), a bypass trust to preserve the benefits of your estate tax exclusion, although this may be handled differently than in the past because of the 2001 Tax Act (Chapter 10). Less common is a testamentary charitable lead trust (Chapter 17). Note that the charitable lead and children's trusts were listed as being both inter-vivos (while you are alive) and testamentary (formed on death). These trusts, like many others, can be formed either while you are alive, or following your death under your will, depending on your needs and goals.

On Starting a New Business or Purchasing an Investment

Some trusts are formed prior to your making a new investment or setting up a new business. For example, say you identify a rental property you want to purchase, and your overall estate and financial plan suggests transferring assets to your children or other heirs or protecting the new investment from malpractice claimants. Before purchasing the investment, it might be advisable to form a trust to own the investment or place the ownership interests in a limited liability company (LLC) that will own the rental property. You can then have your trust purchase some or all of the investment or own some or all of the LLC.

EXAMPLE: Paul and Pauline Parent found a rental property that he thought would have excellent prospects and cash flow. Paul gifts $60,000 of cash that they would have used as the down payment to purchase the rental property to the trustees of the trusts he established for his three children. The trustees could then use this money as the down payment to purchase some portion, or all, of the rental property (or to contribute to the capital of the LLC formed to purchase the property). The trust would then own a portion or all of the rental property. The trust would receive a portion of the rental income. This income could be accumulated or paid out to or for the benefit of the children. The appreciation in the value of the rental property, to the extent owned by the trust, would not be part of Paul or Pauline's estates. Having a trust formed to own a portion of the rental property can protect the property from creditors, yet still permit the family some measure or control over the property and the income it has generated.

Type of Beneficiary

Trusts can be established to benefit any type of person or cause. You can set up a trust to benefit yourself. A revocable living trust is an excellent tool for planning for your own disability. It can also help avoid probate. You may wish to use a trust to insulate your assets from creditors or protect assets from estate and GST taxes. A dynasty trust can achieve this and other goals.

Several types of trusts can be set up for your spouse. These include a marital trust to protect your spouse after your death and a marital trust formed while you are alive to which you transfer assets to benefit your spouse, save estate taxes, and protect the assets from your creditors. There is also a special marital trust if your spouse is not an American citizen.

Numerous different trusts are used for children. A special trust can be used to make gifts to children under the age of 21 and still qualify for favorable tax benefits. Where a special needs child is involved, a trust can be used to protect the child while preventing the loss of government benefits.

A wide array of trusts can be set up for charity.

Purpose of the Trust

Trusts can be classified by the purposes for which they are formed. Although tax benefits are a primary purpose for many trusts, most trusts have important nontax benefits. Because of this, even if your estate will no longer be subject to estate tax because of the changes made by the 2001 Tax Act, trust planning remains essential for most people.

Charitable trusts are designed to provide income, gift, and estate tax advantages, to defer when an heir may receive an inheritance, inculcate philanthropic values, and benefit certain charitable organizations (Chapter 17).

Marital trusts are designed to protect a spouse, manage assets, assure the ultimate distribution of assets to the persons you choose, and qualify transfers of assets in the trust for the gift or estate tax unlimited marital deduction. This could include a Qualified Terminable Interest Property (QTIP) or a B trust, Qualified Domestic Trust (QDOT) (see Chapter 14).

Perhaps the most commonly used tax-oriented trust is the exclusion, credit shelter, or bypass trust. This is used to take advantage of the exclusion available to every taxpayer (see Chapter 14). It can also provide important income tax savings, asset protection, and asset management even if the estate tax is unlikely to affect your family.

Trusts can be designed to avoid creditors and claimants. In addition to the asset protection of each of the trusts previously noted, a trust can be specifically used to protect assets from loss of Medicaid benefits (Chapter 18). Domestic asset protection trusts, in addition of a foreign trust, can be used for wealthy taxpayers to shelter assets from claimants.

Powers of Trustees

Trusts can be classified by the scope of powers given to the trustees. For example, the trustee can be required to pay the income of the trust to a single beneficiary (*income* or *simple* trust). In other trusts, the trustee may be given the flexibility to accumulate the income and only pay the income when the trustee deems it appropriate (*accumulation* trust). In some cases, the grantor may wish to give the trustee broader powers to address future uncertainty. In these trusts, the trustee may be permitted to distribute trust income and principal among various beneficiaries in any manner the trustee determines (*sprinkle* or *discretionary* trust).

Many trusts contain restrictions that prevent the beneficiary from assigning their interests in advance. For example, the beneficiary cannot purchase something and assign future distributions to the seller to pay for the item purchased (*spendthrift* trust).

Trustees can be given the power to buy, rent, or mortgage real estate, operate a business, or almost any other type of management control. Alternatively, the powers of the trustees over the assets can be more limited (Chapter 6). Specific powers that enable a trust to hold stock in an S corporation, or to buy insurance, can be included. Such trusts might be classified or labeled as an *S corporation* or *insurance trust*, respectively.

Grantor's Control

Another method of categorizing trusts is by the degree of control that the person setting up the trust (the grantor) can exercise. If the grantor retains the total right to terminate or change the trust, the trust is called *revocable*. Living trusts are perhaps the most common revocable trust.

If the grantor relinquishes the right to change or terminate the trust, it is said to be *irrevocable*. Where tax considerations are important, the trust is likely to be irrevocable.

The distinction between revocable and irrevocable is not absolute. The grantor may be permitted very limited rights under even an irrevocable trust. For example, the grantor may be permitted a limited right to replace an institutional trustee with another institution.

Some trusts are structured so that they are irrevocable and assets transferred to them are considered outside your estate for gift and estate tax purposes (i.e., the transfer of assets is a completed gift). However, the income from these trusts can remain taxed to you even though it's an irrevocable trust whose assets won't be taxed in your estate. These trusts are called *defective* or *grantor* trusts.

Assets Held

The types of assets transferred to a trust can be used to characterize different trusts. Trusts that hold insurance are commonly used to protect the insurance proceeds from estate tax (Chapter 19). Special trusts to hold real estate or stock of S corporations, are frequently used (Chapters 21 and 22). A voting trust can be used to hold stock of a closely held corporation (Chapter 21) (*voting trust*).

Powers of the Beneficiaries

Although the beneficiaries are generally passive and the trustees make most decisions, the beneficiaries can be afforded several powers. A beneficiary may be given the right to require the distribution of certain amounts of principal each year from the trust (often this is limited to what is called a *five and five power*) (Chapter 5).

A beneficiary may be given the right to designate where the assets of the trust will eventually be distributed (power of appointment) (Chapter 5).

A beneficiary may be given a limited right to replace a trustee, for example, with an independent replacement trustee (e.g., a bank or institutional trustee).

Beneficiaries may be given the right to withdraw part or all of the annual gifts made to a trust up to some maximum amount such as $10,000 (the amount that can be given away in any year to one beneficiary without gift tax consequences). This is done to enable gifts to the trust to qualify for the annual gift tax exclusion. Such trusts could be called *annual*

OVERVIEW OF TRUSTS 21

demand power or *Crummey power* trusts (the latter title is after the famous court case that approved this tax technique).

Since almost any type of trust can give the beneficiaries any or all of these powers, the beneficiaries' rights, although important to any trust, are not a practical category to organize later discussions of different trusts.

CHOOSING A TRUST THAT FITS YOUR OVERALL PLAN

Deciding what trust or trusts are necessary to meet your goals is not a choice you should make in a vacuum. You should coordinate your selection and use of any trust with each of the following factors.

Your Financial Plan

Before making any decision, you must thoroughly review your present and anticipated future financial position. The health, educational, and other needs of you, your family, your loved ones, and others whom you feel responsible for must be evaluated. For example, if you are going to establish Section 529 college savings plans for your child or grandchild, a trust for the same beneficiary may be unnecessary.

Your Will

The use of many trusts should be coordinated with your will. In fact, many of the trusts that are appropriate for you may be included in your will. If you use a pour-over will (a will that distributes some or all of your assets to one or more designated trusts), that trust must be coordinated with your will. The trust should have provisions permitting the trustees to accept, or reject, assets from your executor under your will. The trust should also be executed prior to the will. If you form a trust for a grandchild while you are alive to hold gifts of a family business, that trust should be coordinated with any trust for your grandchildren included in your will (e.g., the use of the GST exemption has to be coordinated to avoid inadvertently triggering GST tax).

Your Power of Attorney

Powers of attorney should be coordinated with your trust planning. A power of attorney is a legal arrangement that permits others to take financial actions on your behalf, for example, when you are disabled. If you establish a trust, particularly a revocable living trust or another type of trust that may not be funded completely, your agent under your power of attorney should be given the specific authority to transfer assets to your trust. Many irrevocable trusts formed during your lifetime require annual gifts to fund them. If you are disabled, your durable power of attorney should authorize your agent to continue your gift plan.

Insurance Planning

Your insurance needs and coverage should be evaluated and coordinated with your selection of a trust. This is critical because a common use of trusts is to own your insurance policies. Insurance trusts to hold insurance policies are only the most obvious issue to coordinate. Your level of insurance coverage can affect your use and selection of other trusts.

EXAMPLE: Frank Father establishes an insurance trust that purchases a $2 million insurance policy on his life. He believes that since his wife will receive the benefit of the $2 million of insurance on his death, only his children, and not his wife, should be made beneficiaries of the credit shelter trust under his will (see Chapter 14).

NOTE: Gene Generous formed an insurance trust to benefit his primary beneficiaries, his three nephews. Because of the large amount of insurance coverage in this trust, Gene has decided not to form education trusts for the nephews while he is alive or under his will. Prior to opting for the insurance coverage, he had debated forming an education trust for each of the three nephews to hold annual gifts of $11,000.

After the 2001 Tax Act, many more taxpayers will be able to name the bypass trust under their will, or simply their estates (the bypass trust will be funded from assets passing through their estates) as beneficiary instead of incurring the expense and administrative burdens of an insurance trust. Speak with your estate planner.

Business Interests

If you want to use a trust as part of a plan to control or transfer ownership of a family business, you should consider the future growth of the business, the wishes of any other partners, and any restriction that a partnership (or other agreement) might contain affecting your transfer of partnership interests to the trust. Bank loan covenants may require that banks which lent the business money must approve transfers. If there are significant leases, the tenant or landlord may have to approve a change in control.

Coordinating Your Plan

The key point to properly plan for the use of any trust is to coordinate the process with your overall financial and estate plan. Your planning should be reviewed with all your advisers—your accountant, attorney, and insurance and investment advisers. Any attempt to plan in isolation is dangerous.

SELECTING THE RIGHT TRUST FOR YOU

The myriad different trusts and trust provisions make the process one that should be completed with professional advice. This book, however, can introduce you to many of the trust arrangements available. The selection of the trusts that may be appropriate for you must begin with a thorough and objective analysis of your personal, financial, estate planning, business, and other goals. You must also review your financial and tax status, and anticipate the current and projected financial and management needs of you and your family. Based on this information, a comprehensive estate and financial plan can be devised. Within the context of implementing this comprehensive plan, appropriate trusts for you can be identified and then implemented. A comprehensive example can illustrate the selection of the appropriate trusts.

EXAMPLE: Gary and Gail Grantor are married. Their net worth is approximately $2.4 million. As a result, their estate planner recommends that they use credit shelter trusts so that each of their estates can benefit from the once-in-a-lifetime $1 million exclusion (the exclusion in 2002 will exempt $1 million of assets from estate taxation; see Chapter 14). Each of their wills thus incorporates a bypass trust. In Gail's will, following Gary's later death, the assets of hers that remain in the bypass trust will be distributed (in part) to her children from her prior marriage. As the exclusion increases beyond $1 million (assuming the 2001 Tax Act provisions are not modified in the future), Gail and Gary may want to limit the amount distributed into a bypass trust, or perhaps alter the distribution provisions to better fit their needs.

Because this is the second marriage for Gail, she wishes to set up a trust for any assets she owns above the $1 million (2002) amount. A marital (QTIP or B) trust is used. This trust will qualify for the estate tax marital deduction so that there will not be any estate tax on Gail's death (Chapters 10 and 14). Following Gail's death, Gary will be entitled to all the income from this trust (principal distributions can vary from none to liberal, depending on their goals). Following Gary's death, the assets from Gail's QTIP trust will be distributed to Gail's children from her first marriage. With this arrangement, there will not be any federal estate tax due on Gail's death. This is because the first $1 million of her estate will avoid tax as a result of her exclusion. Amounts above $1 million are included in a QTIP trust, which will be exempted from tax on Gail's death by the unlimited estate tax marital deduction (but the QTIP assets remaining will be taxed in Gary's estate when he dies). Further planning can be done by allocating the GST exemption to either or both trusts and having some portion of the assets pass on in further trust to later generations.

EXAMPLE: To protect his family, Gary has a $2 million term life insurance policy. If either Gary or Gail owned this policy, it could create a tax cost on the death of Gail or Gary, depending on the year the remaining partner dies, the exclusion in effect for that year, and their other assets. Life insurance is not tax free. The solution—have a life insurance trust own the policy (Chapter 20).

Because Gail and Gary's children are minors, their parents have provided trusts for their children in their wills. These trusts name a succession of close and trusted friends to handle the financial affairs of their children in the event that both Gail and Gary die while their children are still young. These trusts are coordinated with the planning for Gail's children from her prior marriage.

If Gail and Gary were concerned about planning for disability and avoiding the expenses and delays of probate, they could each transfer their assets to a revocable living trust. If this approach is used, the bypass and QTIP trust could be included in each of their living trusts.

CONCLUSION

Trusts are a valuable and flexible tool that can provide substantial benefits for meeting estate, financial, personal, tax, and business goals. This chapter has defined trusts and how you can use them. With this background, we can next explore the components common to most trusts, which will set the framework for your evaluation of different trusts.

2 THE TRUST DOCUMENT: BASIC BUILDING BLOCKS

Many trusts are made up of similar components. Understanding these common components, the basic building blocks of a typical trust, will help you work with trusts and assure that any trusts you ultimately use will be best tailored to meet your needs. If you are named a beneficiary (i.e., you will receive some benefit) or a trustee (the fiduciary managing a trust) of a trust set up by someone else, understanding the basic building blocks will make it much easier for you to read the trust documents and understand your rights and responsibilities as a beneficiary or trustee under that trust. Finally, the format used to explain these basic building blocks is the same order of discussion that will be used in Part Two of this book to explain, in detail, the provisions of many trusts.

NOTE: An exception to this building block approach exists for several primarily tax-oriented trusts. Although similar concepts are found in these trusts, they are often modelled after IRS forms. Although your estate planner may make additions to the sample IRS forms, he or she is likely to follow the IRS recommendations quite closely. Thus, a charitable remainder trust drafted by an estate planner, might closely parallel the model IRS form, and then at the end include supplemental provisions addressing the issues noted in this book (e.g., additional trustee powers).

BUILDING BLOCK 1: INTRODUCTORY PARAGRAPHS

The introductory paragraphs to your trust will typically list the name of the grantor establishing the trust (if it is your trust, this will generally be you), and the initial trustee (or trustees, if there are more than one). This introductory paragraph demonstrates three of the five essential elements of a trust discussed in Chapter 1: a grantor, a trustee, and the intent of the grantor to form a trust.

Preparer's Signature

The lawyer preparing the trust document will often sign his or her name on the top. In some states, this is required for the trust to be recorded. Even if you do not intend to record the trust, you may wish to have the lawyer's signature included in the event that the trust has to be recorded at some future date in a state where such a requirement exists.

Tax Identification Number

Almost any time you do anything with your trust (e.g., open a bank account or change an insurance policy owned by the trust), you will be asked for the trust's tax identification number. A practical approach is to have the tax identification number received from the IRS for the trust noted on the top of the first page of the trust. This number can be obtained by completing IRS Form SS-4 and calling the IRS or mailing the form to the IRS.

NOTE: The first page of most trusts will include the date of the trust, the name of the trust, the name and address of the grantor (the person setting up the trust), and the names and addresses of the initial trustees (the persons managing the trust). Along with the tax identification number, these are the key facts that any bank or other person using or relying on the trust will have to know.

Selecting a Name for Your Trust

One of the first steps is to select a name for your trust. For most people, the use of the last name is a convenient means to identify the trust. Use of a last name makes it easier for banks, accountants, attorneys, and others to properly handle your trust and matters relating to the trust and your personal planning.

Also, consider using a name that is sufficiently descriptive of the trust and its functions to make it easy for you, your family, and professional advisers to work with the trust. This becomes particularly important if you set up several trusts. Since you cannot know what additional trusts you may form in the future, plan ahead.

NOTE: Tom Taxpayer sets up a grantor retained annuity trust (GRAT) in 2005 (Chapter 21). The trust is called "The Tom Taxpayer 2005 Trust." If this were Tom's only trust, the name used might be reasonable. However, in 2006, Tom sets up a second GRAT and calls it "The Tom Taxpayer 2006 Trust." In 2007, Tom sets up an irrevocable life insurance trust (Chapter 20). The trust is called "The Tom Taxpayer 2007 Trust." This is confusing since the names are so similar. Tom might consider the following names instead: "Tom Taxpayer 2005 GRAT," "Tom Taxpayer 2006 GRAT," and "Tom Taxpayer Irrevocable 2007 Life Insurance Trust." These names are clearer and more descriptive.

The Date of the Trust

The introductory paragraph of your trust lists the date the trust is established. The date is important for a number of reasons, which we discuss next.

Gift Implications

The date your trust is established is particularly important because assets cannot be transferred to the trust prior to that date, the trust cannot transact business prior to that date, and tax results may depend on that date and the date assets are transferred to the trust. Where you wish to make gifts to a trust prior to the end of the year to use your annual $10,000 (as indexed $11,000 in 2002) per person gift tax exclusion, the trust must be established prior to year end. Every taxpayer is entitled to give away up to $11,000 to any other person during each tax year without incurring a gift tax. When setting up this type of trust, it is best to set it up soon enough before the end of the year so that you can open a bank account and make an initial deposit. This will help demonstrate to the IRS that the trust was in fact properly formed prior to the end of the year. If you set the trust up too close to year end and wish to transfer stock to the trust, you might miss the year-end deadline and lose the benefit of the current year's $11,000 exclusion.

Revocable Living Trust

If you combine the use a will with a pour-over provision (i.e., a direction that assets from your estate be "poured into," or transferred to, your trust), the trust should not have a date after the date of your will. A pour-over will transfers assets to your trust; then the trust document includes the details as to which beneficiary is to receive which assets (see Chapter 8).

Who Is the Grantor?

Who should be the grantor of the trust? Generally, there is little issue since the grantor is usually the person setting up the trust and contributing most of the assets to the trust. Still, careful consideration must be given to who is named grantor, because the identity of the grantor can have important implications, depending on the circumstances of a particular trust:

- The grantor of most trusts (the revocable living trust and other "grantor" trusts exceptions) should usually not also serve as a trustee or successor trustee, to avoid the trust's assets being included in the grantor's estate for tax purposes. However, if the increased exclusion of the 2001 Tax Act do become effective, you might wish to reconsider this if you are certain your estate won't be taxed.
- The grantor is often assumed to be the person transferring assets to the trust.

- The grantor of certain irrevocable trusts (e.g., insurance trust, child's trust, grandchild's trust) should not be a beneficiary of the trust.
- The powers and rights which the grantor can continue to hold over the trust are often severely restricted. In most irrevocable trusts, one of the few powers that the grantor can retain, without causing the trust assets to be taxable in the grantor's estate, is a limited power to replace an independent trustee with another independent trustee.

Who Should Be Listed as Trustees of Your Trust?

The introductory paragraph will name the initial trustee (or co-trustees) for your trust. Successor, or alternate, trustees will be named in later provisions of the trust. You should carefully consider the following factors in determining who to name as trustee:

Purpose of the Trust

If the trust is an irrevocable life insurance trust, designed to remove insurance proceeds from your estate, you cannot be a trustee. Further, there is likely to be very little activity in the trust prior to the death of the insured. For example, the only functions may be to receive an annual gift, issue a Crummey power notice (see Chapter 10), and write a check to pay the insurance premium. Your accountant, or a business associate, may be an ideal choice until the insured's death. Other persons could be named to take over at the insured's death, when managing assets, making distribution decisions, and so on, will be required. The norm remains, however, to name trustees to serve while the insured is alive and continue after death.

If you are establishing a trust for a minor (instead of a Section 529 college savings plan), you will probably make annual or more frequent gifts to the trust. Depending on the facts, such a trust might grow quite quickly in size. A key criterion for a trustee of such a trust might be investment acumen.

If the trust is a voting trust for a business interest, your partners in the business may insist that you, or you and they jointly, serve as trustees. The provisions of any existing business agreement you are party to may govern who can serve as trustee. Carefully review estate tax implications to such an arrangement with your tax adviser.

If the trust is a revocable living trust (sometimes called a *loving trust*), you may be both the grantor and the trustee (Chapters 4 and 6). However, many professionals prefer that you serve as a co-trustee with another person to facilitate the hand-off of control in the event of your illness or death.

Duration of the Trust

The likely duration of the trust is an important factor to consider in determining who should be a trustee, and in how many successor trustees to name. For example, if your youngest child is age 19, and you wish to have a trust established to last until he reaches age 25, you might be comfortable naming one of your parents as a co-trustee. However, if your child was just born and the trust you wish to fund will remain in existence until your new-born child reaches age 35, your parents may not be an ideal choice. Younger trustees, or perhaps a bank or institutional trustee, would be appropriate to consider. If you name elderly parents as trustees, you should name several younger people, or perhaps an institutional trustee, as successor trustees. If you are establishing a perpetual or dynasty trust, the time frame of "forever" suggests that an institutional trustee should be considered, or if not a de-tailed and flexible mechanism to appoint future trustees should be included.

Different Phases of Your Trust

In some instances, it may be appropriate to name different trustees for dif-ferent phases of your trust. For example, if you establish a revocable living trust, you and a close friend or family member may be the initial trustees. It may not be wise to be the sole initial trustee—legal issues of merger could affect your trust, and in the event of disability, there is no other currently serving trustee to take over quickly. If you become disabled, your spouse or partner may be your successor. After the death of you and your spouse, the trust may continue for the benefit of your minor children. If this occurs, you may name two co-trustees: one with investment acumen to manage the chil-dren's investments and the other a guardian or close family member who knows the children on a personal level and is familiar with their needs.

BUILDING BLOCK 2: ASSETS TRANSFERRED TO YOUR TRUST

As explained in Chapter 1, identification and transfer of property to your trust is one of the five essential elements of every trust. Merely identifying the assets to be transferred to your trust is only one step toward accom-plishing the goal of funding your trust. The legal ownership (title) of the assets must actually be transferred to your trustees to hold in their capac-ity as trustees. This can require a deed to transfer real estate, a bill of sale, and physical delivery to the trustee of tangible property (e.g., a painting), a change in the registration or title of a brokerage account, and so forth.

The decision as to what assets should be transferred to your trusts must be carefully addressed to meet your goals. This decision requires consideration of income, gift and estate tax issues, asset protection con-cerns (the asset transferred should not itself likely be subject to claims), economics (e.g., which asset is most likely to appreciate), personal prefer-ences, and so on. These matters are addressed in detail in Chapter 3, "Transferring Assets to Your Trust." If the asset is real estate, will a mort-gage or lease be affected? If the asset is personal property, must you change the insurance coverage or pay a local transfer tax? There are a host of issues to consider, which is why asset transfers should be reviewed with an attorney in advance.

Do not assume that only the person named as the grantor can transfer assets to the trust. If you set up a trust for your children, as grantor, your parents, for example, can also contribute assets to the trust. One of the recommended provisions to include in many trusts is a provision permitting other persons to contribute or transfer property to the trust, if the assets are acceptable to the trustee. It is often advisable to give the trustee discretion to reject accepting assets. For example, what if the assets have adverse tax or legal consequences? This could occur if a rental property that someone sought to transfer to the trust was not practical to manage, or worse, had a leaky oil tank or other hazardous waste involved.

BUILDING BLOCK 3: THE GRANTOR'S POWERS AND RIGHTS UNDER THE TRUST

As mentioned earlier, the grantor is the person forming and usually funding (giving assets to) a trust. In most revocable living trusts, the grantor will retain substantial rights and powers over the trust and the property transferred to the trust. In other *inter-vivos* (set up during the grantor's lifetime) trusts, the grantor may have few, or no, rights or powers over the trust. The nature and extent of these powers will depend on the objectives of the trust and the type of trust involved. For example, when the trust is formed to remove assets from your estate, you cannot retain any significant powers over the trust that could taint the trust as included in your estate. However, the exclusion amount is increased following the 2001 Tax Act to $1 million in 2002, and eventually to $3.5 million. As a result of the amount of the exclusion, the tax may cease to be a concern for many taxpayers, so you may retain powers that would include the trust in your estate.

If you establish a domestic asset protection trust to protect assets from creditors, you will limit, although not always as severely as for a tax-motivated trust, your rights as grantor to the trust assets and your powers to make decisions affecting the trust assets to avoid creating opportunities for creditors to attack the trust.

If the trust involved is your revocable living trust, you will probably retain total control over the assets and trust since the assets will be included in your estate for tax purposes and will likely be reachable by any creditors or claimants in any event.

BUILDING BLOCK 4: BENEFICIARY DESIGNATIONS AND RIGHTS

Beneficiaries are the last of the five essential trust elements. Every trust must identify the persons who are to benefit from the trust assets during each phase of the trust.

CAUTION: The beneficiaries of a trust must almost always be people or charities. Only a few states permit pets to be named beneficiaries of a trust. At least one of the state statutes that permits pets to be beneficiaries of a trust gives the court considerable latitude to review the trust if the assets transferred to the trust are excessive.

The provisions that affect a beneficiary can be quite simple as illustrated in the following example.

EXAMPLE: I, Gary Grantor, hereby transfer $10,000 to Terri Trustee to hold in trust for the benefit of Mary Minor, as beneficiary. The trustee shall pay the income from this money to or for the benefit of the beneficiary until the beneficiary reaches age 25. At such time, any assets remaining in this trust shall be distributed outright (i.e., without further trust) to John Smith.

CAUTION: The listing of beneficiaries left an important gap as a result of poor drafting. What happens if Mary Minor dies before reaching age 25? Can John Smith receive the assets immediately? The trust is not clear. Every trust must clearly delineate who should be a beneficiary, when, and what they can receive. Possible "what if" scenarios should be addressed.

In many trusts, however, the provisions concerning beneficiaries are far more detailed and complex. You may name alternate beneficiaries. For example, if the primary beneficiary, Mary Minor in the example, were to die, other persons could be named beneficiaries before John Smith is to receive the remainder.

Some trusts may give the beneficiary the right to demand that certain payments be made to them, or for their benefit. This is discussed in detail in Chapter 5, "Designations and Rights of Beneficiaries."

Many trusts name a group or class of people as beneficiaries and give the trustee discretion as to when and how to distribute income, principal, or a unitrust or total return amount, among the various beneficiaries. These trusts are called *sprinkle* or *discretionary* trusts.

BUILDING BLOCK 5: FIDUCIARIES AND QUASI-FIDUCIARIES—APPOINTMENT AND POWERS

Positions and Titles

These provisions of a trust document specify who should serve as trustee, and the various powers, rights, and administrative obligations of the trustees. Less commonly, trusts may name other fiduciaries or quasi-fiduciaries. These might include a trust protector who is given a limited number of specific, but important powers, such as the right to change the trustees and the state where the trust is located (law and situs). Some

trusts might designate a person other than the trustee to make investment decisions. This person is sometimes referred to as an *investment adviser*. Finally, some trusts may appoint a person or group of people
(*committee*) to determine when and how to make distributions (payments) from the trust. The *trust protector, investment adviser,* and *distribution committee* are sometimes referred to as *quasi-fiduciaries* since
they do have fiduciary responsibilities, like a trustee, but they do not
have the broad scope of authority and state law governing their positions.
In many states, the law pertaining to quasi-fiduciaries is new and perhaps uncertain. Some states, like Delaware, have dealt extensively with
quasi-fiduciaries.

Successor Appointments

Although you named the initial trustee and quasi-fiduciaries in your
trust, you should always name alternate (successor) trustees and quasi-
fiduciaries in the event that the initial persons cannot continue to serve
(e.g., health matters). If you cannot name sufficient successors, consider
establishing a mechanism to name a successor. For example, all beneficiaries over age 25 could be given the right to appoint an independent fiduciary or quasi-fiduciary. The trust protector can be given the right to
appoint a successor trustee if none are serving. If all your efforts fail, a
court will have to step in and appoint a successor trustee or quasi-fiduciary.
This is unlikely to be a result you will want.

Details as to how each of the trustees and quasi-fiduciaries should serve,
and what rights and powers each has, must all be provided in the trust
document. Although most laypersons skip through these provisions
quickly as "boiler plate" (i.e., standard in all trusts) this can be a substantial mistake. This is especially dangerous when any quasi-fiduciaries are
named since these positions are less well defined in many state's laws than
are trustee positions (see Chapter 6).

BUILDING BLOCK 6: DISTRIBUTION PROVISIONS

The distribution provisions of your trust are vital to make certain your
wishes are carried out. In prior building blocks sections, the beneficiaries
were clearly identified, the trustees and possibly quasi-fiduciaries, who
manage the trust, were named, and the powers and rights the trustees
have were specified. But how should the trustees (or distribution committee) use the powers given to them to distribute trust income and/or assets
to the beneficiaries you have named? That determination is the objective
of the distribution provisions of the trust.

Distribution provisions are generally not simple. For example, in years
past, many trusts provided that income would be paid out annually or
more frequently. *Principal* (the actual assets of the trust) may have been
held for the *remainder beneficiaries* (the beneficiaries who receive their

interests after the initial phase of the trust). However, modern investment theory has resulted in trusts generally investing for *total return* (i.e., current income and appreciation or capital gains). Thus, for a trust to merely state that income should be distributed currently may not be workable. How can you invest trust assets to satisfy both the current income beneficiary and the remainder beneficiary?

Similarly, every trust contains rules stating if and under what circumstances the principal of the trust can be distributed.

EXAMPLE: You transfer $75,000 to a trust. This amount is the principal of the trust. The trustee invests this amount in common stocks. The trust earns $2,300 of common stock cash dividends. This is income of the trust. The difference between income and principal is not always so clear. When there is a stock dividend paid, or a cash payment for fractional shares if a stock split occurs, will this be characterized as principal or as income? Either the trust can provide detailed rules as to how these decisions should be made, or local law (the *principal and income act* in your state) will make the decision.

The provisions of your trust that provide for how and when income and principal should be distributed are extremely important.

EXAMPLE: You are divorced and remarried. You establish a trust for the benefit of your second spouse during her lifetime. On the death of your second spouse, the assets will be divided among your children from your first marriage. You name a close family friend as trustee. Any receipts that are characterized as income will be distributed to your second spouse during her lifetime. Any receipts that are characterized as principal will be allocated to your children from the prior marriage. The distinction is obviously important. Further, the clearer your trust is about the rules of allocating receipts between income and principal, the less likely your trustee will be embroiled in difficult problems.

Further questions and issues must be addressed. When should principal be invaded? Should the trustee use the trust assets in a child's trust to pay for college? If so, what about graduate school? What if assets are available in an education IRA or Section 529 college savings plan. Which assets will be used first? Should restrictions be placed on the distribution provisions to protect the trust assets from the beneficiary's creditors? The decisions are as varied as your wishes (see Chapter 8).

BUILDING BLOCK 7: SPECIAL PROVISIONS OF YOUR TRUST

Many trusts include specific clauses that make your trust a particular type of trust. Your trust may require special provisions to address the unique characteristics of the beneficiary, or the special nature of the assets to be held in the trust, or other special circumstances. These provisions give the trust its unique classification or characteristics. Several of these are discussed next.

Insurance Trust

An insurance trust can take many forms, depending on the purpose for which it is established, the persons to benefit, and when those benefits should be distributed. These decisions, however, are similar to those made for many types of trusts. To facilitate a trust's holding insurance as an asset, there are several important provisions concerning the trustees' power to deal with insurance companies and related matters that should be added. A marital savings clause is also common. (See Chapter 14.)

Qualified S Corporation Trust (QSST)

An *S corporation* is a corporation which is, for federal (and some state) income tax purposes, treated in a manner similar to a partnership or limited liability company. It generally avoids the corporate-level tax, with income, gains, losses, and so forth passing through to the shareholders and being reported on their personal tax returns. Where a trust owns stock in an S corporation, several requirements must be met to prevent the corporation from losing its favored tax status as an S corporation. Generally, all income must be distributed to a single beneficiary for a trust to be a QSST shareholder in an S corporation. Thus, the provisions of your trust governing when income and principal can be distributed must meet these requirements and the trustee should be given several specific powers to facilitate dealing with this special asset (see Chapter 21). Consider an *electing small business trust* (ESBT) as an alternative.

Charitable Lead or Remainder Trust

These trusts are formed to achieve specific tax advantages. The provisions of the trust governing the distribution of income and principal must conform strictly to applicable IRS requirements or the intended tax benefits will be lost. The documents governing these trusts are generally modeled very closely after suggested IRS forms (see Chapter 17).

Marital Trust

There are several key exclusions from the federal gift and estate tax, a major one being the right to transfer unlimited assets to your spouse or to special types of trusts for your spouse (assuming she is a U.S. citizen). If you wish to protect the assets put aside for your spouse, while still qualifying for the marital deduction, you can place those assets in a marital trust. However, to qualify for the marital deduction, the trust must meet the requirements of the federal gift or estate tax marital deduction. The most common spousal trust that meets these requirements is a *Qualified Terminable Interest Property Trust* (QTIP trust). One of the basic requirements is that all of the income from that trust must be distributed, at least annually, to your spouse. The income distribution provisions of your trust must conform to these requirements of the tax law for you (in the case of a gift to such a trust) or your estate (in the case of a marital trust funded on your death) to qualify for this deduction. (See Chapters 10 and 14.)

Dynasty Trust

A perpetual or *dynasty trust* is a trust that is intended to last forever. As such, the trust must be formed in a state whose laws permit a trust of infinite duration and have trustee provisions (and perhaps other quasi-fiduciary provisions) that facilitate a trust lasting for so long. The special provisions that make a dynasty trust work will affect almost every major set of trust provisions, and often will create new provisions unique to this type of trust.

References to Further Discussions

The previous provisions demonstrate how the income and distribution provisions of your trust may have to address the specific character and nature of the assets transferred to your trust, the purpose of your trust, tax planning, and other factors. These matters are addressed in detail in Chapter 8, "Distribution of Income and Principal, and Miscellaneous Provisions," and in Parts Two and Three.

BUILDING BLOCK 8: TERMINATION OF YOUR TRUST

Most trusts are not intended to last forever. Even a dynasty trust intended to last indefinitely should still include some leeway in case the trust principal shrinks to the point where maintaining the trust is impractical. Every trust should include some provisions addressing if, when, and how the trust should end.

A major determinant of when a trust ends is the distribution provisions, when the principal is to be paid out. If your trust provides that all assets must be distributed on the child-beneficiary's attaining age 35, then the trust will end shortly thereafter. The trust must end because it will have fulfilled its purpose and will no longer have any assets. Perhaps the only steps to be performed after the final payment to the beneficiary pursuant to the terms of the trust will be an *accounting* to the beneficiaries (an analysis of all financial transactions demonstrating that the final payment is correct) and a final income tax return.

A trust may end, however, at an earlier date than the final (residual or contingent) beneficiary reaching a particular milestone (such as graduating from college). You can, for example, give the trustee the power to terminate the trust if it should become so small as not to be economical to manage. This matter is explored in Chapter 25, "Trust Termination."

BUILDING BLOCK 9: MISCELLANEOUS TRUST PROVISIONS

There are several important provisions that are included in most trusts, including definitions of key terms in your trust document (if not defined in earlier provisions of the trust), specification of which state law should govern, the situs of the trust (the state or country in which the trust should be deemed located), and several technical legal provisions governing how your trust document should be interpreted in the event there are ever questions as to what should be done. These matters are reviewed in Chapter 9, "Miscellaneous Trust Provisions and Exhibits."

BUILDING BLOCK 10: SIGNATURE AND EXHIBITS

Trusts created under your will must comply with the laws of your state laws that govern how wills must be signed. Trusts created while you are alive (inter-vivos) will have to conform to your state's laws governing trusts, and if none address this issue, then your state's laws governing how contracts must be signed (since trusts are contracts). Similarly, the trustee may need to sign the trust documents to accept the trust.

CAUTION: You may have to coordinate the date your trust is signed and the date certain assets are transferred to your trust. This is especially important when specific tax results are intended. Speak to your estate planner and be certain that you follow up on any steps you assumed responsibility for.

Signatures often need to be notarized. Sometimes this is not done because of time constraints or other problems. In such cases, the signatures may be witnessed by one or two witnesses. Check with your attorney about state law requirements.

A schedule is usually attached to a trust listing the assets transferred to the trust. In many situations, this may list only a nominal initial deposit (perhaps $100) to start the trust, with the primary assets being transferred at a later date. Be cautious, merely listing an asset on the schedule is often insufficient; you may have to take additional steps to properly transfer ownership to the trust. (See Chapter 3.)

NOTE: To transfer insurance, you must complete the forms from the insurance company to change (for an existing policy) or designate (for a new policy) the trust as owner and beneficiary. Merely listing the insurance policy in a schedule attached to the trust will not complete the transfer and will probably not bind the insurance company.

CONCLUSION

This chapter summarized the key components of a typical trust. The chapters that follow provide greater detail, giving you the tools to begin understanding and working with trusts. This summary helps your understanding of the relevance of any particular part of a trust document to the overall purpose of the trust.

3 TRANSFERRING ASSETS TO YOUR TRUST

The assets you transfer to your trust (the trust property, or *res*) are one of the five key elements essential to every trust. The selection of the assets for a particular trust is critical to the planning process, to the provisions included in the trust document, and to the eventual operation of the trust.

- Certain types of property require that special provisions be included in the trust document to deal with them, for example, insurance and stock in an *S corporation*.
- Special expertise on the part of the trustee may be required for other assets. For example, stock in a closely held business may imply a need for a trustee with relevant business experience. Many institutions will not serve as trustees of a trust holding substantial private business interests, or will only serve as an administrative trustee (i.e., not responsible for the business).
- A large securities portfolio could indicate a need for a trustee with investment expertise, or for naming an *investment adviser*. (See Chapter 7.)
- If you establish a trust under the laws of a particular state (e.g., a dynasty trust formed in Alaska), you cannot transfer real estate in another state to the trust since the real estate may be subject to the laws of the state in which it is located, and not the laws of the state where the trust is based.
- The nature and quantity of the assets transferred is also critical. If you hope to use a trust to avoid probate, then every asset of yours which would otherwise require probate to transfer, should be transferred to your trust.

CAUTION: This is not nearly as easy as many seminars and "how-to" books imply. A pension, other retirement asset, insurance policy, made payable to your estate could then require your will be probated. A lottery winning, business asset your partners will not permit you to transfer, and so on, could all prevent you from achieving a no probate goal. (See Chapter 12.)

This chapter considers these and other questions, and also discusses the methods to transfer various types of assets to your trust.

FUNDED AND UNFUNDED TRUSTS

A trust can either be *funded* or *unfunded* (*stand-by*). A funded trust is a trust to which you transfer assets now. For example, if you wish to set up a trust for the benefit of your children, you will probably transfer assets to the trust each year. An unfunded trust is a trust to which no assets are transferred when the trust is formed. You may transfer a nominal amount of cash, perhaps $100, to such a trust in order to activate the trust and open a bank account. Unfunded trusts have many uses. For example, if you wish that the assets in your estate be poured over into a trust, you could establish a trust that has no assets, but which will later receive the assets from your estate.

SHOULD YOU TRANSFER ASSETS TO YOUR TRUST?

How you fund your trust may in part be determined by the nature of the trust you are setting up. If the trust is being set up to provide management of your assets if you are disabled, it could be funded to assure continuity once you become disabled. Alternatively, the trust could be funded by the agent appointed under a durable power of attorney in the event of your disability. A power of attorney is a document in which you designate a person as your agent and authorize him to take care of specified matters, such as financial, legal, and tax matters, for you. If you wish to use a trust to avoid probate, the trust should be funded with all assets to accomplish its objective, since only assets transferred to the trust before your death will be assured of avoiding probate (see Chapter 13). If you have real estate in several states, it can be advantageous to avoid probate in the states other than where you reside (called *ancillary probate*). This can be accomplished only if the real estate located in states other than where you live (where you are *domiciled*) is transferred to your trust or into limited liability companies or other entities (which should convert real estate which would be subject to ancillary probate into intangible personal assets that should not be subject to ancillary probate).

HOW TO TRANSFER ASSETS TO YOUR TRUST

When your trust is intended to own assets, two steps are typically used to transfer assets to a trust. First, the assets should be listed in the trust document (or in a schedule attached to the trust document) as trust property. Second, the assets should be formally transferred to the trust. For real estate to be transferred to your trust, you must have a new deed completed listing the trust as owner. For interests in a family limited partnership (FLP), the partnership agreement should be signed by the trustee, the schedule attached to the partnership agreement (or the body of the agreement, depending on your lawyer's style) should be amended to indicate the trust as the owner, and in many cases the attorney should have the prior owner (i.e., you) sign an Assignment of Partnership Interests document to transfer ownership. Each type of asset has its own unique issues that you should have your attorney help you address.

WHAT TYPES OF ASSETS SHOULD BE TRANSFERRED TO YOUR TRUST

Almost any type of asset can be held in trust. The assets can be *tangible* (equipment, buildings), *intangible* (stocks, bonds, patents), *real* (buildings, land) or *personal* (equipment, paintings). The decision as to which specific assets to transfer to what type of trust, however, can be much more complex.

Deciding what assets should be transferred to your trust, or trusts (you may need more than one), must start with an assessment of your overall financial and estate planning goals, the nature and value of your assets and the likely appreciation of those assets, your current and future cash needs, and so forth. A few examples will illustrate:

EXAMPLE: You are a retired widower and concerned about managing your money and financial affairs. Your estate consists of a condominium worth $675,000 and marketable securities worth $800,000, for a total estate of $1,475,000. It may be appropriate to transfer all of your assets into a revocable living trust. You will continue to manage your assets while you are able. When you are no longer able to, a mechanism is in place for your chosen trustees to immediately assume management responsibility. Your estate could avoid probate (if that was a concern of yours), possibly saving your heirs expenses and delays. In this scenario, all assets could be transferred to your trust. The problem with the above plan is that it may not be complete. You have not addressed a potentially substantial estate tax cost (depending on the year you die, the exclusion available in that year, and how much your estate value will appreciate). You probably will not wish to give away or encumber your securities since you are probably living off the income. You might use a *Qualified Personal Residence Trust* (QPRT) to remove the value of your home from your estate at a substantially discounted rate (see Chapter 22). Thus, you could transfer your securities to a living trust and your house to a QPRT. Determining the assets to transfer first requires the identification of the overall plan.

EXAMPLE: Tom and Tina Taxpayer are a couple in their forties who have an estate valued at approximately $2.8 million. This consists of $800,000 of rental real estate, $1,000,000 in a family limited partnership; $250,000 equity in their home; and $750,000 in certificates of deposit, bonds, and stocks. The Taxpayers' estate is in excess of the amount that can be shielded by the $1 million exclusion (as of 2002) to which each of them is entitled (see Chapter 10). The Taxpayers wish to begin a gift program whereby they will give gifts to trusts for their children to reduce their combined estate to approximately the $2 million level where no federal estate tax will be due. The investment real estate or noncontrolling interests in the FLP, are likely to be the preferable assets to use for the gift: The parents may still exert significant control over the asset and the real estate or FLP may be the assets most likely to appreciate, so a gift of real estate and/or FLP interests will remove the most future appreciation from their estate. An alternative may be to transfer the real estate to a limited liability company (LLC) and make gifts of membership interests in the LLC directly to the children, or to trusts established for the children. This can limit liability, assure a greater measure of control (with either Tom or Tina serving as manager of the LLC), and—most importantly—qualify gifts to the trusts for discounts for lack of marketability and lack of control. Gifts to children, however, should be coordinated with gifts to Section 529 college savings plans, gifts to insurance trusts, and other gifts that may exhaust the Taxpayers' annual gift exclusions.

EXAMPLE: The Youngcouples are in their early thirties and have a combined estate worth approximately $150,000. However, the husband, the sole bread-winner, has a $2.5 million term life insurance policy. If the husband establishes an irrevocable life insurance trust, and transfers the life insurance, and all incidents of ownership in the insurance to the trust, the couple will have effectively eliminated any potential estate tax (assuming the husband survives for three years after the transfer). The trust will provide for the management of the substantial insurance proceeds in the event of the husband's untimely death. The insurance trust, if written with a spendthrift provision, offers a measure of protection for the insurance proceeds from the wife's and children's creditors, or if the wife remarries.

The type of trust can also have an effect on your selection of assets to transfer to a trust. For example, if your trust is revocable, you can change the trust at any time. Therefore, there is less concern about which assets you transfer to the trust. You can always get them back. If the objective of your trust is to provide for you in the event of your disability, then it may be advisable to fund the trust with some amount of liquid assets to ensure immediate continuation of income in the event of your disability. Remaining assets can be transferred by someone named as your *agent* (attorney-in-fact) under a *durable power of attorney.*

Always investigate the costs of, and possible legal restrictions on, transferring particular assets to a trust. Real estate transfers may cause you to incur transfer taxes, recording fees, and mortgage or deed taxes; require a new title insurance policy; trigger a call of your mortgage; give a tenant the right to cancel a lease; and so forth.

Business and investment interests may have restrictions on transfers. For example, investment limited partnership interests may only be transferable with the consent of a general partner which may be withheld for any reason. Stock interests in a family or other closely held business may be restricted so that they cannot be transferred without the approval of the board of directors or a majority of other shareholders. Interests in a professional corporation (e.g., a medical or law practice) may be illegal to transfer to any nonprofessional (including a trust). Don't despair, however, there may be more creative ways to address the issue. For example, while the interests in a professional practice itself may not be transferable, it may be possible to transfer the building in which the practice is located, the equipment, and perhaps other assets to a trust.

EXAMPLE: Terri Taxpayer is a doctor and quite concerned about the risk of expensive and unwarranted medical malpractice claims. She makes a gift of all her equipment and the building in which she operates her practice to an irrevocable trust for the benefit of her children. She then leases the equipment and building back from the trust at the current fair rental rate, as established by an independent appraisal. If the transfer is made sufficiently in advance of any claim, it may be possible that the assets held in the trust for her children will escape unscathed. Further, this plan may be advantageous from an estate planning perspective by removing assets from Terri's estate. Finally, there may be income tax savings if the children are in a lower tax bracket than Terri and income from the trust is distributed to them (and the *kiddie tax* doesn't apply).

Whenever an irrevocable trust is involved, it is important to exercise caution since the transfer generally cannot be undone once completed. Before transferring assets to an irrevocable trust for the benefit of someone else (e.g., a child, grandchild, or other heir) be certain that, even in the worst-case financial scenario, you will not need the assets in the future.

For certain tax-oriented trusts such as a *grantor retained annuity trust* (GRAT) or a *charitable remainder trust* (CRT) it might seem preferable for the assets transferred to be income producing in order to make the required periodic payments. Raw land might seem inappropriate since no income is generated. However, in many cases, stock paying small or no dividends is ideal for transfer to a GRAT if substantial appreciation is anticipated. Shares of stock can be transferred back to you in lieu of cash in order to meet the periodic payments. In a CRT, non-income producing property is commonly transferred. The charity that receives it can sell the property without incurring capital gains taxes. Further, a FLIP-NIMCRUT type of CRT can be used. This is a specialized type of CRT designed to accept non-income producing property so that no payments are made to you initially, but after the property is sold, larger payments would commence. Thus, be careful in making generalizations about how a trust should be funded. What might seem intuitively best is often not. Consult with an estate planner for guidance.

Finally, it is important to consider when your trust will be funded. Where the trust is established under your will, few steps may be required (other than signing the will) before your death. However, you may have to change the ownership (*title*) of assets from joint ownership to your name (or your spouse's name) alone so that, upon your death, the assets will pass through your estate into the desired trust. If this is not done, the assets will pass to the surviving joint owner by operation of law, skipping your estate and potentially making ineffective any trust planning under your will. For testamentary trusts, your executor may decide what assets to transfer to the trust after your death. It is generally advisable not to specify in your will which assets are to be transferred to which trusts, unless special circumstances necessitate it. If you do, and the asset values fluctuate, or the asset named is sold or destroyed prior to your death, it can become quite burdensome for your executor to address the legal problems thus created (see Chapter 10).

HOW TO TRANSFER ASSETS TO YOUR TRUST

Once you have decided which assets to transfer to your trust, you and your attorney must complete the necessary steps and documentation to properly transfer those assets. The steps that must be taken will depend on the current ownership arrangements of each of the assets involved. The following discussion highlights some of the considerations. Since custom, practice, and law can vary from state to state, it is important to consult with an attorney in your area. (See www.laweasy.com for sample generic forms.)

Real Estate

Real estate can be transferred to your trust by properly completing a quit-claim or gift deed from the current owners to the trust. It is important to review your prior deed (the deed transferring the property to you) to ascertain exactly who the present owners are and how their names appear. If you are not the sole owner, you will have to obtain the consent and signatures of the other owners. Also, if there will be owners other than your trust, you should carefully consider how this will affect the management or use of the property.

EXAMPLE: You own 25 percent of a rental property. Three friends each own the remaining 25 percent interests. You give your property interest to a trust for your domestic partner. This trust will now own 25 percent of the property while your three friends will continue to own the remaining interests. There should be a partnership agreement between the four partners (i.e., the three friends and the trust) governing the ownership, use, financing, sale, and other aspects of the property.

There are several important ancillary considerations when transferring real estate:

- You may need a new *title insurance* policy in the name of the trust in order to retain your coverage. Title insurance insures against claims that you do not own the property. For example, someone sues you, claiming they had purchased a portion or all of the property in the past, or that they have an *easement* (right of way) over your property, or some other ownership interest. The title company will protect you. Where there is a transfer of title to a new person, such as your trust, the title company may require that the trust purchase a new policy. In other cases, only a nominal fee will be charged to add the trust as an additional insured on the policy. You should be certain this matter has been properly resolved with the title company in advance, and the costs considered.
- Be certain that the liability and fire insurance policies are properly amended to reflect the names of the new owner, your trust, and its trustees.

- Mortgage recording fees and taxes, real estate transfer taxes, and recording fees for the deed should all be considered. In some situations, the costs will be so significant that your planning may change.

CAUTION: Inquire as to whether the transfer of real estate to your trust may trigger a property tax reassessment or a change to a different tax rate. If your property is presently undervalued, this could result in a substantial increase in taxes.

- If there is a mortgage on the property, you should have your lawyer review the current mortgage and note documents. These documents may require that the mortgage be repaid when the property is transferred unless the lender consents otherwise. This may not be a simple matter to resolve. Many mortgages are sold, and often resold, in the secondary markets. It may take some effort just to identify to whom you should even ask the question. Occasionally, mortgages permit the transfer of equity to certain varieties of trusts. If so, you may have limited, if any, formalities to address.
- You should also review any potential income tax consequences with your accountant prior to the transfer. A transfer of encumbered property can sometimes have adverse and costly income tax consequences. The rules are complex, so consult an income tax expert before making any changes.
- If the property is being used by you personally before the transfer (e.g., a vacation home owned initially by you), you may have to sign a lease with the trust to have the legal right to continue using the property (once you transfer the vacation home to the trust, you don't own it and therefore you may have to pay rent to use it). You must pay a fair market rental for this use. Where the trust is a revocable living trust for your own benefit, a lease won't be necessary because for tax purposes you will continue to be treated as the owner of the property. For a qualified personal residence trust (QPRT), you won't have to pay rent to live in your house during the trust term, but you will have to pay rent following the completion of the trust term. There are other exceptions.

Bank Accounts

Call your bank. They will provide you with the necessary forms, including signature cards. The bank will also probably ask to see the trust agreement. You will also need to have a federal tax identification number for the trust to open a bank account in the trust's name. You will have to order new checks with the name of the trust. Also, it will be the trustee who will have to sign the checks after the transfer of the account to the trust. Ask the bank for details as to any formalities they may require.

Securities

If you own stocks or bonds in your own name, you will have to contact the transfer agent for the security and obtain the necessary transfer forms, such as a stock power. Complete the forms and return them with the stock or bond certificates. The transfer agent will re-issue the certificates in the name of the trust.

CAUTION: Never send any original stock or bond certificate through regular mail. Always use certified or registered mail, return receipt requested, so that you will have proper records in the event the securities do not arrive. Also, be certain to make photocopies of all documents before sending them.

For some transfers, you may be requested to provide a guarantee or verification of your signature. This can be troublesome, particularly for the infirm seeking to establish a trust to manage their assets, because this will require a separate trip to the bank.

NOTE: Open a brokerage account and transfer the securities to the account. Once the securities are held by the brokerage firm in an account in your name, it will be dramatically easier for your broker to change the name of the entire account to the name of your trust. The broker, however, will likely require the same documents noted above for the transfer of bank accounts.

Partnership or Limited Liability Company Interests

Partnership and *limited liability company* (LLC) interests are transferred by signing an *assignment of partnership interest* form. You must carefully review the partnership agreement (or operating agreement in the case of an LLC) prior to making any transfer. The agreement may prohibit any type of transfer. It may require the approval of some or all of the other partners (or members), or perhaps the general partners (or managers). In some states, certificates may have to be filed at the state or county level. The *partnership (operating)* agreement may require that you pay the legal and filing fees to complete the necessary filings.

CAUTION: Carefully ascertain whether your attempted transfer of a partnership interest could trigger mandatory buy-out provisions contained in the agreement. This is critical because some buy-out agreements could then require you to sell your interests to the other partners (members). Verify with your tax adviser that your transfer, when aggregated with other recent transfers, will not cause a technical termination of the partnership (LLC) for federal income tax purposes.

Stock in a Closely Held Corporation

The transfer of stock is accomplished by complying with any requirements of a shareholders' agreement, articles of incorporation or by-laws, and signing a stock power authorizing the transfer of the particular stock on the corporation's books. You will have to surrender your stock certificates. These will be canceled and retained by the corporation. The corporation will then issue new stock certificates in the name of your trust. The changes will be noted in the corporation's stock transfer ledger. In most closely held corporations, you will also obtain minutes of the board of directors, or a unanimous consent of all shareholders and directors, authorizing the transaction. The trustee will probably have to sign a copy of the corporation's shareholders' agreement, agreeing to be bound by the terms of the agreement. The corporation may require a legal opinion that the trustee has the authority to hold the stock.

If the corporation is an S corporation, your trust must meet the strict requirements in order not to jeopardize the favorable tax status of the corporation (see Chapter 21).

Furniture, Art, Jewelry, and Other Tangible Personal Property

Ownership of these types of assets is demonstrated by a signed *bill of sale.* If the transfer is a gift, a *gift declaration* is often signed as well. This is a statement, usually signed by the donor, witnessed, and notarized, indicating that the transfer of stock is a gift (rather than a sale or other type of transaction). This is particularly important if you wish to prove to the IRS that certain assets were transferred to the trust at a certain time and as a gift. (See www.laweasy.com for a sample form.)

CONCLUSION

Selecting the right assets and then properly transferring them to your trust is critical to make your trust accomplish your desired goals. Proper formalities must be observed to make the transfers effective. Most of these transfers will require the assistance of a professional (broker, accountant, real estate attorney, corporate attorney, or estate planner).

4 GRANTOR'S RIGHTS AND POWERS

The grantor of a trust is also referred to as the *settlor* or *trustor*. This is the person who sets up the trust and generally the person who transfers most of the assets to the trust. Typically, there is only one grantor. However, in some states, the custom is to have a joint revocable living trust in which both spouses may be grantors. In other cases, such as a survivorship (also called *second to die*) insurance trust, both you and your spouse may be listed as grantors.

GRANTOR'S POWERS DETERMINE TYPE OF TRUST

When setting up a trust, it is important to carefully review any right or power which you, the grantor, will have under the trust agreement. The powers and rights of the grantor are very important to consider. They can dramatically affect the tax consequences of the trust, the level of control the grantor has, the degree of protection from claimants which the trust will provide, and other important aspects of the trust.

The powers which the grantor should, or should not, retain over the trust will vary depending on the type of trust involved. The discussions later in this chapter summarize some of the key powers typically held, or not held for many common trusts.

YOUR RIGHT AS GRANTOR TO REVOKE OR MODIFY THE TRUST

A *revocable trust* is a trust which you form, but over which you retain (in the trust agreement) the right to modify, change, or revoke. Revocability of the trust has profound tax and legal implications. If you can revoke the trust, or can make substantial modifications to it, the assets of the trust will be included in your estate for gift and estate tax purposes. If your goal is to minimize estate taxes, this is unlikely to be an appropriate manner to structure the trust. On the other hand, if you are using a trust to assure management of your assets during disability and to avoid probate, there may be no reason not to retain the unlimited right to modify the trust. This is the case with revocable living trusts (see Chapter 13).

Revocable Living Trusts

The most common revocable trust is the revocable living trust. Since these trusts are not intended to be completed transfers for gift and estate tax purposes and are not meaningful for protecting assets from creditors, there is really no limit to the control you can have. Be certain to have a specific provision in your revocable living trust stating that it is revocable. Under the laws of many states, if your trust doesn't specify that it is revocable, it will, by law, be treated as irrevocable. When determining whether your trust should be revocable or irrevocable, remember that on your death the trust becomes irrevocable. Further, if you are disabled, you may no longer have the legal capacity to revoke your trust. Thus, your trust will become irrevocable at that point. It is important to have a provision in your trust defining when you should be considered disabled. Finally, every trust you establish may have several trusts incorporated in its trust agreement. For example, if you establish a revocable living trust to manage your affairs in the event of disability and to avoid probate, that trust may include a credit shelter trust, a QTIP trust, and so forth. These trusts, included in your revocable living trust agreement, will become effective on your death when they are effectively irrevocable. So just because the main trust is revocable, does not mean that it cannot include trusts which are more commonly considered irrevocable.

Trusts under Your Will

You cannot have any ongoing control over trusts established under your will since these trusts, although documented while you are alive, are not formed until following your death. These are called *testamentary trusts*. However, you can change the provisions of any testamentary trust by changing your will. You always have the right to change your will if you haven't signed a contract with someone (typically a second spouse or partner) that you won't change certain provisions in your will. You also must have sufficient awareness and ability (in legal terminology, capacity) to change your will. Thus, even testamentary trusts can be changed prior to your death.

CAUTION: The 2001 Tax Act created tremendous change and uncertainty. The exclusion amount is supposed to increase substantially, then the estate tax is eliminated and carry over basis rules instituted, and then the estate tax is reinstated. The best plan is to revise your estate plan periodically to address these changes. But if you rely on this "wait and see" attitude instead of trying to have a complex and comprehensive will done now, you face the risk noted above. If you become incompetent (due to age or illness), you won't be able to revise your will. Everyone must weigh the current cost of a more comprehensive will against the risks of not being able to update it.

Irrevocable Trusts

Most tax-oriented trusts, including typical insurance trusts, child's trusts, grandchild's trusts, grantor retained annuity trusts, and charitable trusts, are structured to be completed gifts for gift tax purposes. Thus, you would not be given a right as grantor to revoke the trust and your control over the trust is limited.

For some foreign trusts, or even a domestic Alaska or Delaware trust, your estate planner may have you retain sufficient rights over the trust to avoid transfers to the trust being treated as completed gifts for gift tax purposes. These situations involve very complicated tax issues that you will have to have a specialist address.

NOTE: Tax results should not be the sole factor in determining the types of powers you as grantor retain over a trust you form. Make sure that your personal, financial, and other goals are considered in the process. For example, if you are concerned about malpractice suits, you may prefer to severely restrict any rights you have to a particular trust to make it less likely for a claimant to be able to attack the trust. Generally, you cannot be a beneficiary of a trust which you establish (i.e., you are the grantor and fund the trust) and have the trust assets protected from creditors under most states' laws. This is because the trust will be deemed a "self-settled" trust and courts will likely pierce the trust to satisfy claims.

Alaska and Delaware are among the few states that have changed this rule. Thus, you can create a self-settled asset protection trust in these states. However, the laws governing these trusts are new and relatively unproven. This is why some estate planners recommend that trusts be established under foreign jurisdictions with more favorable laws to accomplish asset protection goals.

Irrevocable Trusts Can Be Flexible

Irrevocable trusts cannot be changed. This, as noted earlier, is important to achieve planning objectives. This does not mean you cannot build flexibility into an irrevocable trust to mollify your concerns about its permanence. Some of the techniques you should review with your estate planner include:

- The right to remove and replace a trustee, such as an independent institutional trustee, can be given to the beneficiaries by vote, and even to you as the grantor.
- You can designate a trust protector who can be given the right to make certain specific changes such as replacing the trustee, changing the situs and state law applicable to the trust, and so forth.
- You can give people you choose powers to designate who should receive the trust assets in the future (called *powers of appointment*).
- The trust can be structured as a *sprinkle trust* so that the trustee can distribute money to anyone on a listing of potential beneficiaries so that whoever is in need can be helped.

Irrevocable trusts are not quite as "carved in stone" as you might think. What happens if you included a myriad of flexible provisions but the circumstances change so dramatically that you really have to change or terminate the irrevocable trust? It may be possible to change the trust if every person with any interest in the trust (grantor, trustees, current beneficiaries, remainder beneficiaries, and perhaps even certain contingent beneficiaries) all agree. This, however, is not a simple matter to achieve, and it may require a court proceeding to accomplish. If the court finds that the purposes for which the trust was created are no longer existent, it might authorize the termination of the trust. Terminating an irrevocable trust prior to the time the trust agreement permits is discussed in Chapter 25. Never rely on this approach at the outset as an affirmative planning tool. If you are not certain that the trust should be irrevocable, consider alternatives to an irrevocable trust.

TIP: In some instances, a *family limited partnership* (FLP) or a *limited liability company* (LLC) can be used to accomplish similar objectives to a trust without having to be irrevocable. The agreement governing the FLP or LLC can be changed by the partners or members, respectively, so long as the terms of the agreement are met (e.g., a requirement that at least two-thirds of the partners or members approve a particular change). Using these entities, the parent or donor can retain substantial control as the general partner in the FLP, or as the manager in an LLC.

Questions to Consider When Planning an Irrevocable Trust

When reviewing the provisions to include in a irrevocable trust, consider the following questions in determining what type of flexibility to include in the document:

- Are you confident in the ability of the trustees and the successor trustees named in the trust agreement to carry out their duties in a professional manner? This concern can sometimes be addressed through rethinking the trustees. For example, perhaps you name an institution and an individual as co-trustees.
- Have the needs of the beneficiaries been adequately provided for? Where you have a trust that is not permitted to pay more than income to the current beneficiary, what will happen if that beneficiary suffers an unforeseen calamity, such as disability? Where the trust is irrevocable, and adequate safeguards and discretion have not been built in, tremendous hardship can result. This is why it is so important to ask many "what-if" questions when planning a trust, and to make the distribution provisions as flexible as appropriate in order to address future uncertainties.
- Can you and those who you are responsible for afford to live comfortably and handle any emergencies that may arise for the remainder

of your lives if you make gifts to irrevocable trusts for children or other heirs?

CAUTION: Too often parents, aunts, uncles, and other seniors are pushed hard by future heirs to establish a trust for the heirs' benefit to remove assets from the seniors' taxable estates, save taxes, and perhaps protect against possible future costs of a long-term illness. Once the assets are transferred to a trust, the senior has no further control. Don't set up such a trust unless you are truly comfortable doing so, and under even the worst case scenario you will be left with sufficient resources to support your lifestyle. No senior can relish the thought of having to ask a child, niece, nephew, or other heir for money.

- Will marriage, divorce, or other major family events require that the trust be changed in order for basic business matters to be conducted, or basic living needs provided for?

EXAMPLE: An obstetrician, concerned about malpractice risks, transfers every asset he owns, except his practice, to an irrevocable trust for his wife, who is a homemaker and thus does not face any particular risk of creditors or other claimants. He even transfers all of the equipment and the office building used by his practice to a trust for his children. He then enters into a lease agreement to rent the use of the equipment from the trust. The trustee of both trusts is an independent trust company, Bigbank. The trusts, in addition to being irrevocable, do not provide any right to the trustee to distribute any income or principal to the obstetrician. Trust distributions can only be made to the wife, and after the wife's death, to the children (and only for expenses that are not the obligation of the obstetrician under local law) under her trust. Distributions can only be made to the children under their trust. The wife and the obstetrician husband divorce. He has virtually no assets as a result of the trust arrangements. To terminate the trust will require the consent of an independent trust company (which may view the premature termination as violating its fiduciary obligations to the minor children), the wife (who, unless forced to do so by the courts, is unlikely to be interested in providing assets to her ex-husband), and the children. How can the minor children consent to termination of the trust? A court proceeding may be required with the court appointing a guardian to act on behalf of the interests of the children. What about the interests of any unborn children—how can they be protected? Even if termination of this trust is possible, which it probably will not be, it will be an expensive and time-consuming task.

GRANTOR (DEFECTIVE) TRUSTS

The gift and estate tax rules are independent of the income tax rules. The differences between the two tax systems create traps for the unwary taxpayer or planning opportunities for the astute taxpayer. Grantor trusts can present such an opportunity. A bit of background is necessary. A *grantor trust* is a trust whose income is taxed to you as the grantor having formed the trust. A revocable living trust is a common example. However, in contrast to a revocable living trust, which you can change at any time, a trust can be irrevocable so that assets transferred to the trust are removed from your estate (i.e., a completed gift for gift and estate tax purposes), yet the trust income may still be taxed to you for income tax purposes. This type of trust is sometimes referred to as a *defective* grantor trust because it is a completed transfer for gift and estate tax purposes without being recognized for income tax purposes.

Income Tax Consequences of Grantor Trust Status

When a trust is taxed as a grantor trust for income tax purposes, the income, gain, and losses of the trust are reported on your personal income tax return. Thus, where the powers you (as grantor) retain over your trust are sufficient, the income earned by the trust will be taxed on your personal tax return, and not on a separate tax return filed by the trust (see Chapter 12). This type of trust is called a *grantor trust.*

Grantor trust status for income tax purposes is not always negative. For example, there generally will not be any income tax consequences to transactions between you (the grantor) and the trust. Thus, if you sell appreciated property (worth more than you bought it at) to a grantor trust, there will be no income tax cost to doing so. This is the basis of a sophisticated trust planning technique involving an installment sale of appreciated assets to an irrevocable grantor trust (IDIT or IDIGT).

Even though a trust is a grantor trust for income tax purposes, it may not necessarily be taxable in your estate for estate tax purposes. The rules are different.

Should Your Trust Be a Grantor Trust or Not?

The option you prefer (grantor trust taxable to you for income tax purposes, or nongrantor trust which files its own income tax return) will depend on the circumstances. In many planning scenarios, you will benefit from intentionally structuring your trust to be a grantor trust for income tax purposes, but not for gift and estate tax purposes. Consider the following:

- If a trust has significant tax deductions that you could claim on your personal tax return, you would want the trust to be a grantor's trust. For example, a charitable lead trust can be structured to be a grantor trust in order to permit an income tax charitable contribution deduction upon formation. A grantor charitable lead trust may then invest in tax-exempt bonds to avoid adverse income taxes in future years.
- If you set up a revocable living trust, it will have to be a grantor trust because you will retain complete power over the assets. Thus, you will have to report all of the income from the trust on your personal tax return since this can significantly simplify the tax reporting requirements (see Chapter 13).

- If you set up a Qualified Personal Residence Trust (QPRT), you will want to be certain it is a grantor trust so that if the trust sells the house, you can qualify for the $250,000 ($500,000 married filing jointly) home sale exclusion and the property tax deduction.
- If you establish a trust for a child, the maximum you can give each year to the trust is $10,000 (indexed for inflation, $11,000 in 2002). To give more to the trust without using up your lifetime exclusion, you structure the trust as a grantor trust. Thus, by paying the income tax on the child's trust, more money remains in the trust, for the child's benefit. The income tax you pay is the economic equivalent of an additional gift, but is arguably not taxable for gift tax purposes (needless to say, the IRS is not thrilled with this concept) (see Chapter 16).
- You may set up a foreign situs asset protection trust to protect assets. You may wish to structure the trust so that the transfer of assets is not a completed gift to avoid the 35 percent excise transfer on certain overseas transfers. If this is done, the assets of the trust could be included in your estate (see Chapter 18).
- If you set up an insurance trust, you want to assure that the insurance proceeds will be excluded from your estate. Therefore, you should be certain that your lawyer carefully drafts the trust to avoid tainting it with powers that would cause its inclusion in your estate. However, the insurance trust, at least in part, is likely to be characterized as a grantor trust for income tax purposes if income of the trust can be used to pay premiums on insurance policies on your life as grantor (see Chapter 19).

Estate and Gift Tax Consequences of a Grantor Trust

As explained earlier (and repeated again here because it is not intuitive or logical), the income tax rules differ from the gift and estate tax rules. You must plan the intended income tax result *and* the intended gift and estate tax result. If you want the assets transferred to the trust to be removed from your estate, you want the gift to be a completed gift. If you retain excessive powers and rights over your trust, the assets you give to the trust won't be a completed gift. They will remain, along with any future appreciation, taxable in your estate (see Chapter 10).

A common goal as the grantor is to retain sufficient powers to have the trust treated as a grantor trust for income tax purposes, but not to retain the powers that would have the trust treated as taxable to you for estate tax purposes. This is a technical tightrope, some aspects of which are described next.

What Makes a Trust a Grantor Trust for Income Tax Purposes?

If you, as the grantor, retain impermissible or excessive controls over the trust, the trust will be treated as a grantor trust for tax purposes. Just in case the concept of grantor trust wasn't complicated enough, a trust can be classified as a grantor trust with respect to the principal portion of the trust or the income portion of the trust, or both.

The following are some of the factors that could cause a trust to be treated as grantor trust for income tax purposes:

- *Right of Grantor's Spouse to Income.* If the trust will pay all of its income to your spouse, or accumulate the income for future payments to your spouse, the trust would be a grantor trust (at least with respect to the income) and would taxable to you for income tax purposes. Any rights that your spouse has will be attributed to you for purposes of this test. If this technique is relied on, consider what happens if your spouse dies. The intended tax status for the trust will be lost.

- *Power to Distribute Trust Assets to Class of Beneficiaries.* A trust may achieve grantor trust status if a related nonadverse trustee is given the right to distribute income and principal among a class of beneficiaries without the distributions' being restricted to maintaining the beneficiaries' standard of living (called an *ascertainable standard*). A party is related or subordinate to the grantor if he or she is a nonadverse party and is also the grantor's spouse, parent, descendant, brother, or sister. Other relatives, such as nephews, nieces, and in-laws, are not considered to be related. A nonadverse party is anyone who is not an adverse party. An adverse party is anyone who has a beneficial interest in the trust, whose interest is substantial, and whose interest would be adversely affected by the exercise or nonexercise of the power held by the grantor or a nonadverse party.

- *Use of Income to Pay Insurance Premiums.* Your trust will be a grantor trust to the extent that the income of the trust is or can be used to pay insurance premiums on your life as the grantor.

- *Right to Loan Money without Adequate Interest or without Adequate Security.* If a nonadverse party can authorize a loan to you the grantor, or to any other nonadverse person, such as your spouse, with either but not both, adequate interest or security, the trust should be characterized as a grantor trust.

- *Right to Add Beneficiaries.* The power held by a nonadverse trustee to add charitable beneficiaries can cause your trust to be taxed as a grantor trust for income tax purposes. However, this means that the trustee could name a charity to receive assets instead of your child.

These rules can apply to a portion of a trust—it is not an all-or-nothing situation. So if you retain the right to appoint the income, but not the principal, of the trust to anyone including yourself, the income will be taxable to you. The principal of the trust, however, may not be considered owned by you. Similarly, if you have the right to appoint one asset, such as a house, or certain bonds in a trust, but not the other assets, only the asset that you can appoint will be considered yours.

A trustee's rights to fees and commissions alone is not sufficient to classify the trustee as an adverse party.

There are certain powers that you, as grantor, can retain over the trust without having the trust income taxable to you. For example, you can have the power to distribute principal of the trust to any beneficiary in accordance with a reasonably definite (ascertainable) standard. You can have the right to withhold income temporarily, such as where a beneficiary is disabled or a minor. If these are the only powers you have over the trust, the trust will not be a grantor trust.

RIGHTS COMMONLY RESERVED OR AVOIDED BY GRANTORS IN SPECIFIC TYPES OF TRUSTS

With this background, you can now consider what types of rights you, as the grantor, would wish to have, or specifically refrain from having, in several common trusts:

- *Qualified Personal Residence Trust (QPRT).* You would reserve the right to live in the house during the term of the trust. Following the end of the trust, you might reserve the right to rent the property for fair rent from the beneficiaries (typically your children). You might serve as a trustee.

- *Grantor Retained Annuity Trust (GRAT).* You would reserve the right to a specified annuity payment (typically quarterly or annually). You might reserve the right to receive additional principal distributions beyond the periodic payment, but this is not common. You might serve as a trustee.

- *Charitable Remainder Trust (CRT).* You, and perhaps your spouse or another, reserve the right to a periodic annuity or unitrust payment.

- *Charitable Lead Trust (CLT).* For a nongrantor CLT you would hold few, if any, rights because the transfer to a charitable lead trust is designed to benefit a charity during its term and your heirs (typically children) after the term ends.

- *Domestic Asset Protection Trust (DAPT).* You might be a discretionary beneficiary and, depending on state law and the manner in which you have structured the trust reserve few or substantial additional benefits. These might include the right to veto distributions if the transfers to the trust are not intended to be "completed" gifts. If the transfers are to be completed gifts, you would restrict your powers considerably.

- *Insurance Trust (ILIT).* If the trust is a survivorship trust (insuring both your and your spouse's lives), you probably would retain few if any rights as grantor. However, if the ILIT is holding insurance on your spouse's life (she would be the grantor), you might be a co-trustee with considerable powers (although the powers you hold to make distributions would be limited) and you would likely be a beneficiary.

- *Child/Grandchild's Trust.* If your spouse was the grantor, you might serve as a co-trustee. Your powers as co-trustee would have to be restricted to avoid inclusion in your estate. If your spouse is grantor, she would not retain any significant powers, to assure that the transfers to the trust were completed gifts.

- *Qualified Terminable Interest Property (QTIP) Trust.* If you form a QTIP for your spouse during your lifetime, you would limit your powers so as to assure that the transfer is complete. You might, however, reserve the right on your spouse's death to be a beneficiary under a bypass trust provided for your benefit following her death.

SHOULD YOU AS THE GRANTOR ALSO SERVE AS A TRUSTEE OR CO-TRUSTEE?

If your trust is revocable, there is no particular disadvantage from a tax perspective for you to serve as a trustee. This is because a revocable trust will probably have no estate tax advantages in any event. Tax-oriented trusts are typically irrevocable and the objective is often (but not always) that the gifts you make to the trust as grantor be removed from your taxable estate. Other irrevocable trusts are intended to protect assets.

If the trust is intentionally structured as a grantor trust for income tax purposes (e.g., a QPRT or GRAT), you may wish to serve as a co-trustee. However, care must be taken so that the powers you exercise do not taint the trust assets as being included in your estate for estate tax purposes through broad trustee powers.

If your trust is irrevocable and not one of the tax-oriented grantor trusts noted earlier, and particularly when a goal of establishing your trust is to move assets beyond the reach of creditors or malpractice claimants, you should generally not serve as trustee or even as co-trustee. If it is inappropriate, for tax or legal purposes, for you to serve as trustee, your spouse should probably also not serve as trustee. This is because your spouse is not considered an adverse party—her powers or actions may be attributable to you. Thus, any adverse tax consequences that would occur as a result of your being a trustee could also occur as a result of your spouse serving as trustee. There are, however, exceptions—when your spouse would commonly serve as trustee. A common example is a trust for a child in which you are the grantor and your spouse a co-trustee. In such cases, the powers and rights that your spouse is given as trustee should be carefully restricted to avoid adverse tax problems. For example, your spouse's rights to distribute trust income or principal may be limited so that she cannot use trust income to discharge her legal obligation as a parent to support the child beneficiary.

CAN YOU AS THE GRANTOR CHANGE OR APPOINT A TRUSTEE?

If your trust is revocable, you will probably serve as trustee. Further, reserving the right to change or remove trustees is not a problem with a revocable trust since the trust is revocable by you in any event. Since most revocable trusts are not formed primarily for tax benefits, reserving this right should not create any problem.

If the trust involved is irrevocable, the situation is different. If you have an unlimited right in your trust to change trustees at your discretion, you may defeat the objectives of setting up your trust. An unrestricted right to remove existing trustees and appoint any person as successor trustee, in your sole discretion, gives you substantial control over the trust because you could dismiss any trustee who doesn't perform exactly as you wish and name one who will. For tax purposes, your right to remove trustees without restriction will be treated as if you have retained the rights of a trustee yourself. If, however, your right to replace a trustee is properly restricted to, say, replacing an independent institutional trustee with another institutional trustee, you can have a limited right to do so without losing the hoped-for benefits of your trust. This power will not taint the tax benefits of the trust. It will not cause the trust corpus to be included in your estate.

CONCLUSION

Always be certain that the trust you intend to establish meets your nontax needs and goals in addition to addressing income and estate tax issues. You should raise each of these issues with your planners. If your trust is revocable, you have substantial freedom to retain whatever rights you wish since the tax results are usually minimal. When tax issues are a primary objective of your trust, you will generally best be served by severely limiting any rights you retain over your trust, to assure that the assets are not taxed in your estate. If protection of assets is an important goal, less control may be best. For some trusts, you walk the fine line of having the trust income still taxed to you, while assuring that the principal assets are not taxed in your estate.

5 DESIGNATIONS AND RIGHTS OF BENEFICIARIES

Beneficiaries, the persons or organizations who will receive the income and principal of the trust, are one of the five essential elements to a trust (see Chapter 1). A number of important issues concerning beneficiaries must be addressed to achieve your goals in establishing a trust:

- Beneficiaries must be clearly designated. Who are they?
- You must determine how and when the beneficiaries should receive distributions. This could be at specific ages, on achieving certain milestones, or simply in the trustee's discretion.
- *Contingent beneficiaries* should be named in the event the primary beneficiaries are not alive when distributions are to be made, or do not wish to accept the benefits the trust bestows on them. When done properly, this can provide important planning flexibility to the beneficiaries.

EXAMPLE: In your will, you leave $50,000 to your aunt Kate. If Aunt Kate dies, this $50,000 would be distributed as part of your residuary estate under your will, or under a comparable provision under your trust, perhaps called *Alternative Distribution.* These are the backstop provisions that address where assets should be distributed if all prior provisions in the document lapse as a result of the death of the beneficiaries (or their unwillingness to accept the distributions). Perhaps if Aunt Kate died, you would prefer that her husband or surviving children receive the money. This can be accomplished with the following, more detailed provision: "$50,000 to my aunt Kate Smith, who resides at 555 Main Avenue, City Name, State Name. If she shall not survive grantor's death, to her surviving spouse. If she has no surviving spouse, then to her children in equal shares. If any child is not then living, or disclaims such bequest, to the then-living issue of such child, per stirpes. If there be no living issue, then this legacy shall lapse." The above provision provides additional planning flexibility. If Aunt Kate and her husband do not need the money, they can file a *disclaimer* (renunciation) in the appropriate court. This will have the legal effect as if they had died before you, so that they can cause the $50,000 to be distributed directly to their children. If a child is, for example, concerned about being sued, he too can file a disclaimer, causing the assets to pass to his children. See the discussion of GST tax in Chapter 11.

- Finally, certain powers and rights can be given to the beneficiaries. These will vary depending on the nature of the trust and your objectives in forming the trust. They may include a right to withdraw contributions (called a *Crummey* or *annual demand* power which is done for gift tax purposes), the right to demand principal distributions, possibly serving as a co-trustee, the right to change trustees, and perhaps other powers as well.

NAMING BENEFICIARIES OF YOUR TRUST

It is often obvious who the primary beneficiaries of your trust should be. Even so, the decision is more complex than most people realize, and can trigger tax or other issues that are easily overlooked.

Revocable Living Trust

If you are setting up a revocable living trust to provide for the management of your assets in the event that you become disabled, you will be the primary beneficiary. You may, however, permit other persons (spouse, children, or others) to be beneficiaries as well. However, distributions to these persons will likely constitute gifts for gift tax purposes. Thus, if those distributions are made to people other than your spouse and exceed $11,000, a gift tax may be due. On the other hand, if you don't name these other people as beneficiaries, your *successor trustee* (the trustee who takes over should you become disabled) won't have the legal right to use trust money to help them (see Chapter 9).

You will also name beneficiaries to receive the trust assets after your death. These may be your family, loved ones, friends, a favorite charity, or anyone else you select. Many people name as beneficiaries a combination of trusts. These could include a bypass trust to sprinkle income among your spouse and children while taking advantage of the exclusion available to your estate, a marital (QTIP) trust for your surviving spouse which will take advantage of the unlimited marital deduction, and trusts for children or other heirs to protect their inheritances until they reach ages which are more appropriate for distribution.

Thus, you, your spouse, and your children could all be beneficiaries of your living trust, although at different times and with different interests.

Trusts for Your Spouse

When setting up a trust for your spouse, or other partner, as described in Chapters 14 and 15, your spouse or other partner will be the primary beneficiary. If the trust is a bypass trust to take advantage of the tax exclusion available to your estate ($1 million in 2002), you may wish to name children or other heirs as beneficiaries along with your spouse. This can provide greater flexibility without sacrificing any tax benefit. However, as the estate tax exclusion increases as a result of the 2001 Tax Act (from $675,000 before the 2001 Tax Act to $1 million in 2002, and eventually to $3.5 million), you may be uncomfortable giving anyone other than your spouse access as a beneficiary to so much of your estate.

If the trust is intended to benefit your spouse and take advantage of the unlimited marital deduction, you may not name anyone other than your spouse to receive income (as opposed to principal) or you will jeopardize the important tax benefits (see Chapter 14).

If the prime beneficiary is not a married spouse, but rather a partner, the marital deduction will not be available. You must then carefully plan with your tax adviser to address this issue (see Chapter 15).

How do you specify who your spouse will be? In most cases, you will name your spouse (". . . to my wife, Jane Doe . . .") in the trust. However, with the 50 percent plus divorce rate, and the increasing use of long-term perpetual (dynasty) types of trusts, more flexibility may be appropriate. You could use what is called a "floating spouse clause." Instead of naming the specific person you are married to at the time the trust is prepared, you instead use general language saying that the beneficiary will be whoever is your spouse at the time the trust is operative. This approach enables you to establish an irrevocable trust while preserving some flexibility in the event of divorce or widowhood and remarriage.

For most marital trusts mentioned earlier, the trust will terminate only on the death of your spouse or partner. Thus, you must carefully designate the successor or contingent beneficiaries.

Trusts for Children or Other Heirs

If you set up trusts for your descendants, your children and/or grandchildren will be beneficiaries. You must carefully delineate who is to be considered a child. Is an adopted person a child for purposes of making distributions from the trust? What about a child born after the trust is established? What happens if a child dies before all distributions are made from the trust? Who should receive the deceased child's share? His or her own children? Your other children (i.e., the siblings of the deceased child)?

EXAMPLE: You name your children as beneficiaries of a trust, but something totally unexpected happens years later, you have another child. Is that child to be a beneficiary? It depends on the language used in the trust. If the trust says ". . . my children, Dick Doe and Jane Doe, only," a future child may not be covered. If instead, the trust says: ". . . my children, Dick, Jane, and Tom, and any later born children," the new child will be included as a beneficiary. State law, as well as the language of your trust, can affect the outcome, but the best approach is to be explicit in the trust agreement to avoid any confusion.

What if you adopt a child after setting up a trust for your natural children? Is the adopted child to be included? You can eliminate all doubt with explicit language: "My children Dick, Jane, and Tom, and any later born or adopted children."

If you set up a perpetual trust, how will your descendants be determined in the future? What about spouses of children and grandchildren? There can be a host of issues to address.

Trusts for Charity

When you form a charitable trust, charities will be among your beneficiaries, or the sole beneficiaries. Often, when naming charitable beneficiaries, there is a presumption that the charity qualifies for the unlimited gift or estate tax charitable contribution deduction. For some inter-vivos trusts the income tax charitable contribution deduction—where you are seeking a current income tax deduction such as a Charitable Remainder Trust—is similarly important. If this deduction is essential for your planning, be certain to verify when establishing the trust that the charitable beneficiary is qualified. Call the charity and confirm the name and principal business address (these can sometimes differ from the common public names) and request a copy of the letter the charity received from the IRS approving tax-exempt status. Save this with your permanent trust papers.

EXAMPLE: You name a charity as a beneficiary: "The sum of $70,000 to the ABC charity located at 123 Main Street, City Name, State Name, for its general purposes." Now ABC is defunct; you have a problem. Better language would be: "The sum of $70,000 to the ABC charity located at 123 Main Street, City Name, State Name, for its general purposes, or to its successor. In the event that such charity no longer exists, or no longer qualifies for the gift and estate tax unlimited charitable contribution deduction, to the DEF charity located at 456 State Street, City Name, State Name, for its general purposes, or to its successor. In the event that charity no longer exists, to a charitable organization named in the discretion of my trustee which has a similar purpose and which does qualify for the gift and estate tax unlimited charitable contribution deduction."

A legal doctrine called *cy pres* can act to preserve an intended charitable bequest, but it is usually preferable to name alternatives. The last clause in the example may also help avoid an unintended problem, or a lapse in a hoped for charitable gift.

When discussing with your attorney the provisions of your trust that relate to charitable gifts, be certain to address the tax qualification issue as well as the naming of successor charities. Also, consider which assets should be used to fund the charitable bequests. There can be advantages to using Individual Retirement Account (IRA) or other pension plan assets to fund your charitable gifts. For Charitable Remainder Trusts, it is advantageous to use appreciated assets to fund the trust since the trust can sell the assets without incurring any income tax.

CAUTION: If the charitable trusts are being formed under your will, have your estate planner carefully review the tax allocation clause of your will. This clause governs which bequests and assets bear the federal and state estate and inheritance tax clauses. Because charitable contributions are deductible, you will generally not wish them to bear any of the tax cost. If they do, you will reduce the amount of charitable deduction by the tax paid, hence increasing the overall tax cost. The result is a circular calculation and often not the economic result you want.

Bequests to charities offer a final opportunity for you to contribute something back to society and to make a final positive and helpful statement to your heirs about what is really important in life. Charitable bequests under a will or as part of a trust send an important message to your heirs. Don't overlook these vital nontax aspects of charitable giving (although the bequest below is nonideally structured from a tax perspective).

SAMPLE TRUST PROVISION: "When my child, Joan Smith, attains the age of 35 years, the Trustee shall distribute 95 percent of the trust estate to my child, outright and free of further trust, and the remaining 5 percent of the trust estate to XYZ charity, for its general purposes, in honor of Joan Smith. It is my hope and desire that the charitable portion of this distribution will set an example for Joan and encourage her further and continued charitable evolvement in the years to come."

HOW SHOULD ASSETS BE DIVIDED AMONG BENEFICIARIES?

If you set up a trust for a single child, the division of assets at the primary level of the trust (i.e., when the child who is the primary beneficiary is alive) is quite simple: Assets will be distributed only to that child. However, in many cases, the distribution mechanism must be more complex to accomplish your goals. For example, if the child is no longer alive, or if the child reaches a specified age and his or her interests in the trust terminate, alternate beneficiaries may then receive the trust assets. How should assets be distributed to a list of alternate or successor beneficiaries? If these provisions are not carefully drafted, tremendous complications could result as a court may have to be involved to sort out who gets what.

Apart from the common mistake of not listing enough beneficiaries and clarifying when successors should receive the bequests, another common problem is phrasing the language controlling the distributions in a manner that cannot work if circumstances change.

EXAMPLE: You contemplate funding a trust with $1 million. After your death, $100,000 will be distributed to each of your four nieces and nephews, and the remainder to your domestic partner, who is your primary heir. Your anticipation is that your partner would receive $600,000. First, this distribution scheme does not contemplate the effects of estate tax. If a $150,000 tax is paid out of the trust (because a portion of your exclusion was used previously), your partner will not receive what you anticipated. What happens if your estate declines to $500,000? If your partner was your primary concern, he or she will end up with little—not your goal. Evaluate the consequences of changes in the size of your trust's assets with your estate planner in formulating the distribution mechanisms you will use.

When preparing distribution provisions, always ask "what-if" questions. What if a beneficiary dies prematurely? What if a beneficiary wins the lottery and doesn't need the money? What if a beneficiary is in the midst of malpractice suit or is incompetent when distributions are to be made? What if the size of the estate or trust increases significantly? What if it decreases? How will expenses and taxes affect the distributions? Explore these and any other relevant issues with your estate planner when crafting trust language, and address any particular concerns which might be relevant to your trust. Alternative approaches can address many of these issues. For example, you can make all distributions discretionary with the trustee. If a beneficiary has a problem or doesn't need the money, the trustee may decide that no distribution will be made. You can set percentage and/or dollar limits on trust distributions.

Another common problem is drafting your trust to make distributions by percentages. Say you have four cousins you are leaving the trust assets to following your death. If your trust says: "Distribute 25 percent to Jane Doe, 25 percent to Tim Smith, 25 percent to Joe Perez, and 25 percent to Susan Chen." What happens if Tim Smith is not alive? Have you only distributed 75 percent of your trust? What happens with the remaining 25 percent? A better approach is to divide the trust estate into shares and sub-shares. If one or more of the bequests *lapses* (e.g., by the beneficiary dying or disclaiming), there is no issue as to the distribution of the assets. The math works.

SAMPLE TRUST PROVISION: Upon my death, the trustee shall divide the trust estate into the equal number of shares required by this provision, and distribute such shares outright, free of trust, to the persons named below. Should any such bequest lapse, then the remaining persons listed shall continue to share in the trust estate in the proportions set forth. The number of shares into which the trust estate shall be divided shall be the number of shares for those beneficiaries listed below, which bequests have not lapsed by the death, disclaimer, or other failure of such beneficiaries named. The following beneficiaries shall take under this provision:

(1) Three and one-half (3.5) shares shall be paid to my son John Smith.
(2) Three (3) shares shall be paid to my daughter Jane Doe.
(3) One (1) share shall be allocated to my grandchildren, (the "Grandchildren's Share") to be disposed of by the provision entitled "Grandchildren Pot Trust," below.
(4) One (1) share to be divided into the number of equal sub-shares which shall be the total number of sub-shares for those charitable beneficiaries listed below. The following beneficiaries shall take under this provision:
   i) One (1) sub-share to the American Humane Society, a not-for-profit corporation.
   ii) One (1) sub-share to the American Cancer Society, Inc., a not-for-profit corporation.

A little extra care and planning in designing the appropriate distribution scheme for your trust can assure that your distributions are made the way you want, to the people or causes you want, and with the least expense and delays. The small amount of extra time and legal fees required to have the provisions completed properly and thoroughly at the outset, and to run through various hypothetical "what- if" scenarios, can have a tremendous benefit to your intended heirs.

HOW SHOULD THE BENEFICIARIES RECEIVE THEIR DISTRIBUTIONS?

It is not enough to merely make sure the right people or organizations receive the distributions from your trust. They must receive it at the right time. This is one of the most complicated and often-ignored aspects of trust preparation. It is ignored because it cannot be done in isolation. You must review your entire estate plan, including all trusts, will distribution provisions, gift planning, and the like to properly address how distributions should be made.

The most difficult aspect of planning distributions, however, is that you must ask tough personal questions: How will the distribution of money affect my child/nephew/heir? Am I giving too much too fast so that I will impair the heir's motivation to become a productive individual? Am I being so controlling that my child or other heir will never develop the maturity necessary to best handle the money involved? Am I being so stingy that my child will resent me forever?

These are not easy questions. Most estate planners do not address these personal imperatives—the answers can hurt! If you do not carefully address these issues, however, all the best tax and legal planning will be for naught.

One approach which has received a lot of attention is called an *incentive trust*. The trustee is directed to pay trust income and/or assets to the beneficiary only when certain goals are achieved. For example, for any year in which the child achieves a grade point of B or better (or the equivalent) at any accredited school, the trustee is directed to distribute say $50,000 to the child. If the child earns $50,000 or more of earned income, then the trustee is directed to match the child's income dollar for dollar. The variations and milestones to warrant distributions are endless. The real question is, do incentive trusts work or do they merely antagonize the heir? There is no correct answer. The solution for you will depend on your particular circumstances and the personality of each heir involved. Incentive trusts raise tough administrative issues. For example, say you have two children. One becomes a world famous artist, but never completes school. The second child coasts through life and third-rate schools with no real goals or accomplishments. Under an incentive trust designed to make distributions based on grade point averages, the highly successful child will not be rewarded, while the mediocre child will be. If your incentive trust makes payments based simply on the beneficiaries' earnings, the trust would reward the child who develops a successful Internet gossip site, while penalizing the child who devotes her life to charitable volunteer work.

EXAMPLE: A child has received such large gifts from her grandparents, and such significant distributions from the trust her parents have set up, that she has never bothered completing college, obtaining a job, doing volunteer charitable work, or making any productive contribution to society. What difference does it make how much tax has been saved? Lack of forethought has perhaps destroyed the child whose welfare was the very goal of the family. Perhaps it would have been better had the grandparents made their gifts in trust and had distributions withheld. Perhaps for this particular child (but not necessarily for her siblings), certain distributions should have been made contingent on completion of a semester of college courses with a specified minimum grade point average.

EXAMPLE: A wealthy family has one child, age 13. They establish a Qualified Personal Residence Trust (QPRT) for their house for a 12-year period. Two years later, they establish a 10-year grantor retained annuity trust (GRAT). These trusts, and other trusts established for their child under their wills provide that all assets be distributed to the child at age 25, which they believe to be an age of sufficient maturity to handle assets. This plan could result in every trust, and thus all of the child's inheritances, being received in a single year. Is this prudent? What if the child is sued, divorces, or has an emotional breakdown? Would it not be more prudent to coordinate each trust and the will, at the planning stage, to spread out the distributions? This would give the child an opportunity to become acclimated to handling ever-larger sums of money, rather than an avalanche all at one time. If there is a suit, divorce, or other difficulty, the assets which at that time remain in trust will still be protected.

Should a minor (whether your child, grandchild, a niece or nephew, or other heir) receive a distribution of a substantial sum of money on your death? Probably not. How should "minor" be defined? Just because someone is 18 and can vote does not mean they have the maturity and knowledge to manage tens or hundreds of thousands of dollars. This is why most trusts provide that children (or adults) under a certain age will receive their distributions through a trust. The income and principal should be distributed in a calculated manner that assures proper care of the beneficiary, while giving the beneficiary reasonable opportunity to acclimate to handing the responsibilities of money.

Any beneficiary who is disabled and unable to handle his financial affairs should have his share distributed into a further trust for his benefit. These important issues are explored in Chapter 15.

Income tax considerations also affect the distribution provisions. Because trust income can be taxed at the marginal tax rates, many trusts provide for the distribution of income to the beneficiaries (see Chapter 12).

TAX CONSEQUENCES OF THE BENEFICIARY'S POWERS OVER THE TRUST

Many trusts are set up for tax benefits. For example, the bypass trust discussed in Chapters 10 and 14 is designed to keep a portion of your estate out of the taxable estate of your surviving spouse. The objective is to use up as much of your exclusion (which exempts $1 million of assets from estate tax in 2002 and is scheduled to increase in future years) and give your surviving spouse substantial interest in the trust as a beneficiary, but without having the assets (corpus) of the trust included in your surviving spouse's estate. How much control can you give your surviving spouse, as a beneficiary of the bypass trust, without having the IRS consider the control sufficient to tax the trust assets in your her estate? This is a question which affects the beneficiaries of many different types of trusts.

Beneficiary Serving as Trustee

If a beneficiary is to be the trustee of a trust, several precautions should be considered. Because this issue is so technical, be certain to review it with an estate tax specialist. If a beneficiary is made trustee, the powers of the trustee should not extend to making decisions concerning the distribution of income or property to herself. This can be accomplished by having the beneficiary serve as a co-trustee with an independent trustee (a bank trust department as an example). The bank will then be given the sole authority concerning decisions to make distributions to the co-trustee who is also a beneficiary. The co-trustee who is a beneficiary will be prohibited from making these decisions. Another option to discuss with your estate planner is limiting the distributions which the beneficiary/trustee can make to herself to those necessary to maintaining her standard of living (an "ascertainable standard"). The bank or other independent trustee can be given a broader power to make almost unlimited distributions to your beneficiaries ("comfort and welfare").

Beneficiary Annual Demand (Crummey) Power Withdrawal Right

Many trusts are set up with the intent that you will make gifts each year to the trust in the future. This is common for an insurance trust so that annual premiums can be paid. It's common for children's education and other trusts when you intend to take advantage of the $10,000 (indexed for inflation $11,000 in 2002) annual gift tax exclusion. This is the amount you can give away each year to any number of beneficiaries without any gift tax consequence. When this common planning is done, you will want to take steps to assure that the trust is structured so that gifts to the trust will qualify for the annual gift tax exclusion. If gifts do not qualify, then any gifts to the trust will use up a portion of your once-in-a-lifetime gift tax exclusion ($1 million which, unlike the estate exclusion, will not increase). Once that gift tax exclusion is used up, gifts will trigger a gift tax cost. These concepts are explained in Chapter 10.

This issue is based on a tax rule that only permits gifts you make to qualify for the annual gift tax exclusion if the gifts are "of a present interest." This means that the beneficiary can benefit from the gift immediately. An outright gift of cash to the beneficiary obviously qualifies. Few gifts in trust qualify because most trusts restrict when the beneficiary can get his hands on the money. A technique is needed to circumvent this dilemma.

The most common solution to this potential gift tax dilemma is to include in your trust an annual demand power (called a *Crummey power* after the court case where it was approved). This power permits your beneficiaries a limited right to withdraw an amount each year equal to the amount of gift made to the trust. When properly handled, this can enable gifts to the trust to qualify for the annual gift tax exclusion.

When this approach is used, following your gift as the grantor/donor to the trust, the trustee must give written notice to the beneficiary of the amount the beneficiary can withdraw from the trust. If the beneficiary does not exercise the right to withdraw the amount permitted within the prescribed time period, say 30 to 60 days, the money or property then remains part of the trust to be distributed as provided under the general trust terms. The beneficiary should sign the notice letter acknowledging that they were informed of the right to withdraw. The trustee should save all of these annual notices.

Beneficiaries' Power of Appointment to Avoid GST Tax

When planning for a large estate where transfers to grandchildren are involved, the generation skipping transfer (GST) tax can be a major concern (see Chapter 11). When assets are transferred to certain types of trusts for which the only beneficiaries are grandchildren (in tax jargon, *skip persons*) a substantial GST tax could be incurred. This tax can be planned for in several ways. First, if the trust is properly structured (see Chapters 11 and 16) annual exclusion gifts of $11,000 to a trust for a single grandchild may remain exempt from GST tax. In other instances, it can be beneficial to allocate some portion of your $1 million (indexed) GST tax exclusion to the trust so that all assets in the trust will remain GST tax exempt (in many cases the tax rules will automatically make this allocation for you—see Chapter 10).

Another approach to avoid the GST tax relates to the powers the beneficiaries are given under the trust. Assume you set up a "pot" trust to benefit your child and his children. A trust which benefits grandchildren can raise GST tax issues. Assume further that you have already used up your GST tax exclusion and want to avoid GST tax on this trust. Using this planning approach, you give your child (who is not a skip person for GST tax purposes) the right to appoint the principal of the trust under his will to anyone he chooses, including his estate and creditors of his estate. This right given to your child will assure that no GST tax will be assessed. This broad right (called a *general power of appointment*) causes the assets of the trust to be included in your child's estate for estate tax purposes. While this GST tax savings will be at the cost of having the assets taxed in your child's estate, it can be less costly overall. For example, your child may have unused exclusion to minimize the tax.

SAMPLE TRUST PROVISION: The following illustrates a general power of appointment to avoid GST tax:

Upon the death of such beneficiary, the trustee shall transfer the principal of the trust to such persons other than child, but including his estate, his creditors, and the creditors of his estate, to such extent, in such amounts or proportions, and in such lawful interests or estates, whether absolute or in trust, as such child may by his or her last will and testament appoint by a specific reference to this power.

Beneficiaries' Limited Right to Replace a Trustee

Another aspect of the powers which a beneficiary can be given under a trust is a right to replace a trustee with a successor independent trustee. This can be an important degree of flexibility to build into any long-term trust. If a bank, for example, is named as trustee or co-trustee, and if the bank's performance is less than optimal, the mere power by the beneficiaries to change to another trustee may motivate the bank to improve its responsiveness. If not, a change can be made.

CAUTION: If you are setting up a trust for children or other beneficiaries, do you really want them to have an unrestricted right to change trustees? Will this cause the beneficiaries to go "trustee shopping" to find the trustee most likely to give them what they want? Will this undermine the trustees' ability to carry out your wishes and instructions as indicated in the trust agreement (and perhaps in your meetings with the trust company and in side letters further detailing your wishes)?

Although perhaps no longer necessary from a tax perspective, some parents and other grantors prefer to restrict when a beneficiary can change trustees. One approach is to permit the beneficiary to change the trustee only if there is a valid reason.

Without some reasonable assurance of an opportunity to manage the trust for a time period that becomes economically feasible, an institutional

SAMPLE TRUST CLAUSE: Upon a unanimous vote of all current income beneficiaries, it shall be permissible to remove a trustee, if one should then be serving, for "cause," as defined by the following thirteen factors:

1. The legal incapacity of a trustee.
2. The willful or negligent mismanagement of the trust's assets.
3. The abuse or abandonment of, or inattention to, the trust.
4. A federal or state charge involving the commission of a felony or serious misdemeanor.
5. An act of stealing, dishonesty, fraud, embezzlement, moral turpitude, or moral degeneration.
6. The use of narcotics or excessive use of alcohol.

7. Poor health such that the trustee is physically, mentally, or emotionally unable to devote sufficient time to administer the trust.
8. The failure by the trustee to comply with a written fee agreement or other written agreement in the operation of the trust.
9. The failure of a corporate trustee to appoint a senior officer with at least five (5) years of experience in the administration of trusts to handle the trust account.
10. Changes by a corporate trustee in the account officer responsible for handling the trust account more frequently than every five (5) years (unless such change is made at the request of or with the acquiescence of the other trustee).
11. The relocation by a trustee away from the location where the trust operates so as to interfere with the administration of the trust.
12. A demand from the trustee for unreasonable compensation for such trustee's services.
13. Any other reason for which a court of competent jurisdiction in the state would remove a trustee.

---

trustee may be reluctant to accept the trust's business. This is because there are substantial up-front costs for an institution to accept a trust. Many institutions will want to have trust officers personally meet all current beneficiaries and spend considerable time getting to know them and understanding their needs. The trust agreement will have to be reviewed carefully to understand the limitations and requirements the new institutional trustee will face. Finally, the financial accounts will have to be transferred from the current trustee to the new institution. This all takes time and incurs expenses. If the institution is not assured of the business from the trust for a reasonable period of time, it may be reluctant to make this investment. Thus, to best protect the beneficiaries of the trust, consider some limitations on a power to remove the trustee. You could address these concerns by limiting the number of times a beneficiary can change a trustee. For example, "Removal and replacement of an institutional Trustee shall only be permitted once in any twenty-four (24) month period by the current income beneficiaries."

Beneficiaries' Right to Withdraw $5,000 or 5 Percent of Principal

Another right sometimes given to beneficiaries is a limited right to withdraw some amount of money from a trust. This might be done to assure the beneficiary access to some cash without having to obtain the trustee's permission. You might be concerned that the person you named as beneficiary may need additional money before the trustee can provide it. If tax considerations were not a concern, you could set any limit you felt would meet the beneficiary's needs without excessively depleting the trust.

NOTE: After the 2001 Tax Act, the increases in the exclusion to $1 million for 2002 and higher in later years (if the scheduled increases materialize) might obviate the need for you to worry about the estate tax. If so, you could set any limit you want. However, the future of the estate tax, including the amount of the exclusion, is uncertain, so you are still probably best off considering tax issues, just in case.

However, since tax considerations are often important, you should consider limiting the beneficiaries' demand rights to avoid adverse tax consequences. If the beneficiary is granted the right to demand principal from a trust which is greater than the larger of $5,000 or 5 percent of the trust assets, the entire amount of the trust's assets will be taxed in that beneficiary's estate. So the common planning approach to achieve the objective of giving a beneficiary flexibility to demand money without triggering a tax problem, is to use a *five and five power.* This permits the beneficiary to demand a distribution in any year of no more than the greater of $5,000 or 5 percent of the trust assets in that year. If the beneficiary's power is limited to this statutory formula, the power will not alone cause all of the assets of the trust to be included in the beneficiary's taxable estate. If the power is anything greater, even $6,000 or 6 percent, as an example, the *entire* trust will be taxable in the beneficiary's estate. The five and five type of provision could be added to a bypass trust to give your surviving spouse (or any other beneficiary) greater comfort in having the assets on your death held in trust rather than given to her outright. This could encourage your spouse to agree to the use of a bypass trust to save estate taxes.

SAMPLE TRUST PROVISION: Grantor's spouse shall have the right to request of the Trustee of this Bypass Trust to pay over to such surviving spouse, upon written request, out of the principal of this Bypass Trust, in each successive calendar year commencing with the calendar year in which Grantor's death occurs, a sum not exceeding the greater of five thousand dollars ($5,000) or five percent (5%) of the assets of the principal of this Bypass Trust valued as of the date of the receipt of such request, provided, however, that only one such request may be made in any one calendar year, and such right to withdraw sums of principal shall not be cumulative from year to year.

CAUTION: Where the beneficiary has a five and five power, her estate could be taxed on the amount of income she could have demanded to be distributed in the year of death, even if the demand for the money is not made. Thus, for some trusts, if the power is not really necessary, it should not automatically be included.

CONCLUSION

Naming the beneficiaries of your trust is usually presumed to be a straightforward task. Unfortunately, this is not always the situation. Great care must be taken in properly identifying your beneficiaries, and in naming successor, alternate, or contingent beneficiaries. Further, you should pay careful attention to how and when each beneficiary can or must receive distributions from the trust. Finally, you must discuss with your estate planner the appropriate powers and rights that the beneficiary should have over the trust to accomplish your personal, tax, and other objectives. Be certain to review the tax implications of each of these matters to avoid costly and unintended surprises. And don't assume that if you don't face an estate tax that these issues will disappear—they won't.

6 FIDUCIARY RIGHTS, POWERS, AND OBLIGATIONS

Fiduciary is a general term that can include trustees (the primary persons who manage your trust) and even other persons who act like trustees, but who are not trustees (quasi-fiduciaries). These can include a *trust protector.* This is a special position sometimes used to provide greater flexibility and control over a trust through authorizing someone to change trustees and make other specified decisions. An *investment adviser* may be charged with investing trust assets instead of the trustee. A *distribution adviser* or *committee* can be charged with making distribution decisions (instead of a trustee), or perhaps merely making recommendations on distributions for a trustee to consider. These quasi-fiduciary positions have begun to be used relatively recently. You must consult with an estate planner as to whether they can be used, their implications under the state law in which your trust is being formed, and whether they will really address your concerns, or just create more complexity.

When a trust has more than one fiduciary or any quasi-fiduciaries, be certain that the rights, powers, and obligations of each are clearly delineated to avoid conflicts and to avoid gaps in decision making (if the trust document inadvertently leaves uncertain which fiduciary or quasi-fiduciary shall exercise a specific power).

Compensation is also critical. If you have several people serving, how will they be paid? Will the trustee's fee be reduced to reflect the fact that someone else is making investment decisions?

The discussion that follows will refer primarily to trustees, since most trusts will continue to be set up with this simpler format. Many of the issues relating to trustees will apply to the quasi-fiduciaries as well. When the term *fiduciary* is used, it is intended to encompass trustees, co-trustees, investment advisers, distribution committees, and trust protectors.

WHO SHOULD BE THE FIDUCIARIES OF YOUR TRUST?

This is the single most important question of this entire book. The success of your trust depends on your making this decision wisely. Who should be your trustee and your successor trustees? Trustees are the persons or institutions (such as a bank or trust company) who manage your trust. The trustees, under the provisions of your state's laws that govern trusts (and the differences between states can be important, so always consult with an attorney experienced with your state's laws), and within the framework you provide your trustees in your trust document, are charged with the responsibility of carrying out the intent of your trust.

There are a number of general factors to consider when selecting a trustee or quasi-fiduciary. Make a list of everyone who could reasonably be a trustee. Prepare this list as quickly as possible, without making judgments or taking off any potential candidates. Try to come up with at least five names. If your partner or spouse can help, have them come up with their own list, independently. Then you can narrow and rank the listing. Some of the concerns you have about potential trustees can be addressed by having them serve as co-trustees, by ranking them after better candidates, limiting their powers or discretion, or using quasi-fiduciaries.

TIP: If you only name one trustee and one successor, if neither can serve (e.g., one moves away and the other is sick or dies), what happens? A court proceeding may have to be initiated by the beneficiaries (or their guardians if they are minors) to have a court select a trustee. Not only is this process expensive and time-consuming, but the records of the trial may be public information. Most importantly, how can a judge who does not know you or the beneficiaries personally select a trustee who will be more to your liking than you could have selected?

GENERAL FACTORS TO CONSIDER WHEN SELECTING A TRUSTEE

Start a checklist of factors for selecting a trustee. Evaluate each person in your "possible trustee" list. If the decision is tough, set up a chart listing each potential trustee and weigh or rank them by factors to come up with your listing. Here is a starting list of factors to consider:

- *Integrity.* No attribute is more important.
- *Common sense.* Unfortunately, this attribute is far from common. Even if your trustee has inadequate skills, if they have the common sense to recognize this and hire the appropriate professionals, all will bode well for your trust.
- *Duplication.* Spouses and partners should carefully consider whether they should name the same fiduciaries in their respective documents. If the couple is one economic unit and the beneficiaries are similar or identical, this can make drafting and eventual administration easier. This means you both will name the same trustees under your respective trusts, the same executors under your wills, and agents under your durable powers of attorney.

PLANNING TIP: Check with your attorney concerning a legal concept called the "reciprocal trust doctrine." If your trust and your spouse's trusts are identical, the law may disregard both trusts. Some practitioners view this as a theoretical issue unlikely to arise on tax audit.

- *Abilities.* Trustees should be selected based on their skills, not based on whether someone left out will be insulted. The job is too important for decisions to be based on such considerations. If you feel someone will be hurt by not being selected, consider writing some explanation or apology in your letter of last instruction (a personal letter you should write to your executor and guardians stating personal preferences, concerns, and the like).

- *Ability to manage assets.* If there is an interest in a business or other difficult to manage asset, consider the specific skills necessary to manage those assets. Alternatively, make sure your trust gives the trustees the power to hire an appropriate adviser or management company, and your trustee has the knowledge to do that. Keep in mind that the primary document to address succession planning for your business is really the partnership, shareholders', or other agreements controlling the business, not your trust.

- *Ability to get along reasonably well with the beneficiaries.* Perhaps more importantly, the trustee has to be able to say no to a request by the beneficiary.

- *No conflict of interest.* Your long-time business partner may be your most trusted friend and the most financially astute individual you know, but if her decisions about the business could adversely affect your family's interests, she is not the choice for fiduciary. An alternative may be to name her co-trustee and prohibit her from making any decisions concerning the voting of the stock in the company. Also, consider whether a buy-out agreement to dispose of the stock may not be the best option. This could leave your trust with cash instead of business interests and eliminate the problem of the trustee having to manage business interests.

- *Business and investment acumen.* Can the person you select be trusted to handle this much money properly? If they do not personally have the investment skills, will they consult proper advisers and use them effectively? These concerns can be addressed to some extent by your involving your brokers and investment advisers as part of your estate planning team, or even naming an investment adviser as a quasi-fiduciary. Don't dismiss a trusted, honest friend or family member who understands your goals and objectives, but does not have investment acumen. The ideal situation may be to combine such person's talents with an institutional trustee (or one of your long time and trusted advisers) which can provide the accounting, investment, and other professional advice.

- *Judgment to determine the needs of your beneficiaries.* The most financially astute person may not exhibit the sensitivity you want toward your beneficiaries. One solution to this dilemma is to name co-trustees. One trustee can have substantial investment or trust management expertise. The co-trustee can be someone who exhibits the personal sensitivity and skills you desire. Together they can, hopefully, do a better job than either would alone. This approach is frequently used with institutional trustees. You may select an institution, such as a bank's trust department, to serve as a co-trustee with a family member. Similarly, you may select friends or family members to serve jointly where their skills and personal characteristics compliment each other. Another alternative is to name a distribution committee that could consist of family, friends, or even beneficiaries.

- *Legal issues with trustee-beneficiaries.* If you name a person who is a beneficiary as trustee, several legal and tax problems can be created. Legally, if the same person is the only trustee and the only beneficiary, there may be no trust (this is the legal doctrine of *merger*). If you have several beneficiaries and only one of them is a trustee, the non-trustee beneficiaries could be put at a disadvantage. This becomes more problematic as the discretionary authority given to your trustee is increased. Tax problems can also affect a trustee-beneficiary. Where a person as trustee can distribute trust assets to themselves as a beneficiary, or to another beneficiary whom they are obligated to support, the entire amount of the trust could be included in their estate for tax purposes.

NOTE: One approach to addressing this problem is to have two co-trustees. In addition, the provisions of the trust that define the trustees' powers can prohibit any trustee who is also a beneficiary from participating in any decision to distribute money to themselves, or to anyone they are obligated to support.

- *The term of the trust is important.* Where you are setting up a long-term trust for young children, or grandchildren, you should consider this time factor in selecting trustees. One approach is to name more successor trustees than you would for a shorter term trust. You may wish to name an institution, such as a bank trust department, as a trustee. Institutional trustees do not get old, cannot die, and usually do not resign. If you prefer not to name an institution initially, you may wish to name them as a final successor trustee in the event that the individuals named cannot serve. Another alternative is to give the trustee the right to name a successor trustee which may include an institution. Thus, if your last-named trustee realizes that there is a possibility of the trust agreement not designating a trustee, he or she can then appoint a successor. A trust protector can also be used to appoint successors.

- *Use discretion and heart in selecting trustees.* For example, assume that you have three children (or siblings, friends, etc.) and you trust one or two of them as trustees, but not all. How will the persons not selected as trustee react? Will you create friction and other problems between the one or two serving as trustee and the one or two who are not? Sometimes, adding a nonbinding comment explaining the appointment to the trust, or in a side letter, can address the potential problem. However, be certain your attorney is comfortable that "fluffy" statements won't create legal entanglements. Another alternative is, don't name anyone from the group as trustees. Use others or even a bank. Consider the following:

SAMPLE TRUST PROVISION: "I select my youngest son, John, as Trustee. I have selected John prior to his older siblings as first choice for Trustee, not out of any lack of love or concern for my other children, but in recognition of his background as an accountant, which makes him best suited for this role."

SELECTING A TRUSTEE FOR DIFFERENT TYPES OF TRUSTS

There are circumstances specific to each trust which should also be considered when selecting trustees. The following text addresses trustee selection for several common trusts.

Revocable Living Trust

For a revocable living trust, the initial trustee is easy: It's you. This is not always the best answer. If you are the sole grantor, trustee, and beneficiary, the legal doctrine of *merger* may apply. This could result in no trust being validly formed under a few states' laws because no different interests have been established. More importantly, is it really practical to be the sole trustee? A major goal in setting up a revocable living trust is to manage your assets and money if you are disabled. How will your trust make the transition from you as the sole (disabled) trustee to the successor trustees? It may be an easier and smoother transition if you name someone as co-trustee initially to serve with you, particularly if you are ill or elderly at the time the trust is formed. If this is done, then the co-trustee will have signed the trust, will have a copy of the signed trust, will be aware of his or her responsibilities, and will have signed the bank and brokerage signature cards in advance. In the event of an emergency or disability, no hurdles will exist to the co-trustee's stepping in to assist you and your family.

Should your spouse/partner or someone else be the co-trustee? Consider naming someone other than your spouse or partner as co-trustee if your spouse or partner travels with you much of the time. If you are injured, they may be with you during the catastrophe. You can name your spouse or partner as the immediate successor. Thus, if an emergency affects you, but not your spouse or partner, they will serve as successor trustee, the same position they would have had if they had served as immediate co-trustee with you. However, if they are affected by the same emergency as you, the initial co-trustee will be in a position to help both of you.

Trusts for Children

If you're setting up a trust for your children, either now (inter-vivos) or under your will, most likely your spouse (if the other parent of your children) will be the initial co-trustee. It is generally preferable that a parent not be the sole trustee of a trust for a child. If the parent makes disbursements from the trust which discharge the parent's legal obligation to support the child, tax problems could be triggered. On the other hand, if the parent is instead a co-trustee, and as co-trustee is prohibited from making disbursements which discharge a legal obligation of support, the nonparent co-trustee can instead make decisions and take actions pertaining to those types of payments. Several successor trustees should be named if the trust will continue for many years (e.g., the child is 2 and the trust ends at age 25).

Qualified Personal Residence Trust

Since this is a grantor trust, you could be a trustee of the trust. However, consider naming a co-trustee. If your spouse is transferring her half interest in the residence to a separate QPRT, she should name a different co-trustee then you to avoid issues of the reciprocal trust doctrine explained previously. This approach will facilitate management in the event of disability, avoid the reciprocal trust doctrine, and help support any claimed discount on the value of the house as a result of each of you transferring noncontrolling interests to your respective trusts (see Chapter 22).

Bypass Trust

When setting up a bypass trust (an A trust), your surviving spouse can be a co-trustee; however, caution should be exercised in making her the sole trustee. This is because the primary objective of a bypass trust is to assure that the assets of the trust are not taxed in your surviving spouse's estate. If your spouse is co-trustee, he or she can be prohibited from participating in decisions that could taint the trust assets as taxable in her estate. If your spouse is a second or later marriage, consider whether an independent trustee should be named to better balance the needs of your surviving spouse and children from another marriage (see Chapter 8).

Qualified Terminable Interest Property (QTIP) Trust

This trust is intended to qualify for either the gift or the estate tax unlimited marital deduction on a transfer of assets, in trust, to benefit your spouse. The value of this trust, however, is then taxed at the death of the surviving spouse. This is why second to die life insurance is often used in estate planning (see Chapter 19). However, the increases in the exclusion scheduled to occur may eliminate tax on the surviving spouse's death.

Since the value of the trust will be included in the surviving spouse's estate in any event, there is less tax concern with naming the surviving spouse a trustee then in a trust, such as a bypass trust, which is intended not to be taxed in her estate. If it is a first and only marriage and the children of both spouses will inherit the assets, there might be little concern over naming the surviving spouse as trustee, and granting her broad powers. A primary objective of the trust will likely be to assure her maximum comfort. However, if a second or later marriage is involved, there may be an inherent conflict in selecting as trustee the surviving spouse who is not a parent of the children who will inherit the remaining trust estate. Similarly, it is often not appropriate to have the children of a prior marriage named as trustees.

Insurance Trust

If a trust may purchase insurance on your life, you should generally be the grantor and should not serve as trustee. If *second-to-die insurance* (pays only on the death of the last of you and your wife) is to be held in a trust, neither of you should be named trustee.

OTHER OPTIONS TO CONSIDER WHEN NAMING A TRUSTEE

Other trusts will face their own unique issues in naming trustees. The previous discussion has summarized important points raised in several types of trusts. Because the selection of a trustee can be so complex from a tax perspective alone, it is essential to consult with an attorney specializing in estate planning. Other techniques to consider are discussed next.

Trust Protector

If you are setting up an irrevocable trust and are concerned about how to address unforeseeable changes, especially changes concerning the conduct of trustees, the use of a *trust protector* may be part of the answer. The protector can be considered to be an intermediary between the beneficiaries and the trustee, with the primary objective of protecting the beneficiaries from, and representing them before, the trustee. A trust protector is a quasi-fiduciary, as discussed earlier, because he can exercise powers traditionally reserved to the trustees. The protector can be empowered to change trustees, change the state or country where the trust is based, and the choice of law provision (i.e., which state or country's laws are to govern the trust). Some trusts provide the trust protector a limited right to add or change the beneficiaries of the trust.

Give Beneficiaries Power to Change Trustees

Another commonly used approach, as previously discussed, is to give the beneficiaries a right to change the trustee periodically. This can be an unlimited right, or perhaps could be limited to the right to replace an institutional trustee with another institution.

POWERS WHICH YOUR TRUSTEE SHOULD BE GIVEN

Your trustees need a broad range of powers to effectively discharge their responsibilities as trustees. State law typically provides an array of powers that trustees have so that these same powers need not be repeated in the trust document. However, attorneys generally prefer to list detailed powers in the trust agreement to assure granting adequate powers and to avoid the need to consult state law to make a determination each time trustees must act. Further, if the trust is moved to another state, the powers granted under state law may change.

CAUTION: The trustee power provisions should not be dismissed as "boiler-plate." If the provisions are too broad, limit them. If certain provisions are too restrictive, you may wish to amend them to be certain that the trustees have the flexibility to address changing circumstances. If the trust has any special goals or assets, the powers should reflect them. If you have farm land, real estate investments, closely held businesses, insurance policies, generation skipping transfer tax concerns, or other unusual considerations, the trust power provisions should be tailored to assure the trustee adequate powers to deal with these matters.

The trustee may have the power to allocate income and principal among the various beneficiaries. This is called a *sprinkle power* (see Chapter 8). The trustee can be granted the power to reserve the right to withhold distributions of income to a beneficiary who is disabled or a minor.

Every trustee, unless the trust agreement specifically says otherwise, is entitled to compensation for serving as a trustee. Beyond immediate family members, no person is likely to serve without compensation. In many, if not most, cases, you really don't want family serving for free either. State laws, in order to prevent abuse, have set maximum fees that may be charged by trustees. Often, the trust agreement is silent and the permissible fees are charged. If an institutional trustee is serving, they may require that approval of their standard fee schedule, and other provisions, be added to your trust. If an institution is named, even as a successor trustee, it is advisable to contact them before signing the trust and consider incorporating the language they require.

To encourage trustees to serve, you may wish to exonerate them for liability where they have acted reasonably and in good faith. An honest error, or poor investment made after reasonable analysis, should not penalize your trustee. State law may affect the extent to which you can relieve a trustee of liability.

POWERS AND RIGHTS THAT YOU MAY CHOOSE NOT TO GIVE YOUR TRUSTEE

There may be a number of powers you don't want your trustee to have. For example, in many cases the trustee should not be given the right to make trust distributions that discharge the legal obligation of the trustee to support a particular beneficiary, such as a child. If this is done, the trust income could become taxable to the trustee and the trust assets could be included in the trustee's taxable estate. A common planning technique is to prohibit the trustee from making any such distributions. Instead, a co-trustee not subject to these problems could make the distributions.

Caution should be exercised whenever you limit a trustee's power for reasons other than tax or legal requirements. If a situation arises and you have prevented the trustee from having the power to act, court intervention may be required.

TRUSTEES' DUTIES AND OBLIGATIONS

Trustees have a substantial number of responsibilities under the typical trust agreement and under state law. These are discussed next.

Duty to Protect Trust Property

The trustee must take all reasonable steps to protect and conserve trust property. Historically, this duty was not delegable. However, recent changes (such as the prudent investor act that permits trustees to delegate investment decisions) have eroded this. Even when delegation is permitted the trustee will remain responsible and must monitor the person retained to assist the trust.

Duty to Make Trust Property Productive

The trustee has a specific duty to make the property of the trust productive, unless the grantor indicated an intent otherwise or it is impractical to do so.

Duty to Be Prudent

The duty of the trustee to be prudent can have an important impact on investment and other actions taken by the trustee. The trustee has a duty to act reasonably and competently in all matters relating to the administration of the trust. This is a standard of conduct, not performance. An amateur trustee is held to the standard based on the care and skill a person of ordinary prudence would exercise in dealing with his own property. A professional trustee who holds himself out as a professional with special skills is held to the higher standard of employing those special skills.

Duty to Carry Out Terms of the Trust

The trustee has a primary duty to carry out the intentions of the grantor as they have been communicated in the governing instrument. This is why one of the first steps any newly appointed trustee must take is to obtain a copy of the trust instrument, read it, and then discuss it with an attorney. Without knowledge of the trust agreement, a trustee is unlikely to be able to fulfill his or her obligations. The duties of any trustee must be viewed in the context of state law as well as the trust document. If there is a contradiction between the two, legal advice should be sought.

Can a trustee deviate from the terms of the trust instrument? Unless it is impossible, illegal, or circumstances have changed considerably, the answer is generally no.

To carry out your duties as trustee, have a periodic polling of beneficiaries to determine their status (e.g., tax bracket) and needs. The input of the grantor is often not binding unless the grantor has expressly reserved the right and power to amend, modify, or revoke the trust (e.g., a revocable living trust).

Self-Dealing Prohibited

If the grantor designated an institutional trustee, the issue of investing in such trustee's own securities (or securities in which it is involved) can be an issue. This is most likely to occur where a pooled investment fund is used for many smaller trust funds.

If a trustee lends trust money to itself, it may breach the duty of loyalty it owes the trust. Even if borrowing is authorized, it can raise issues of impropriety. What if the trustee, an institutional fiduciary, invests directly in debt instruments issued by it or its parent company? What if the common trust fund make such an investment? What should occur if the trustee receives, as part of a portfolio, stock in itself? It generally appears that it is preferable for the trustee not to invest in its own stock, and if it inherits stock, to obtain an authorization from the beneficiaries, or the grantor, if the trust is a revocable trust, to retain the stock.

Is a Trustee Permitted to Earn a Profit?

A trustee is in a *fiduciary* position (i.e., a relationship of trust and responsibility) with respect to the beneficiaries and the trust assets (*corpus*). As such, trust law has historically prevented the trustee from earning any profit from the trust, other than the trustee fees provided for under the trust agreement or state law. This is one of the reasons for requiring a trustee to account for all trust income and assets.

Trustee's Authority to Retain Agents

Trustees have a general duty to the beneficiary not to delegate to others the doing of acts which the trustee can reasonably be required personally to perform. A trustee has the power to perform every act which a "prudent person" would perform for the purposes of the trust including employing attorneys, auditors, investment advisers, or agents to advise or assist the trustee in the performance of his administrative duties. There is a general trustee's duty to avoid conflicts of interest when hiring agents (the trustee should probably not hire his wife as a broker). It is generally inappropriate for a trustee to make any type of profit, other than the trustee fee, from serving the trust. A court order may be required where the transaction involves a profit to the trustee.

Retaining Investment Advisers and Agents

The Prudent Investor Act passed by many states (see Chapter 7) will result in many trustees delegating investment authority to a money manager. This is a significant departure from the historical circumstances (mentioned in the preceding paragraph) of not delegating. Trustees should be careful in that improper delegation will leave the trustee liable for the errors and omissions of the investment adviser hired. If the adviser doesn't reasonably diversify the trust's investments, you as trustee, may get sued. There must be adequate supervision by the trustee.

To be prudent in selecting an adviser, trustees should participate in setting trust investment objectives, and routinely monitor the advisers' performance. Where this is properly done, the trustees should not be liable for delegating to advisers.

Duties Owed by Trustee to Trust and to Beneficiaries

The trustee owes a duty of loyalty to the trust and to the beneficiaries. The trustee has a generic duty to administer. This means that the trustee should do what is necessary for the good of the trust and those interested in it. As a trustee, you owe the beneficiaries loyalty and impartiality.

Self-Dealing Issues Affecting Trustee

If you hire yourself, or a related person (an investment company you own) to perform a service which an independent agent (e.g., a realtor, accountant, or attorney) could also perform, you could be guilty of "self-dealing."

It is generally better to employ an unrelated person unless the trust agreement expressly permits the employment of a related one. Even if the trust permits you to do so, you may want to disclose in writing to the beneficiaries the reasons why you want to hire a related person. Perhaps by using an accounting firm you work with, you can better and more economically manage trust matters. Have the beneficiaries agree in writing if feasible.

CONCLUSION

Naming trustees is often the most difficult and important decision to be made when planning any trust. The powers and rights of the trustees are extremely important and should be reviewed with care to assure that your trust will function as closely as possible to what you desire. If you are contemplating accepting the position of serving as a trustee, not only must you be familiar with the trust instrument and the powers you have, but you must also have an understanding of your obligations and responsibilities as a trustee. This chapter outlined some of the many concepts affecting trustees.

7 INVESTMENT STANDARDS AND DECISIONS

With the tremendous fluctuations in the stock market having wreaked havoc with many portfolios, it should be obvious that one of the most important aspects of managing a trust is investing the trust money wisely. This is not only a question of finance; it is a question of law. The provisions contained in the trust agreement can dramatically affect how trust assets must be invested. State law, and in particular a law called the *Uniform Prudent Investor Act,* can also have substantial influence over what is permissible. If you are serving as a trustee, you must be familiar with both. If you are setting up a trust, you must review how your trust agreement should modify, if at all, the state law governing the trust's investments.

PLANNING TIP: Involve your financial planner or other investment professional in the process of reviewing language proposed for a new trust, or in helping you interpret and implement the investment provisions of an existing trust. This task really requires the coordination of both your attorney and investment professional.

Consider the following illustration of the difficulties that can be created by not addressing trust investment provisions.

EXAMPLE: Most trusts provide that income should be paid to a current beneficiary, for example, your spouse. On the eventual death of your spouse, the remaining trust assets are to be paid to the remainder beneficiaries, say your children from a prior marriage. The trustee may be permitted to invade principal for medical or other emergencies (in other situations, but not this example, the trustees may be given wide latitude to invade trust principal). If the trustee invests for total return, which is what modern investment theory would advocate, what should be paid to your spouse? Total return investment strategies seek to maximize after-tax return inclusive of current income (dividends and interest) and capital gains. But if this results in little current income and mostly appreciation, your spouse will be severely penalized for the benefit of your children. This may not be your intent.

The example illustrates why it is so important to analyze and coordinate investment and distribution provisions of your trust, and to be certain that they reflect your goals for the trust.

UNIFORM PRUDENT INVESTOR ACT

The modern trend in state laws affecting trusts is the Uniform Prudent Investor Act, which provides that the trustee investing and managing assets owes a duty to the beneficiaries of the trust to invest as a prudent investor would with consideration to risk, return, diversification, beneficiary needs, taxes, and other relevant factors. While this may seem like common sense to any investor, historically the trustee was obligated to preserve trust principal. This was a very different standard that ignored modern investing theory and created a host of problems.

The uniform prudent investor rule is a default rule that may be expanded, restricted, eliminated, or otherwise altered by express provisions of the trust instrument. Thus, reading state law in isolation is insufficient. You must interpret, as trustee, both state law and the trust agreement and see how they interact. If you are contemplating establishing a trust, you should consider what aspects of your state's law you need to address in your trust agreement. Because so many states' laws are changing, or may change in the near future, it is best to err on the side of addressing investment matters in greater length in your trust agreement.

OVERVIEW OF THE UNIFORM PRUDENT INVESTOR RULE

The standard of determining investment prudence is based on the portfolio as a whole, rather than on individual securities. Thus, investing in any particular type of security will, in states adopting this modern view, no longer be deemed imprudent. Under older investment laws, the merits of each individual investment were determined independently.

EXAMPLE: Under modern portfolio theory as adopted in the newer uniform prudent investor acts, if you invest trust assets in a diverse mix of, say, 30 securities (or several diversified mutual funds investing in different asset categories) several of the individual securities or funds might be quite risky if evaluated in isolation. But, when these risky assets are combined as part of a diversified investment strategy, they can be demonstrated to actually lower the risk of the portfolio as a whole. Under the Uniform Prudent Investor Act, this type of investment would be appropriate. Under older versions, since these were risky investments individually, a trustee could be held personally liable for investing in them if they declined in value.

Be careful, however, if the grantor prohibited investing in a particular type of security, such as derivatives or options, in the trust agreement. The trustee will still be bound to that restriction.

The trade-off between risk and return is a central consideration of the trustee's investments. No class or type of security is per se impermissible, if it fits within the overall investment plan and is, as part of such plan, prudent. Assets will have to be diversified (modern portfolio theory) unless a specific reason not to is present.

If you, as the grantor setting up a trust, want a particular investment to be retained, such as a family business, you should state that you do and provide guidelines as to when it can be sold.

Investment management can be and should be delegated if you don't have the expertise. Under the new rules, a trustee must have a comprehensive investment plan for the trust which considers the facts and circumstances affecting the trust. If you are a trustee, protect yourself and have an investment professional prepare a written plan.

ASSET ALLOCATION

Diversification of the trust's investments through asset allocation is an essential component to any thorough trust investment plan, and hence to your duties as a trustee.

Asset allocation is the process of identifying the asset classes in which a particular trust should invest, and then allocating the trust assets to those asset classes through an analysis of rates of return, risk tolerance, and other factors, such as liquidity needs. Modern portfolio theory, in very general terms, assumes that the investment markets are efficient. Therefore, the decision as to which asset categories investor capital is allocated is more critical than picking specific assets (e.g., stocks) within any particular category. Selecting asset categories that have negative correlation (e.g., when one rises the other tends to fall) can minimize risk while achieving the desired level of return. The relationship of asset categories can be indicated by their correlation. A correlation of +1.0 indicates assets whose values move in perfect tandem. A correlation of −1.0 indicates assets whose values move in opposite directions. The technical term used to describe the relationship between asset categories is their *co-variance*. Co-variance is a measure of the likelihood of the assets to move in the same direction and the momentum of their likely movements.

Studies have demonstrated that more than 90 percent of the risk of a portfolio can be explained by the allocation of assets. Where a portfolio is diversified among asset categories, approximately 90 percent of the risk can be viewed as market risk, while only 10 percent or less of the risk of that portfolio will be specific risk of a particular stock.

Through an analysis of the co-variance of particular assets and the expected return of those assets, a portfolio can be constructed that theoretically minimizes the risk faced by the investor attempting to achieve any particular level of return. By optimizing this relationship, in theory, an investor could earn greater returns than on his or her present portfolio while reducing risk.

FACTORS THE TRUSTEE SHOULD CONSIDER

The trustee must invest and manage trust assets as a prudent investor would, considering the purposes, terms, distribution requirements, and other circumstances of the trust. To do this, however, the trust should provide some clear directions. Many trusts do not do so, instead relying on general and vague provisions. To best assure that your beneficiaries are treated as you wish, if you are setting up a trust as grantor, provide guidance to the trustees. This guidance should be flexible enough to enable the trustees to deal with circumstances that may be unforeseeable at the time the trust is completed. If your directives are very specific (e.g., "The trustee shall never sell the family business"), you may create costly problems. If you wish that consideration be given to retaining the family business interests so long as any family members work in the business, or may work in the business within five years, indicate this in the trust agreement. This latter approach is more specific, provides clearer guidance, and most importantly gives the trustee flexibility to sell the business if your real objective, family employment, is not presently met and is unlikely to be met in the foreseeable future.

Can the Trustee Reconcile Prudent Investor Rule Diversification with Special Trust Objectives?

The trustee is required to diversify the investments of the trust unless it is reasonably determined that because of special circumstances this is not preferable. This creates a potentially difficult situation for many types of trusts. Consider the following example concerning one type of trust, an insurance trust.

EXAMPLE: Insurance trusts are often silent about their primary objectives because of tax considerations. For example, if a beneficiary other than the decedent's/insured's estate receives the insurance proceeds (e.g., an insurance trust) but the proceeds are subject to an obligation to pay estate taxes, debts, or other charges enforceable against the decedent's estate, the insurance proceeds will be taxable in the decedent's estate. If the insurance trust requires the trustee to pay the estate tax due from the decedent's estate, such language would violate the above rule and cause the inclusion of the insurance proceeds in the decedent's estate even though they were not payable to the executor. If the insurance trust is then silent, how is the trustee who is fully aware of the grantor's objectives to justify compliance with a prudent investor rule? For example, if the trustee maintains a substantial cash position to have funds available to lend to the grantor's estate, or to purchase assets of grantor's estate, can the fiduciary be surcharged for the cash position? Can the fiduciary be held liable for the loan to the grantor's estate since it is not diversified, and the risks-reward relationship is not favorable? Will the situation be affected by the fact that the beneficiaries under the insurance trust differ from the beneficiaries of the estate?

How Does Investment Delegation Affect Trustee Fees?

If a trustee retains an investment adviser and pays his fees from the trust, should the trustee's fees then be reduced? With a myriad of fee, expense, and other compensation arrangements for investment professionals, how should these additional costs be addressed? Unfortunately, in many instances the law is unclear or evolving. If you are setting up a trust that contemplates the trustee's hiring an investment professional, discuss with your attorney flexible options to deal with the compensation issue.

CONCLUSION

Trust investment provisions are vitally important for all to consider. Since the law in this area is complex and changing, it is important to consult an attorney to avoid problems. When forming a trust, your goals for the trust investments should be carefully evaluated and documented in a manner flexible enough to meet your goals without unduly restricting your trustee. When serving as a trustee, you must evaluate your obligations under the trust and state law. You should then document in writing the investment decisions made.

8 DISTRIBUTION OF INCOME AND PRINCIPAL

The trust provisions governing how and when trust income and assets should be distributed are one of the most important and fundamental trust provisions. What standards should be used to determine how and when one or more beneficiaries should receive benefit of trust income or assets? What special rules should apply to restrict these distributions? How does the specific nature of certain type of trusts affect the distribution standards for that trust? Should an incentive distribution plan be used to motivate beneficiaries to be goal oriented? Should an income payout or a total return payout (e.g., 4 percent of trust principal paid each year in quarterly installments) be used? This chapter addresses these and related issues concerning trust distributions.

TYPE OF TRUST AFFECTS DISTRIBUTION PROVISIONS

The manner in which income and assets (the principal, corpus, or res) should be distributed will depend to a great extent on the type of trust and the purposes for which the trust was formed.

Revocable Living Trust

A revocable living trust is established to assist in managing assets in the event you as the grantor become disabled, minimizing publicity and avoiding probate (see Chapter 13). There is no tax benefit to a living trust during your lifetime. Although a bypass trust and marital or QTIP trust can be included in a revocable living trust, these do not take effect until your death. Thus, there is generally no concern about restrictions on distributions to you. (It's your money!) As the grantor, you will typically reserve every right to amend or revoke the trust. Therefore, you will have total control over distributions. You can get what you want and when you want it. Typically, if you become disabled, other persons will take over as trustee. In this event, the provisions of your revocable living trust will govern how income and principal should be distributed.

CAUTION: If distributions are made to persons other than the grantor and the grantor's spouse, gift tax consequences must be considered.

If you are disabled, you might wish to mandate a standard for distribution. If your children or other heirs are the successor trustees who take over if you are disabled, you might want to assure that they at least maintain your standard of living or make specified minimum distributions to you. You may not want to rely solely on their largesse to pay your money to you. What if your son-in-law encourages your daughter to spend less on you to enhance her inheritance?

Following your death, the manner in which income and assets of your trust will be distributed will depend on the distribution provisions (which may include various trusts) your living trust provides for. A revocable living trust can incorporate almost any *testamentary trust* (a trust funded on death).

Bypass Trust

The purpose of a bypass (or A trust) is to provide your surviving spouse with income and certain principal invasion rights without the assets of the trust being taxed in her estate. The assets transferred to the bypass trust preserve the $1 million exclusion to which your estate is currently entitled (2002).

Bypass trust distribution provisions have as a primary goal limiting distributions to your surviving spouse at least enough to avoid the bypass trust assets being taxed in her estate. Other than this tax parameter, there is considerable flexibility in the distribution provision you include in a bypass trust. Many bypass trusts give the trustee the discretion to "sprinkle" distributions at any time and in any amount among a class of beneficiaries. This group of beneficiaries, selected by you when you have the bypass trust document drafted, might be limited to only your spouse, or can include your surviving spouse, children, and even other persons.

Where a bypass trust is formed to serve as beneficiary for pension or retirement assets, such as an Individual Retirement Account (IRA), special distribution provisions must be used that address the pension tax rules.

QTIP (Marital) Trust

A qualified terminable interest property (QTIP, marital, or B) trust is the most commonly used trust intended to benefit a surviving spouse and to qualify for the unlimited gift and estate tax marital deduction (i.e., you can transfer an unlimited amount to a spouse without tax). Your spouse must be a United States citizen or special rules apply.

Why use a marital trust? It can provide professional management, limit your spouse's access to the money, provide protection from creditors, and more. One major reason is so that you can assure that on the death of your surviving spouse the assets which you gave her will go to your children (or other heirs), and not to her second husband, or to the children of her second marriage. To achieve these goals, the distribution provisions will adhere to the tax law requirements for this benefit (see Chapter 14). A major requirement is that all income be distributed to your surviving spouse annually. This is an overriding distribution provision for any QTIP trust.

Minor Children's Trust

Distribution provisions of a minor's trust will largely depend on your goals as the grantor establishing the trust. Often, whether implied or explicitly stated, many child and grandchild or other minor beneficiary trusts are intended to assist in covering the cost of college and graduate school. In light of the enhancements of Code Section 529 college savings plans in the 2001 Tax Act, fewer trusts will be set up for children and grandchildren as people rely more on these plans, which do not require a trust.

Most child and grandchild trusts give the trustee broad discretion to distribute money for the health, education, and maintenance of the child. In other cases, some parents prefer to limit distributions until certain ages or events (e.g., the child graduates from college) to encourage the child to be productive. In some plans, assets are held in the child's trust for life with limited distribution provisions to protect the assets from creditors and to permit the assets to be transferred to later generations without incurring gift, estate, or GST taxes.

Qualified Personal Residence Trust (QPRT)

The distribution provisions of this specialized type of trust are simply that you have the right to live in the house. If the house is sold, in order to comply with technical QPRT tax requirements, the distribution provisions must mandate that a periodic annuity be paid to you from the sale until the termination of the trust (see Chapter 23).

Grantor Retained Annuity Trust (GRAT)

This tax-motivated trust is intended to reduce gift tax costs on large transfers. Therefore, the distribution provisions are drafted almost entirely to comply with tax law requirements during the term of the trust. Thus, you as the grantor will be paid the requisite annuity amount every month, quarter, or year (whichever payment period is specified in the trust). The payments will be made either at the beginning of the period or at the end of the period, again as specified in the trust agreement. The rate of annuity payment will be calculated in accordance with a formula set forth in the tax regulations (see Chapter 21).

Irrevocable Life Insurance Trust

If a trust is established as an irrevocable life insurance trust, other than the Crummey or annual demand power notices (see Chapters 5 and 10), there are unlikely to be any actual distributions prior to the death of the insured. This is because the typical insurance trust contains little by way of assets other than the insurance policies involved (see Chapter 20).

Charitable Trusts

If you establish a charitable remainder trust (CRT), periodic payments to you from the trust will be made in accordance with either a statutory annuity payment or uni-trust amount. A charitable lead trust (CLT) is a similar concept except that the payments are made to the charity during the term of the trust. Since, like the GRAT, these are tax-motivated trusts, the distribution provisions are drafted primarily to comply with tax law requirements. The rate of the payment can be determined by you when the trust is established and will help determine the tax consequences of the trust (see Chapter 10).

Qualified Subchapter S Trust (QSST)

If stock in a subchapter S corporation (the most common form for closely held businesses) is transferred to a trust, that trust must meet strict tax requirements in order to be a shareholder of an S corporation. If these requirements are not met, the tax benefits of an S corporation are lost. The most common trust used for this purpose is a qualified subchapter S trust (QSST). This trust requires that all income generally be paid out annually to a single beneficiary. The rigidity of these rules will thus largely govern the distribution provisions of a trust owning stock in an S corporation (see Chapter 21).

TRUST POWERS GOVERN THE DISTRIBUTION OF INCOME AND ASSETS

Many of the most important provisions governing how income and assets can be distributed from your trust will be included in the powers granted to your trustees. These include the right of a trustee to defer distributions to a beneficiary under a disability, the right to make emergency or special distributions of trust assets in the event of the beneficiary reaching a milestone or facing changed circumstances (such as for education or to assist a beneficiary in purchasing a home), and to terminate the trust if the balance of trust assets is so small as to make it uneconomical to continue administering the trust. In addition to these administrative powers of a trustee which can affect distributions, there are several important discretionary powers that may be given to a trustee, depending on the nature of the trust, and that can affect distributions.

These discretionary trust provisions can provide different standards for determining the trustee's authority to make distributions. The standards to be used in your trust will depend on tax, legal, and personal considerations. For example, where the trustee is completely independent, you may prefer that the standards give the trustees the widest latitude to distribute any amount of income earned by the trust, or principal of the trust, to the beneficiaries as could reasonably be necessary for the comfort and welfare of the beneficiaries. Where a beneficiary is a trustee (or the parent or spouse of a beneficiary), however, this type of broad standard could result in the trust assets being included in that trustee's estate. The usual response to this is to limit the power of such a trustee to make distributions.

For example, if a trustee is a parent of the beneficiary, consult your attorney about limiting distributions by the parent/trustee to those which do not discharge the parent's legal obligation to support the child. If a beneficiary is a trustee, consider limiting the trustee/beneficiary's right to make distributions to those necessary to maintain his standard of living (an "ascertainable standard"). This standard could be that distributions be made only for the health, education, and maintenance of the beneficiaries in accordance with their current standard of living. This is a more restrictive standard, but it does have the benefit of mitigating potential tax problems. Many people setting up trusts are also comfortable with such a standard because their primary goal is often to provide for basic living needs, not an extravagant lifestyle.

The general trust distribution standard can be combined with a right given to the beneficiary to withdraw the greater of $5,000 or 5 percent of the trust principal in any year. This limited withdrawal right won't create tax problems and gives flexibility to this latter type of trust arrangement (see Chapter 5).

YOUR FINAL WISHES FOR DISTRIBUTION OF YOUR ASSETS

Your personal feelings and concerns are a major factor in determining how assets will ultimately be distributed from your trust. You may wish to have assets tied up in trusts for years to protect the ultimate beneficiaries from their own excesses, divorce, creditors, and other unknowns.

EXAMPLE: A parent, concerned about his daughter's erratic marital history after four divorces, decides to leave her share of his estate in trust until she reaches age 60. Until that time, she will be entitled to the distribution of all of the income annually, and only so much of the principal as the trust company named as sole trustee deems necessary for her health, support, and maintenance.

Other people setting up trusts take a very different view. They may have had their own assets tied up in a trust for many years and been uncomfortable with the result. They may then choose to have all assets remaining in their trust be distributed to each child upon reaching age 18. Generally, however, neither of the above extremes is appropriate.

SPENDTHRIFT CLAUSE

This is one of the most common trust provisions, and often one of the most talked about. A spendthrift provision is intended to limit, to the extent the law permits, the beneficiary's assigning trust assets in advance of a distribution. It also limits creditors' ability to attach assets in the trust.

If you, or your spouse, set up a trust for your own benefit, the courts will be far less likely to respect a spendthrift provision. This is because the law is loathe to accept a self-funded trust as a means of protecting assets in the trust from your creditors. However, where such a provision is included in a trust created by someone else for you (e.g., your parents leave your inheritance in a spendthrift trust for your benefit), it can have important asset protection benefits. Another alternative for a self-settled trust is to form it in a state that has changed its laws to expressly permit such trusts, such as Alaska or Delaware. These changes enable you to set up a trust in the United States to protect your assets while enabling you access, albeit restricted, to the trust assets. These trusts are often called *domestic asset protection trusts* (DAPTs).

Including this type of provision in a trust can provide important protection against creditors of the beneficiaries, but the barrier is not impenetrable. Where creditors provide necessary items, such as food, clothing, and shelter, state law permits these creditors to force the trustee to reimburse them from trust assets by exercising available discretionary powers. The IRS, as may be expected, may pierce a trust, even one with a spendthrift provision, to claim back taxes.

NOTE: The laws concerning the effectiveness of spendthrift provisions vary from state to state. If creditor protection for your beneficiaries is an important concern, be certain to review the matter with a local attorney.

SPRINKLE (DISCRETIONARY) POWER OVER DISTRIBUTIONS

A sprinkle power is nothing more than its name implies—the power of the trustee to sprinkle income or assets wherever the trustee determines the funds are needed. For example, you could require your trustee to distribute all of the income each year from a children's trust to all of your children. Alternatively, your trustee could be given the power to sprinkle the income among your children in any manner deemed appropriate. Thus, if no unusual circumstances were present, the trustee may simply divide the proceeds equally. However, if one child had special medical needs, or was pursuing a graduate degree while the others were working, the trustee could direct distributions to the child in need. This can be an extremely effective device to use in a trust since it builds in flexibility to enable the trustee to address circumstances that may not be foreseeable when the trust was first formed.

A sprinkle power can create a number of serious issues. Where a trustee is also a beneficiary, it can be inappropriate for such trustee to exercise a sprinkle power. Some commonly used trustee powers specifically prohibit any trustee from participating in any decision concerning any distribution to that trustee (see Chapter 6).

NOTE: Carefully consider the type of trust involved before using a sprinkle power. For example, where the trust is intended to be a QTIP (or QDOT) trust for your surviving spouse, the use of a sprinkle power would disqualify the trust for the estate tax marital deduction, and would create a substantial tax cost. This is because all of the income from such a trust must be payable to your spouse.

CONCLUSION

How and when income and assets of your trust may (or must) be distributed are vital to achieving your tax, financial, personal, and other goals. To accomplish your objectives, the distribution provisions of your trust must be carefully reviewed and coordinated.

9 MISCELLANEOUS TRUST PROVISIONS AND EXHIBITS

In addition to the main provisions of a trust governing the assets transferred to the trust, the naming of the beneficiaries, describing how distributions are to be made, and the rights and powers of the trustees, there is a need for a number of additional provisions, often erroneously ignored as *boiler plate* (standard provisions which don't change) which help make the key provisions of your trust work. These provisions should not be overlooked. Although they may appear at the end of a trust agreement, they are nevertheless important.

THIRD-PARTY RELIANCE

For your trust objectives to be carried out, the trustee will have to conduct business with several unrelated people, banks, brokerage firms, insurance companies, real estate firms, and others. To facilitate these dealings, and the operations of the trust, the trust agreement could give these third parties assurances that they will not be sued or held accountable for good faith efforts to work with the trustee.

These trust provisions may go further to make clear that the bank, brokerage firm, or other third party will not be required to assure that the proceeds of any transaction with the trustee are applied as required under the trust, or to inquire into the appropriateness, validity, or propriety of any transaction. The trust should limit the third party from having any obligation or liability to anyone other than the trustee. A bank should not be responsible for the trustee's misappropriating trust assets or for misinterpreting trust provisions. The bank or other third party should be fully indemnified in distributing any assets of the trust in accordance with the directions of the trustee.

RULE AGAINST PERPETUITIES

The *rule against perpetuities* is a technical legal provision that is designed to prevent trusts for lasting indefinitely into the future. This legal principle provides that if a trust continues for longer than some period specified by state law, the trust could be illegal and could be terminated. A typical state law might be that a trust cannot exist for more than the life of a beneficiary (or other key person) alive when the trust is formed (a "life in being"), plus 21 years. To prevent this problem, many trusts include a provision that requires that if the time period of the rule against perpetuities is violated, the trust will terminate and the trust assets will be distributed to the then current income beneficiaries.

This provision is intended to make any trust cease prior to the time at which it would violate this rule. The laws differ from state to state so if you wish to have a trust last for an extended period of time, you should consult with an attorney specializing in estate planning in your state.

Some states and foreign countries have eliminated any such restrictions to encourage people to set up trusts based in their jurisdictions, designed to continue for generations (dynasty trusts).

When a state has eliminated its rule against perpetuities and assured no state income tax on trusts, this can present a powerful opportunity to benefit future generations. The savings in state taxes, even if minor when compared to the federal income tax rate, can compound to huge savings over a period of 50 years or longer. Trusts formed in those states to take advantage of these benefits are often referred to as *dynasty trusts* since they are often structured to continue for many generations.

DEFINITIONS

Every legal document, and trusts are no exception, contains numerous definitions. It's really a matter of style, not law, where these are placed in the document. Some attorneys have a definition section in the beginning of the document, some at the end. Other attorneys prefer to define a term the first time it is used. Many documents evolve over time to some combination of these. Certainly not every term needs to be defined.

Many terms have commonly understood meanings and thus are not defined, unless there is a unique application to your trust. For example, terms like *tangible, real property*, and *personal property* have generally recognized meanings and might not be defined with a specific provision. However, if you have special or important items of property, they may be addressed individually, or with greater specificity. For example, a scientist or inventor with many different intellectual property interests, or an artist with a collection of self-made paintings, sculptures, and other items, might want to give each one special attention (they can also present special estate tax problems as a result of something called income in respect of a decedent, or IRD). Other terms are defined in your state's statutes. However, even if a term is defined by state law, many attorneys may still include a definition in the document. Where this is done, the definition in the document is readily available for the trustees to rely on and apply; this can simplify trust administration. In other instances, the definitions in the document are included to specifically override state law provisions that may not be as favorable or appropriate.

Specialized Definitions Tailored to Your Trust

For example, a common planning technique, where a closely held business is involved, is to restrict who the trustees can be for that business interest. The trustees may be governed by the provisions of a shareholders' agreement or other document independent of the trust. A frequently used legal drafting technique is to define a specific word or phrase as having a meaning helpful to carry out your personal planning.

EXAMPLE: Abe, Bob, and Cathy, three siblings, own ABC, Inc., and several related businesses started by their parents. They sign a shareholders' agreement. The shareholders' agreement permits each of them to transfer their stock to a trust for the benefit of their minor children, if certain restrictions are adhered to. They each use this right to pursue their own personal estate planning goals. However, if the shares are transferred, they can only remain voting shares so long as the shareholders constitute a majority of the trustees of the trust holding the shares. Abe establishes a trust to transfer some of his shares to his children. Abe's wife, Lynn, serves as a co-trustee with Bob and Cathy so that the trust shares can remain voting. When each of the siblings prepares their revocable living trust, they will probably create a defined term to identify all of the family business interests. Thus, wherever in the trust that defined term appears, its meaning will be understood. For example:

ABC, Inc., and any other business, whether a corporation, limited liability company, partnership, or other form, owned 80 percent or more by Abe, Bob, and Cathy, and involved in widget manufacturing or any related or ancillary business, shall be referred to as the "Business."

Income and Principal

Income and *principal* are extremely important to define. The following example illustrates this.

EXAMPLE: Tom is the income beneficiary of a trust. He is to receive all income until he reaches age 35. At that time, the trust is distributed to Jane. The trust is invested in a single stock, XYZ, Inc. XYZ, Inc., declares a cash dividend. This is clearly income and is paid to Tom. Later, XYZ, Inc., declares a stock dividend. If it is defined as income, then it is paid to Tom. If it is defined as principal, or a capital item, it is held in trust for the benefit of Jane. The differences to the two beneficiaries can be substantial.

State law can provide a definition of income and principal and these laws, such as the Uniform Prudent Investor Act described in Chapter 7, are changing to more flexibly address modern investment planning. Your trust can also include a definition. For example, cash dividends can generally be assumed to be income and not principal. All corporate distributions in shares of stock (whether denominated as dividends, stock splits, or otherwise, and cash proceeds representing fractions thereof) of any class of stock of any corporation will be considered principal. Dividends on investment company shares attributed to capital gains could be characterized as principal whether declared payable at the option of the shareholders in cash or in shares or otherwise. Liquidating dividends, rights to subscribe to stock, and the proceeds of the sale thereof, and the proceeds of sales of unproductive or underproductive property can be classified as principal.

Should there be any apportionment of the proceeds of the sale of a specific asset of the trust as between principal and income because such asset may be or may have been wholly or partially unproductive of income during any period of time? In many cases, this will not be done. Should this rule be varied depending on whether the asset was real or personal property, or tangible or intangible? Are there any special assets in the trust that should be addressed in a manner different than the general rule? How should the trust allocate between principal and income the depreciation, depletion, amortization, obsolescence, intangible drilling expenses, and similar or related charges generated by an investment in an oil drilling, natural gas, or other investment? Should the allocation simply be left to the discretion of the trustee? If this is done, the trustee must make the allocation in a reasonable and prudent manner that is impartial to the beneficiaries. While this may appear easy, it will not mollify the potential friction between beneficiaries with differing interests or the trustee attempting to mediate. Often it is best to provide a definition which, if included in the trust, will serve as the instructions for the trustee to follow.

What is the relationship of the investment policies of the trust, distribution provisions, and the income and principal definitions? If the trust is invested for a total return (i.e., maximization of aggregate economic gain which includes dividends, interest, capital gains, and even unrealized appreciation) how will the distribution provisions be affected? For example, if there is a current beneficiary to receive all income, and only income, while the principal is to be paid to the remainder, these various provisions should ideally be coordinated.

DESIGNATION OF SITUS AND STATE LAW

The provision governing the choice of law contained in the typical trust agreement is given little thought. A typical clause could read: "The validity, construction, and effect of the provisions of this Trust shall be governed by the laws of [insert the name of your state]." In other situations, the conclusion should not be viewed so simply.

For foreign situs or domestic, asset protection trusts, the provisions governing situs, and applicable law should provide a mechanism to change the situs and the choice of law in the event of unforeseen changes. This differs from a typical choice of law provision that establishes a permanent choice of law. For example, if the laws of the host country or state change unfavorably, the trust protector, in connection with the trustee, could designate a new jurisdiction and choice of law.

What if the designated state enacts unfavorable state tax laws? What if the beneficiaries and trustees all relocate to another part of the country? Thus, in some situations, in can be useful to grant the trustee authorization to change, without court approval, the situs and governing law of the trust.

SECRECY AND NONDISCLOSURE PROVISIONS

A typical foreign trust will include secrecy and nondisclosure provisions to assure privacy. The trustee, however, may request a waiver of this with respect to inquiries by the U.S. government or its agencies. This is not as common in a domestic trust. Where any type of nondisclosure provision is used, exceptions will have to also be made to permit a trustee who is named a party in a lawsuit to defend himself.

ANTIDURESS CLAUSE

This clause permits the trustee to ignore instructions given to it under duress or coercion, for example, when a court which does not have jurisdiction makes a demand, directly or indirectly, on the trustee. This type of provision is common in foreign asset protection trusts.

FLIGHT CLAUSE

Foreign asset protection trusts generally allow the trust to be moved to another jurisdiction, as mentioned previously. This may also be accomplished through a *flight clause.* If a creditor is successful in gaining access to the assets of a foreign asset protection trust through a court having jurisdiction over the trust, the trust is capable of quickly fleeing to another foreign location. If the host country enters into a bilateral trade, tax, or other treaty with the United States, information reporting and other provisions of such a treaty could jeopardize the insulation provided by the foreign trust. A shift of the trust location, and trust assets, to a jurisdiction without such a treaty could assure retention of these benefits.

ANCILLARY DOCUMENTS

You should not forget that there are many ancillary documents essential to the operation of your trust that must be completed for your planning to be successful. This can include many different documents used to properly transfer legal ownership (title) of assets to your trust (see Chapter 3). Also, when any business or investment assets are involved, additional assets from deeds, to limited liability company operating agreements, and the like may be necessary or appropriate (see Chapters 21 and 22). Form SS-4 will have to be filed to obtain a tax identification number for the trust (see Chapter 11). Insurance company forms may have to be completed (see Chapter 20). As for many trusts, especially inter-vivos trusts with a tax orientation, a gift tax return, Form 709, will be required.

CAUTION: Carefully review with all of your professional advisers, attorney, accountant, insurance agent, securities broker, or financial planner what ancillary documents are necessary. Do not rely too heavily on a checklist, since every trust will differ at least somewhat.

CONCLUSION

This chapter reviewed several of the more technical and formalistic provisions included in many different types of trusts. Be alert to these items and address them in the planning process with your attorney if they could be important to achieving your goals.

Part Two

TAX CONSEQUENCES
OF TRUSTS

10 PLANNING FOR THE GIFT AND ESTATE TAX

There are many reasons to set up and use trusts. Saving transfer (estate, gift, and GST) taxes is only one reason. Protecting assets, assuring assets are distributed when, to whom, and how you want, providing professional management, managing assets if someone is disabled, and a myriad of personal reasons justify setting up trusts. If the publicity given to the 2001 Tax Act has you believing trusts are no longer necessary, reconsider what trusts really accomplish.

Saving gift and estate taxes is a key goal if your assets are, or may become, valuable enough that a tax might apply. These taxes are costly—they start at 37 percent and quickly rise to 50 percent and more! Although the 2001 Tax Act will reduce the maximum estate and gift tax rates to 45 percent in 2010, the rates still remain high until the estate tax is permanently repealed in 2010, if that ever actually happens. Even if the estate tax is repealed, the gift tax will remain at 35 percent. While far less burdensome than currently, it remains costly. Finally, in light of the tremendous financial, budgetary, and other uncertainties, it is not clear what the future may hold for gift and estate taxes. Therefore, prudent planning is required to minimize the gift, estate, and other taxes you and your heirs may face, no matter what Congress decides to do. Trusts have been one of the key planning tools to minimize or eliminate gift, estate, and GST taxes. After the 2001 Tax Act, they actually become more important planning tools for many.

To use trusts to minimize or eliminate gift and estate taxes, you must understand the basics of the gift and estate tax. To obtain tax benefits with trusts, the trusts will almost always be irrevocable (i.e., you will not have the right to change or revoke the trust after it is signed). Since these types of trusts cannot be changed, the income, gift, and estate tax implications, as well as other aspects of the trust (e.g., who the trustees are, when beneficiaries should receive distributions, and the like) should all be carefully planned for in advance. This chapter provides an overview of the gift and estate tax, with an emphasis on how they affect trust planning.

OVERVIEW OF THE TRANSFER TAX SYSTEM

The transfer tax system actually consists of three separate, but related, taxes:

1. *Gift tax,* which is a tax assessed on gratuitous transfers of assets while you are alive. The gift tax is discussed next. Even if the estate tax is repealed after the 2001 Tax Act, the gift tax will remain indefinitely.
2. *Estate tax,* which is assessed on transfers of assets following your death (e.g., assets bequeathed under your will).
3. *Generation skipping transfer (GST) tax,* which is assessed on transfers made during your life or following your death to people two generations below yours, such as grandchildren (or trusts for the benefit of such people) (see Chapter 11).

These three federal taxes are all based on your transfer of assets. While the rates of each of these taxes are extremely high, and will remain high for years after the 2001 Tax Act, there are many exclusions, deductions, and other planning benefits.

The three federal transfer taxes—gift, estate, and GST—can be distinguished from the inheritance tax assessed by many states. An inheritance tax is not a tax assessed on your transfer of assets. Rather, it is a tax on the recipient when property is received.

CAUTION: The 2001 Tax Act phases out the credit which had been paid by the federal government to states to share estate tax revenues. The result will be that states will either increase inheritance taxes, or find other taxes to make up for the lost revenues.

THE GIFT TAX

The gift tax is a tax charged on your right to give away assets during your lifetime. Although in everyday usage the term *gift* implies a donative intent, tax law does not require that you had the intent to show this. All that the tax laws require to trigger the gift tax is that you transfer your assets and get back less than full payment of value (consideration).

A Gift Must Be Complete for the Gift Tax to Apply

No taxable gift is made until the gift is *completed.* This means the donor must transfer beneficial interest in the assets to the recipient (donee) and must give up control over the asset. You must part with sufficient control over the assets so that the gift is completed and you cannot retract the gift. The gift must be *beyond your recall*. The delivery of the gift property should also be completed. If you make a gift to a trust for the benefit of your nephew, determining whether the gift is complete will involve not only an analysis as to whether you have consummated each of the steps necessary to transfer the asset to the trust, but the terms of the trust will have to be evaluated as well. For example, if you have substantial control over the trust, the gift may not be complete. If you are a trustee, or if you have reserved significant powers, such as the right to terminate the trust, the gift may not be complete.

Is it better that the gift be completed or not completed for gift tax purposes? It depends on the circumstances and your goals.

NOTE: Incomplete gifts have been used as an intentional planning technique when setting up many different types of trusts. Transfers to a foreign asset protection trust may intentionally be structured so that you retain sufficient powers to avoid a completed gift. If this is not done, you may face, in addition to a gift tax, a substantial excise tax applicable to transfers of assets to foreign countries. (See Chapter 18.)

If your goal is to remove the value of an asset from your estate, you will want the gift to be completed. Further, if your intent is to use the annual $10,000 (indexed for inflation $11,000 in 2002) gift tax exclusion, you will want to be certain that the gift is completed in a particular tax year.

What Is the Value of the Gift Made?

Once you have determined that the transfer is a gift, and that the gift has been completed, you must determine the value of the gift. The value of the gift is often quite obvious where you give cash or stock in a publicly traded company (e.g., IBM, GM, and the like). However, in many situations, the value of the gift will not be simple. These more complex valuation situations can also present the best tax-planning opportunities.

The value of a gift is the fair market value of the asset given on the date the gift is completed. Fair market value is defined as the price which a willing buyer would pay for the asset when purchasing it from a willing seller, where neither the buyer or seller were under any unusual pressure or obligation to consummate the transaction.

If the gift is residential real estate, a written appraisal from a local real estate broker or appraiser is essential. If the gift is commercial real estate, a certified appraisal report should be obtained. The reports should address comparable property sales, replacement cost, and the income capitalization method of valuation.

If the gift is an interest in a closely held business, a written analysis from a business appraiser should be obtained. The analysis should address each of the factors discussed in a ruling published by the Internal Revenue Service, Revenue Ruling 59-60. The appraiser should be very familiar with this ruling and other valuation law. The report should evaluate hard assets (accounts receivable, property, plant, equipment, etc.) and soft or intangible assets (such as goodwill, customer lists, customer loyalty, trademarks, and patents). The analysis should also make adjustments for any transactions that were not arm's-length (on the same basis if the parties had not been related). For example, if you control a family business, you could take a salary and perquisites (company car, travel, etc.) which are substantially in excess of that which an unrelated hired employee would have in a similar situation.

Four Exclusions to Avoid Gift Taxation

There are four exclusions that can be used to avoid the gift tax. One or more of these can be a foundation for how you plan gifts to the trusts that you establish during your lifetime.

The Annual $10,000 Gift Tax Exclusion

You can give away up to $10,000, to any person, without incurring a gift tax. This amount is indexed for inflation ($11,000 in 2002). You can make this type of gift to as many people as you want to during each calendar year. You can give away $11,000 every year to the same person so that over a number of years substantial gifts can be given to the same person. This is called the *annual gift tax exclusion.* For a large estate, the $11,000 limit may not sound large, but it can be substantial when used to the maximum extent feasible.

EXAMPLE: Tom and Tina Taxpayer have three children. Each child is married and has two children. Tom and Tina set up trusts for each of their six grandchildren. Tom can give $11,000 to each of the six trusts each year. Tina can give $11,000 to each of the six trusts each year. Thus, the Taxpayers can give $132,000 per year to trusts for their grandchildren. In two years, they can give $264,000. Since the $11,000 gifts can be made in each calendar year, the Taxpayers could make gifts of $132,000 on December 31 and $132,000 on January 1. Thus, they could give gifts to trusts for their grandchildren in excess of a quarter-million dollars in two days.

When gifts are made to a trust, rather than outright to the intended donee, special requirements must be met for the gifts to qualify for this exclusion.

If you make gifts to a Code Section 529 college savings plan, a special exception to the $11,000 per year rule permits you to make five years' worth of gifts in one year. You and your wife together can thus give anyone's Section 529 plan $110,000 in one year without adverse gift tax consequences. This is a considerable advantage Section 529 plans have over trusts.

Exclusion for Medical and Tuition Payments

You can pay unlimited amounts to a qualifying educational institution without incurring any gift tax. A qualifying educational institution is one that normally maintains a regular faculty and curriculum and normally has a regularly enrolled body of students. You can also make unlimited payments for medical care if paid directly to the person or organization providing the medical services. To qualify for the exclusion, tuition and medical payments must be made directly to the providers.

Marital Deduction

Gifts made to a spouse, who is a U.S. citizen, or to a special marital trust (e.g., a QTIP trust) for a spouse, in any amount, are not subject to gift tax. A less common transfer that also qualifies for the marital deduction (i.e., no tax) is to give your spouse a life estate with a general power of appointment. This means the spouse would have the right to the income or use of the assets for her life. The spouse will also have the right to designate who should receive the property following her death.

If your spouse is not a U.S. citizen, the maximum gift that can be made without incurring a gift tax in any year is $110,000. Any amount over that, or any amount given at death, will only qualify for the marital deduction if made to a special trust called a qualified domestic trust (QDOT) (see Chapter 14).

If your partner is not legally your spouse, the unlimited gift tax marital deduction will not be available and a large transfer will trigger a tax. Special planning will be required (see Chapter 14). For nonmarried couples with large estates, tax planning, even after the 2001 Tax Act, will remain vital.

Charitable Deduction

An unlimited gift tax charitable deduction can permit you to give any amount of property to a qualified charity. For trust planning, large gifts to charities will usually be as a charitable remainder unitrust (CRUT) or as a charitable remainder annuity trust (CRAT) (see Chapter 17). In some cases, you may want to provide a gift to benefit your spouse through a QTIP, and at her death have the trust funds distributed to charity (see Chapters 14 and 17).

This gift tax charitable contribution deduction is independent of the income tax benefits of a charitable gift. You can avoid gift tax and obtain an income tax deduction when you use a charitable remainder trust.

Special Rules Affecting the $10,000 Gift Tax Exclusion

The $10,000 annual exclusion (indexed to $11,000 in 2002) is one of the cornerstones of planning for gifts to trusts. Many taxpayers only make gifts up to $11,000 per person each year to avoid taxable gifts (or as explained next, to avoid using any of their $1 million [2002] exclusion). To take maximum advantage of the annual gift exclusion when planning trusts, consider the following suggestions.

Gift Splitting

Everyone can give away $11,000 per year per donee (recipient). Thus, a husband and wife can together give away $22,000 per year per donee. Do they each have to write out a separate check (or transfer assets separately)? No, a special rule, called *gift splitting*, permits a couple to jointly give away $22,000 per year without worrying about which spouse wrote out the check or owned the asset given to the trust. You can make a gift and have your wife join in the gift so that two $11,000 annual exclusions can reduce the value of your gift to zero for gift tax purposes. To qualify, you and your wife must be married, you both must be citizens or residents of the United States, your wife cannot remarry during the remainder of the year if you die or divorce after making the gift, and both of you must agree (consent) to this tax treatment for the particular gift and for all gifts made by either of you during that particular year.

> **NOTE:** If you choose to gift split you must file a gift tax return, Form 709. Be certain to review this with your accountant before April 15.

Gifts to a Trust

Two issues are raised by gifts to a trust. Who are the donees of the gifts and does the annual $11,000 per donee exclusion from gift taxation apply? When you make a gift to a trust, the beneficiaries of the trust, and not the trust, are considered to be the recipients of the gift.

> **EXAMPLE:** You give $20,000 to an insurance trust that purchases insurance on your life. Your two children are the trust's beneficiaries. This is treated as if your children were each the recipient of a $10,000 gift. You can't then make additional direct gifts of $11,000 to each of your children and have those additional gifts also protected from gift tax by annual exclusion as well. You will have given more than the maximum $11,000 to each child in that year. The fact that one gift is directly to your children, and the other indirectly to them as beneficiaries of the insurance trust will not enable you to double your tax-free gifts. You can, however, gift an additional $1,000 ($11,000 – $10,000 given to the trust).

The $11,000 annual exclusions are only available to offset gifts that meet a technical requirement of "present interest" gifts. This means that the recipient of the gift must have the current use and benefit of, and access to, the gift. For example, if you receive $11,000 in cash, this is clearly a gift of a present interest since you can take the funds and apply them in any manner you wish. Gifts of a future interest do not qualify for the annual exclusion. This includes *reversions* and *remainders* (you receive property at some future date, for example, after the life beneficiary dies, or after a fixed number of years) for which you will not have the right to possess or enjoy the property until some future date.

EXAMPLE: You transfer assets worth $11,000 as a gift to a trust which was established years ago for the benefit of your child. If the child cannot use or benefit from the gift until the money is distributed at some unknown future date (perhaps in the sole discretion of the trustee), the gift will not qualify as a gift of a present interest. Therefore, you won't be able to use the $11,000 annual exclusion to offset the value of the gift. The result is that you will have to use up a portion of your remaining $1 million gift exclusion. If your exclusion has been fully used, you will have to pay a gift tax on the $11,000. Had you transferred the assets directly to the beneficiary, you could have avoided paying a gift tax, or using up any of your exclusion. However, directly giving the cash to the child would not enable you to protect the money from the child's creditors or his or her own spending habits.

Most gifts made to trusts will not meet the present interest requirement because most trusts are drafted to preserve the assets of the trust for future use by the beneficiary. An additional step must be taken to assure that gifts you make to these types of trusts will qualify as a gift of a present interest and will therefore not trigger a tax or use of your exclusion.

NOTE: Qualifying for the $11,000 exclusion is not relevant to many types of trusts. Assets of a revocable living trust are fully taxable in your estate (subject to the use of credit shelter and marital deduction planning) so qualifying for the annual exclusion would not make sense. Grantor retained annuity trusts (GRATs), grantor retained unitrusts (GRUTs), and qualified personal residence trusts (QPRTs) are structured so that the gift tax annual exclusion will not apply to gifts to those trusts. Thus, in funding these trusts a portion of your unified credit would be used. Charitable trusts similarly do not qualify for the annual exclusion.

One way for a gift to a trust to be a gift of a present interest qualifying for the $11,000 annual exclusion is for these requirements to be met: (1) The trust should generate an income flow, (2) some portion of the income must go to the trust beneficiaries, and (3) the amount of income the beneficiaries will receive must be ascertainable.

EXAMPLE: You make a gift to a trust for your two daughters. The trust requires all assets to be fully and productively invested and that all income be paid out to the two daughters each year. On the death of the last daughter, the trust is paid to your grandchildren. The income interest of your daughters, determined on an actuarial basis, might qualify as a gift of a present interest.

Another approach used in some trusts for children under age 21 is for the trust to meet the requirements of Code Section 2503(c) so that the present interest requirement can be ignored until the beneficiary attains the age of 21 (see Chapter 16).

The most common alternative is to use an annual demand power. This is often called a *Crummey power* after the court case in which the court sustained the taxpayer's argument that a gift to a trust, where the beneficiary had an opportunity to withdraw the funds currently, but did not elect to do so, qualified as a gift of a present interest, and hence for the annual gift tax exclusion. The trust must give the beneficiary a reasonable opportunity to withdraw the money. This is accomplished by having the trustee give written notice to the beneficiary that the withdrawal right for monies contributed exists and that the beneficiary has the right to send in a written request demanding the money be distributed. Have the beneficiary sign the notice acknowledging receipt.

Since an audit of a trust may not occur for many years, it can be difficult to keep track of all the Crummey notices you have sent. You may wish to provide your accountant a copy to retain in the permanent tax file for your trust (where he or she maintains a copy of the trust, tax election information, and similar documents). This will also alert your accountant to any gift tax return filing requirements. The trustee should retain a copy in his or her gift files as well.

If you are planning any irrevocable trust (e.g., life insurance trust or a child's trust) to which you will make gifts, you should carefully review these complex Crummey power rules with your estate planner and set up a procedure for who will handle sending and saving them. If this notice is required to be given, but is not provided to the beneficiaries, the transfers or gifts to the trust may not qualify for the annual $11,000 gift tax exclusion.

CAUTION: If you have existing irrevocable trusts to which you are making gifts, and you have not been issuing Crummey notices for each gift, consult your tax adviser immediately. Some tax advisers had their clients issue a single notice to the beneficiaries when the trust was formed, and had the beneficiaries waive the need for future notices. The IRS has ruled that this is not sufficient and that annual notices are required. If you have not been making notices, it may be advisable to begin doing so for the current year's gifts. Your estate planner may also suggest that if the notices were given verbally in prior years, that everyone involved sign an affidavit confirming this.

A gift to a trust will qualify for the annual $11,000 gift tax exclusion up to the amount that the beneficiary (e.g., your child in a children's trust) can withdraw each year from the trust. Even if the beneficiary does not exercise this right, so that the money or other assets remain in the trust, the existence of this right enables you as donor to avoid any gift tax or use of your exclusion.

Exclusion

If you make a taxable gift in excess of the exclusions available, there is one last, but substantial, tax break available to offset any gift tax that would otherwise be due. This break is called your *exclusion* and it is the corner-stone of estate and trust planning for most taxpayers.

Gift and Estate Tax Rates after 2001 Tax Act

Year	Top Estate Tax Rate	Top Gift Tax Rate	Estate Exclusion Amount
2002	50%	50%	1 million
2003	49%	49%	$1 million
2004	48%	48%	$1.5 million*
2005	47%	47%	$1.5 million*
2006	46%	46%	$2 million*
2007	45%	45%	$2 million*
2008	45%	45%	$2 million*
2009	45%	45%	$3.5 million*
2010	Repealed	35%	N/A*
2011	55%	55%	$1 million

* The gift tax exclusion is limited to $1 million, but the estate and gift tax exclusions remain unified so that a use of your gift tax exclusion will reduce dollar for dollar the estate tax exclusion remaining available to you.

The gift tax and the estate tax are largely integrated and will remain so until 2010 when the estate tax is to be repealed (if it happens). They share many similar concepts, in particular a single exclusion. This exclusion can permit anyone to give away up to $1 million, in aggregate, in assets during their lifetime (as gifts) or at death (e.g., under your will). In 2004, the estate tax exclusion is scheduled to increase to $1.5 million and eventually to $3.5 million in 2009. However, the gift tax exclusion will remain at $1 million. When the estate tax is repealed in 2010, the gift tax exclusion will still continue, at the same $1 million level. The gift tax rate will be the same as the maximum income tax rate.

EXAMPLE: In the year 2005, you give away $900,000. You can still give away $100,000 ($1 million – $900,000) without incurring a gift tax. If you die before making any more gifts, your estate will be entitled to a $600,000 exclusion [$1,500,000 exclusion available in year 2005 – $900,000 previously used]. The gift and estate tax exclusion remain unified, only the limit on lifetime gifts is lower.

You can give away up to $1 million above the $10,000 annual exclusion amounts without incurring tax.

EXAMPLE: Paul Parent, a widower, has made no gifts before the current tax year. Paul gives $11,000 to each of his three children on January 10. No gift tax is due and none of Paul's unified credit is used. This is because Paul's gifts are each offset by the $11,000 annual exclusion available on gifts to each recipient. On June 1 of the same year, Paul Parent gives each of his three children an additional $200,000. The annual exclusion has been used up on the January gifts. Therefore, he will use up $600,000 (3 gifts × $200,000 per gift) of the transfers which can be offset by his $1 million exclusion. In the next year, Paul pays $64,036 for tuition and medical expenses of his children and grandchildren direct to the educational institutions and medical care providers. No portion of his unified credit or annual exclusion is used because these gifts qualify for the special exception described for medical and tuition payments. Paul dies four years later, having made no additional gifts. Paul's estate can use his remaining exclusion of $400,000 [$1 million – $600,000] to offset the tax on $400,000 of assets passing under Paul's revocable living trust.

The previous example also illustrates how the gift and estate tax are so closely related. You really cannot plan for one and not the other. In addition, when planning with trusts, you need to consider the impact of the gift tax rules, the nature of the trusts established, and the consequences to your overall plan.

EXAMPLE: Tom Taxpayer makes gifts to his partner of $551,000. The first $11,000 is tax free as a result of the annual exclusion. The next $540,000 [$551,000 total gift – $11,000 annual exclusion available] is a taxable gift. Since Tom has not used any of his exclusion, no tax is currently due. However, Tom will have exhausted a portion of his exclusion so that $460,000 [$1,000,000 – $540,000] remains to be given away without a gift tax.

In the next year, Tom establishes a grantor retained annuity trust (GRAT) contributing 40 percent of a family limited partnership which owns $4 million of real estate, for the benefit of his son (see Chapter 21). The gift tax value of the GRAT is only $650,000 (as a result of discounting and the GRAT time value of money concepts explained in later chapters). No portion of the annual exclusion is available for a gift to a GRAT so the full value of the gift offsets Tom's remaining exclusion of $460,000. Because Tom's remaining exclusion is smaller than the gift tax value of the gift to the GRAT, Tom will have thus made a taxable transfer to his trust of $190,000 [$650,000 taxable gift – $460,000 gift for which exclusion is still available to offset the tax]. A gift tax will be due. Tom will have to pay the gift tax and file a gift tax return, Form 709, by April 15 of the next calendar year. If Tom dies in 2003, there will not be any exclusion remaining to offset any tax then due. If Tom dies in 2004 or later, the scheduled increases in the exclusion will be available to offset tax on his remaining assets owned at death. Tom should have weighed the benefit of deferring a portion of the gift until the exclusion increased.

The gift tax is vital to consider when planning to use most types of trusts. Although the tax can be extremely costly, careful planning and judicious use of the exceptions and other special rules can dramatically limit the tax. Even after the 2001 Tax Act, this type of planning should be pursued. Why waste your exclusion unnecessarily when you cannot know with certainty the future of the gift and estate tax, the size of your estate, and a host of other factors that might affect you or your loved ones?

THE ESTATE TAX

The estate tax is a transfer charge assessed on property owned by you on your death. The actual tax, however, is much broader and more complicated.

Why is this complex tax so important to plan for? Estate tax rates can reach as high as 50 percent (60 percent when certain phase-outs are in effect prior to the 2001 Tax Act). Even though they are to be reduced to 45 percent, the rates remain high so that planning will remain important. The real rates can be even higher when state transfer taxes are considered. As noted earlier, state inheritance and related taxes may increase as a result of the 2001 Tax Act changes phasing out the tax remitted by the federal government back to the states.

These high rates are even costlier if the generation skipping transfer (GST) tax is added on. Planning to minimize this tax burden is essential if you want to pass on the maximum amount of assets to your heirs.

A key to minimizing estate (and other) taxes is the proper use of trusts.

EXAMPLE: For most taxpayers, the proper use of a bypass trust to fully utilize the exclusion available to both spouses, a marital trust (QTIP or QDOT), and perhaps an irrevocable life insurance trust, can eliminate most or all estate taxes, protect assets from second and later marriages, keep creditors at bay, provide professional management, and more. However, if you do not have a spouse, a QPRT, GRAT, or a common law *grantor retained interest trust* (GRIT), or other trust, techniques may be used instead to eliminate the estate tax burden.

EXAMPLE: You are considering using a grantor retained annuity trust (GRAT) to give interests in a rental property to your children. The use of the GRAT, as explained in Chapter 20, will discount substantially the value of the gift for gift tax purposes. However, if you don't survive the term of the trust, the entire value of the rental property will be pulled back into your taxable estate. As an alternative, your estate planner suggests transferring the rental property to a family limited partnership and make gifts to your children. Gifts made in this manner would be removed from your estate no matter how long you survive. To discuss these options with your estate planner, you need to understand how the estate tax works.

What Is Included in Your Gross Estate?

To determine the estate tax on your estate, your executor must identify all property and property interests that are included in what is called your *gross estate* for federal estate tax purposes.

NOTE: Don't confuse *taxable* estate with *probate* estate. *Taxable* estate means assets that will be subject to estate tax on your death. *Probate* estate refers to assets that must pass through the probate process on your death. Thus, if you set up a revocable living trust and transfer all of your assets to the trust, your probate estate may be nonexistent. However, your taxable estate may be substantial since it will include all assets in your trust. Insurance, IRAs, pension assets, and jointly owned property may all pass to your heirs without becoming part of your probate estate. However, each can be part of your taxable estate.

Your gross estate is the sum of the values of all assets or property owned, or in which you have an interest, on your death. Generally, your gross estate includes all property, whether real estate, personal property, or intangible property, to the extent the estate tax rules require that this property be included in your estate.

CAUTION: Many taxpayers substantially underestimate the size of their taxable estates and as a result fail to take the steps necessary to avoid estate taxes. Most taxpayers simply do not feel as "rich" as the IRS and the estate tax laws view them. Your house may have appreciated substantially, but is not a spendable asset so long as you live in it. Life insurance owned by you can be included in your estate, but while you are alive, you certainly would not view the death benefit as an asset. Pension assets are often not felt to be as valuable as they actually are because until retirement they are often not accessed, and post retirement they are often drawn down periodically, and not viewed as a spendable asset. Thus, you could have a substantial estate for federal tax purposes without actually "feeling" wealthy.

Assets included in your gross estate include any interest that you had in property at the time of your death which is included in your probate estate. For example, a bonus you were entitled to at the time of your death is included in your gross estate. If you contracted to purchase real estate and died prior to consummating the purchase, the value of the contractual right to the property is included in your estate.

Property interests to be included in your estate are very broadly defined. Property that you gave away during your life can be required to be included in your gross estate in some cases. For example, if you transferred property, say to a trust but retained the right to the income, or even the right to designate who will obtain the income, these assets will be taxed as part of your gross estate. If you gave property to another person or a trust for them, but they could only obtain the right to use and enjoy that property after your death, the entire value of the property is included in your estate. If you transferred property but reserved the right to change who will have the right to enjoy that property, this will also be included in your estate. This can be a problem if you set up a trust hoping to remove assets from your estate, but you retain too many powers to control the eventual distribution of the assets in the trust.

If you have a general *power of appointment* over property (you could designate who would get the property including your estate or creditors), the value of that property is included in your gross estate. Powers of appointment can be extremely tricky to plan for. Not only are the rules quite technical, but in some instances it is very difficult to even identify if and where you have been given such powers. These powers can exist not only in trusts

---

EXAMPLE: Your uncle established a trust for his children. Following the death of the last of his children, he gave you the power to appoint the trust assets to any person or any number of people you designated by a clause in your will specifically referring to the power. Since you were not a beneficiary of the trust for many years while your cousins were alive, how can you find out about this power to even plan for it?

---

you have created, but in trusts other people have created even if you are not listed as a beneficiary of the trust.

Joint property presents another costly trap for many taxpayers since many mistakenly believe that joint ownership removes assets from their estate. Joint assets are not included in your *probate* estate since they pass on the death of the first joint tenant to the surviving joint tenant automatically. However, the value of these assets is included in your *taxable* estate. In fact, the tax law presumes that where the joint tenants are not spouses, the entire value of the joint property is taxable in the estate of the first joint tenant to die, unless the surviving joint tenant can demonstrate that he or she contributed to the purchase of the asset. For a qualified joint tenancy with a spouse, only one-half of the property is deemed taxable in the estate of the first joint owner. This special rule is not applicable where the spouse is not a U.S. citizen.

Certain transactions that occurred within three years of your death are "pulled back" into your estate for tax purposes. These include:

- Gift tax paid on gifts made within three years of your death (the value of the gifts is not pulled back in unless one of the other special provisions pull it back in). So if you made a large taxable transfer to an irrevocable trust and died two years later, the amount of gift tax you paid is added to your estate.
- Life insurance policies that you transferred. This can occur when you set up an irrevocable life insurance trust but die within three years of transferring the policy to the trust.
- If you have a reversionary interest or a power to revoke, amend, or terminate property interests, and if you actually revoke the power within three years of your death, the value of the property involved will be taxed in your estate.

EXAMPLE: If you form a trust but retain the unlimited right to revoke the trust or replace the trustee, the value of the trust assets will be included in your estate. If you revoke this power and die less than three years later, the value of the trust will still be included in your estate even though you did not hold this power at death.

Assets in Your Estate Must Be Valued

Once the assets to be included in your taxable estate are identified, as discussed earlier, you must value them. The fair market value of the assets at the date of your death is the amount to be included in your gross estate. This is the price at which the property would change hands between a willing buyer and a willing seller, neither being under any compulsion to buy or to sell, and both having reasonable knowledge of the relevant facts.

A number of special valuation rules which should be considered. We discuss these next.

Special Use Valuation

Real estate is generally valued at its highest and best use. For example, you owned land you used as a tree farm, which could be developed as a subdivision. If no special rules apply, the land would have to be valued as if it were to be sold to a developer. This result can create hardships. It could burden your family farm excessively to require application of the general rule. It could force your heirs to sell the farm to pay the tax. Thus, the tax laws permit the executor to elect to value the land based on its current use, up to a maximum decrease in the value of the gross estate of $750,000.

Alternate Valuation Date

The date at which the valuation must be made also has to be determined. In most cases, it is the date of your death on which values are set. Your executor (and perhaps the trustee of your revocable living trust) has the option to elect to value all assets as of the date six months following the date of death. This is called the *alternate valuation date.* This election could be useful in the event that there is a decline in the value of key assets following death (e.g., a stock market crash between the date of death and the date the estate tax return must be filed).

Deductions, Expenses, and Credits

Your estate is allowed deductions for funeral expenses, debts, administrative costs, legal and accounting fees, and casualty or theft losses. Certain claims against your estate can be deducted, as can qualifying charitable contributions. There are a number of credits that may also be applied to reduce your estate tax. These include a credit for prior transfers, for death taxes paid to your state (subject to phase-out and eventual elimination by the 2001 Tax Act), and so forth.

Who Pays the Estate Tax When Trusts Are Used?

The estate tax, even after the 2001 Tax Act, will remain substantial for many millions of taxpayers' estates. A key question you must address is: Who will pay the tax? Which trusts or other beneficiaries under the will should bear the tax burden? Most wills include tax allocation clauses to address this. The following discussion illustrates the importance of addressing tax allocation matters with your estate planner.

One of the most common estate tax planning benefits is the unlimited marital deduction. This deduction is available on gifts and bequests to a spouse who is a U.S. citizen. Qualifying marital gifts or bequests can be made outright (i.e., directly to the spouse) or in a special marital trust, called a qualified terminable interest property (QTIP) trust. When a QTIP trust is used, the assets in the trust qualify for an unlimited estate tax marital deduction on the death of the first spouse. On the later death of the second spouse (i.e., the spouse that was the beneficiary of the marital trust) these QTIP trust assets are generally taxable in the estate of the surviving spouse. Unless the will of the surviving spouse explicitly provides to the contrary (which usually it will not, at least not intentionally), the executor of the surviving spouse's estate will recover any estate tax payable with respect to the QTIP assets, from the QTIP trust, or the beneficiaries of the QTIP trust. This should be the result if the surviving spouse's will is silent. This will be the result where the surviving spouse's will directs that the QTIP assets bear their own tax.

EXAMPLE: Husband dies and is survived by Wife-2. Husband's estate is allocated to $1 million (2002) to a bypass trust with the $1 million balance to a QTIP trust, income to Wife-2 for her life, and on her death, to issue of Husband and Wife-1, his children from his former marriage. On Wife-2's later death, her estate consists of $1 million, plus the QTIP assets. Assume the estate tax is assessed at a flat 50 percent rate. If the tax was $1 million, $500,000 would be paid out of her assets passing to her children and $500,000 would be paid out of the QTIP passing to the children of her deceased Husband's former marriage.

What if the wife's will was unartfully drafted to include a generic tax allocation clause that provided that all taxes should be paid from the residuary of the estate (the residuary is what is left after specific distribution provisions are completed). Would that language override the presumption that the QTIP trust should bear its share of the tax? If it did, then the husband's children from his prior marriage would receive the entire QTIP trust, undiminished by estate taxes. Wife-2's estate would bear the entire $1 million tax, so that her children from her prior marriage would inherit nothing ($1 million estate less $1 million in estate taxes). Fortunately, the law won't permit this unintended tax result. The right to recover estate tax from a qualifying terminable interest property (QTIP) marital trust will be waived only if the language in the decedent's will specifically states that this shall occur. The point remains, however, that planning for which assets and bequests bear tax, is critical to planning.

CONCLUSION

The gift and estate taxes are complex and broad transfer taxes that can substantially affect the type and nature of trusts that you may choose to use. A properly planned gift and estate tax program almost always including trusts is an essential step for any large estate. Even if your estate is not large, it would be advisable to consider gift and estate taxes when planning. Otherwise, you could waste valuable benefits (e.g., your exclusion) which will be needed in the future if your estate grows. Planning is also important because many taxpayers simply don't realize how the IRS views their estate.

The judicious use of annual exclusion gifts, with particular attention to the problems created by gifts to trust, can enable you to transfer substantial assets out of your estate at little or no tax cost. The careful planning of assets transferred to irrevocable trusts, and the proper restriction of the rights and powers that you retain in those trusts, can provide outstanding opportunities for reducing your potential estate tax cost while still providing you some comfort and assurance as to how those assets will be used and the many other benefits that trusts can provide.

Considering the complexities and the usually substantial amounts involved, always review the gift and estate tax issues with your tax adviser.

11 PLANNING FOR THE GENERATION SKIPPING TRANSFER TAX

The gift and estate taxes, described in Chapter 10, are not the only taxes to face on making gifts using trusts. The generation skipping transfer (GST) tax is an expensive and complicated transfer tax that can affect wealthy taxpayers making transfers by gift or at death to grandchildren, other people, and trusts, whom the tax laws consider to be more than two generations beyond the donor. GST tax considerations are even broader and can affect planning for those that don't quite consider themselves Rockefellers.

EXAMPLE: You work as a physician and are quite concerned about malpractice. You are also on your third marriage and wish to protect assets. Finally, if managed care doesn't get the better of you, you hope in the future to have a substantial estate. Any of these reasons can make trust planning for your family important to consider, and GST planning, even though your estate is not huge, can be important. You form a dynasty trust for yourself and all of your descendants. You ask your parents to amend their wills and instead of leaving you directly whatever they intended to bequeath (you don't have to address with them what you are getting), you ask that they instead bequeath it to your dynasty trust. This trust will safeguard your assets from malpractice claimants, your third and any future spouses, and estate taxes on your death if your estate grows as hoped. GST tax exemption will have to be allocated on your parents' estate tax return to the bequests they make to you. Thus, GST tax planning is relevant even though your parents' estates may not be subject to estate tax on their death, and your estate at present isn't that large. The benefits of this type of planning are tremendous.

The GST tax is charged on every gift or other transfer of property that meets the requirements of being a generation skipping transfer. The GST tax is calculated as a flat 50 percent tax rate on the taxable amount of a generation skipping transfer (55 percent prior to the 2001 Tax Act). The rate will be reduced each year to match the maximum estate tax rate applicable after the 2001 Tax Act (see the chart in Chapter 10).

The purpose of the GST tax is to equalize intergenerational taxation of property transfers where planning is attempted to avoid the estate tax. The GST tax was designed to prevent the very wealthy from passing assets through many layers of generations, free of transfer tax, often through the use of trusts.

To understand how to implement the many planning opportunities using trusts to minimize or eliminate GST tax, it is essential to understand the basics of how the GST tax works. Once the basics are explained, the planning opportunities are examined in detail.

HOW THE GST TAX WORKS

You are entitled to an exclusion from the GST tax, similar to that available under the gift and estate tax. The exclusion in 2002 and 2003 is $1 million, indexed for inflation. For 2004 through 2009, the GST tax exclusion is the same as the estate tax exclusion in the chart in Chapter 10. After 2009, the tax is eliminated (supposedly). Once it has been determined that you've made a taxable generation skipping transfer, the GST tax must be calculated. The first step is to determine the value of the property involved. The property is generally valued at the time of the transfer occurred. However, if the transfer was a direct skip (explained next) and the property was included your gross estate, the special valuation rules your estate uses (e.g., alternate valuation date or special use valuation) will apply to the GST as well. Where the GST (e.g., a gift to a trust for your grandchildren) also triggers a gift tax, the amount of GST tax you pay is also treated as a further gift subject to the gift tax. Wow, they tax you on paying a tax!

The GST tax is assessed at a flat rate equal to the maximum estate tax rate, 55 percent in 2001, 50 percent in 2002 and declining to 45 percent in 2009 as provided in the 2001 Tax Act.

Overview of Transfers That Trigger the GST Tax

The GST tax can apply to a broad range of property transfers, including transfers of property in trust (e.g., a gift to a trust established for all of your grandchildren), life estates (e.g., a child has the right to income from the property for life and on the child's death a grandchild receives the property), remainder interests (e.g., a grandchild receives the property after the death of a child and the termination of the child's life estate in the property), and so forth.

For the GST tax to apply, a GST "taxable event" must occur. This requires a *generation skipping transfer*. The simplest example is where you give your grandchild property. More technically, the GST tax applies where there is a transfer of property to a person who is considered to be a member of a generation at least two generations below the generation of the person making the gift.

EXAMPLE: You're generation 1. Your child is generation 2. Your grandchild is generation 3. Assume that your spouse sets up a irrevocable trust for one of your grandchildren and makes a gift to the trust of $45,000 of stock. This gift would trigger GST tax consequences. This is because the gift is for the benefit of a member of a generation at least two generations below your generation. A gift from your spouse to your child of the same amount would not cause the GST tax to apply (but there could be a gift tax).

Some basic definitions must be explained to discuss the complicated GST tax. These include the three events which can cause the GST tax to apply. These are a direct skip, a taxable distribution, and a taxable termination. It is necessary to understand the term *skip person* before explaining each of these three rules.

Who Is a Skip Person?

A *skip person* is a person who is two or more generations below the generation of the person making the gift or establishing a trust. This could include your grandchild, or a trust for the benefit of your grandchild. A trust is considered a skip person where no distributions can be made to nonskip persons. A nonskip person is a person who is less than two generations below the generation of the person making the gift (e.g., your child or sibling).

EXAMPLE: A bypass trust is formed under your will for the benefit of your surviving spouse and descendants. Descendants include grandchildren who are skip persons. However, your spouse and children are nonskip persons so that the trust is not a skip person. This doesn't mean that GST tax is not a consideration. What it does mean is that the initial transfer to the trust is not a transfer to a skip person so that the GST tax will not be due immediately. If distributions are later made to a great-grandchild, who is clearly a skip person, GST tax may apply.

While a grandchild or later descendant is obviously a skip person, the law is unfortunately much broader and more complex. A skip person can include any individual (not only a direct descendant) who is more than a specified number of years younger than the person setting up the trust or making the gift. For nonlineal descendants, a generation is considered to be 25 years. A person born within 12.5 years (i.e., half of the 25 years) of your birthday will be treated as being of your generation. A person who is more than 12.5 but less than 37.5 (i.e., 12.5 + 25 years, which is considered a generation) is considered to be in the same generation as your children would be (assuming you had children). Persons who are more than 37.5 years younger, are skip persons, considered to be in the same generation as your grandchildren would be (assuming you had grandchildren).

EXAMPLE: Gary Grantor, age 73, never married and has no children. His will provides that his estate will be distributed one-half to his partner and one-half to his four nephews. His nephews are ages 22, 23, 25, and 39, respectively. If Gary died, the distributions to the first three nephews could trigger GST tax consequences. The fourth nephew is deemed to be in the same generation as a child of Gary would be.

Taxable Transfer 1—A Direct Skip

A direct skip is a transfer of an interest in property, which is subject to the estate or gift tax, to a skip person (or to a trust for the benefit of a skip person). A direct skip occurs, for example, if your will leaves a car to a grandchild. If a trust is created and all trust income is accumulated for a number of years without distribution, but eventually the trust benefits only skip persons, a direct skip occurs and a tax is assessed.

The GST tax for a direct skip, when no trust is involved, is to be paid by the person making the transfer (the donor, or if it is a bequest under your will, your estate). If the transfer is made from a trust, then the trustee will have to pay the tax.

EXAMPLE: You transfer property to an *irrevocable* (cannot be changed) trust for the benefit of your grandchildren. If the transfer is a gift for federal gift tax purposes, and a direct skip, it will trigger the GST tax. If, however, you retain sufficient powers over the trust, or alternatively give sufficient powers to your children over the trust (so that the trust will be taxable in their estates), the GST tax won't apply. These two techniques: (1) your retaining powers over the trust, or (2) giving your children (i.e., a nonskip person) sufficient powers over a trust, are two additional planning techniques that can be used to accomplish personal goals while avoiding the GST tax.

A direct skip is a tax-exclusive calculation. This means that if you as donor pay the GST tax on a gift of assets (a direct skip) to your grandchild, the amount of GST tax you pay will not be considered an additional gift for GST tax purposes. While this sounds far from generous, for some of the GST transfers described next, the GST tax is calculated on a "tax-inclusive" basis so that the payment of GST tax triggers more GST tax!

A special exclusion from GST taxation is a direct skip where a child has died. If your child dies and you make a gift to the child of your deceased child (i.e., your grandchild), no GST tax will be assessed. Thus, your child will not be considered a nonskip person. The 2001 Tax Act liberalized this benefit somewhat.

Taxable Transfer 2—A Taxable Distribution

Where there is a distribution of property or money from a trust to a skip person, the GST tax may apply.

EXAMPLE: Your spouse sets up a single trust for the benefit of your two daughters and their three children (i.e., your grandchildren). Any distribution by the trustee to any of the three grandchildren will result in a *taxable distribution* subject to GST tax. The grandchildren are all considered skip persons for purposes of the GST tax since they are two generations below you, the grantor of the trust.

PLANNING TIP: Your GST and trusts planning may encourage you to set up trusts for your children that can make taxable distributions to your grandchildren. This could occur where you've used up your $1 million (indexed) exemption. If you set up a trust solely for the benefit of your grandchildren, the transfer would immediately trigger the GST tax. Since this tax is so onerous, it's always best to defer it. Deferral of the GST will let the assets in the trust continue to grow. If the trust names your children and grandchildren as beneficiaries, and the trustee has the power to sprinkle income to any of these beneficiaries, the GST tax can be deferred until the trustee actually makes a distribution to one of the grandchildren, or the children all die. If you've set up a GST exempt trust to use your $1 million (indexed) GST exemption, your trustee could be making generous distributions to your grandchildren from that trust before tapping the expensive (from a GST tax perspective) money in the sprinkle trust.

The GST tax on a taxable distribution is based on the fair value of the property transferred, reduced by any expenses incurred in connection with determining the GST tax. If the GST tax is paid out of a trust, the amount of tax paid is treated as an additional distribution subject to the tax. The GST tax on a taxable distribution is charged against the property that was given, unless specific provisions are made for a different treatment. The transferee (your grandchild in the previous examples), however, is liable to pay the GST tax.

When a GST-taxable distribution occurs, the tax basis (what you as the grantor paid for the property transferred to the trust) is increased. The increase is for the portion of the GST tax attributable to the excess of the fair market value of the property above its tax basis. However, the increase cannot increase the tax basis to more then the value of the property.

If income from a trust is distributed to a skip person, the GST tax as a taxable distribution will apply. However, the recipient can deduct the GST tax paid on the income distribution on his or her personal income tax return.

Taxable Transfer 3—A Taxable Termination

A *taxable termination* is a transaction that will trigger the GST tax. This occurs when the interests of a beneficiary of a trust (e.g., your child who is entitled to trust income while he is alive) terminates (e.g., your child dies) and a grandchild then receives the principal of the trust. This could occur as a result of a death, lapse of time (e.g., the trust runs only until your child reaches age 60, at which time the trust ends and your grandchild receives the money), or release of a power. This will be considered a taxable termination resulting in a GST tax.

EXAMPLE: You create a trust. Income is paid to your child for his life. On your child's death, the principal passes to your grandchild. On the child's death, when the child's interest terminates, a taxable termination will occur triggering the GST tax. The GST tax would be in addition to any gift or estate tax paid when the trust was created. If the trust does not terminate but rather just makes a distribution to the grandchild, the rules for taxable distribution instead apply. There can be important differences depending on which rule applies. These differences are quite technical (e.g., tax basis adjustments) and should be discussed with your tax adviser.

Several exceptions can prevent incurring the GST tax in these situations. A common planning technique is to cause the trust assets to be taxed in a nonskip person's estate.

EXAMPLE: If, in the above example, your child was given a general power of appointment over the property (i.e., the right to designate who should inherit the property on his death), the property would be taxed in the child's estate and no GST tax would be due. This is because the power of appointment would constitute an interest in the property as required under the above exception. This could be advantageous, especially after the exclusion increases according to the 2001 Tax Act. Your child may be able to use the increased exclusion to avoid any estate tax while simultaneously helping prevent GST tax on the trust termination.

The GST tax on a taxable termination is payable by the trustee of the trust. The amount of tax is calculated based on the value of all property to which the taxable termination occurred, reduced by expenses, debts, and taxes. The tax is quite burdensome because it is a "tax-inclusive" transfer tax. This is similar to the estate tax. What this means is that there is no deduction for the tax paid.

EXAMPLE: If the trust were $1 million, and a 50 percent (2002 tax rates) GST tax applied, the tax would be $500,000. Thus, the tax is assessed on the same dollars used to pay the tax (i.e., on the full $1 million, including the $500,000 of it which is tax). These are dollars that never pass to any beneficiary.

Of modest relief is that when a taxable termination occurs, the tax basis of the assets involved is "stepped-up." This is similar to what happens when assets are included in an estate.

EXAMPLE: In the above example, if the donor/grantor who set up the trust had a $1,000 tax basis (investment) in the $1 million asset transferred to the trust, if the asset were sold, there would be a $999,000 taxable gain for income tax purposes [$1 million value − $1,000 tax basis]. When the child beneficiary of the trust dies and a GST tax is incurred as a result of a taxable termination, the tax basis of the asset is increased (stepped-up) to its $1 million fair value so that there is no income tax gain if the asset is sold. After 2009, if the estate and GST tax are repealed as planned under the 2001 Tax Act, the carryover basis rules will apply and a different result will occur.

Caution: If any portion of the GST tax is avoided by use of the $1 million GST exemption discussed later, the basis adjustment is reduced.

Disclaimers Can Trigger GST Tax

Disclaimers are a common post-death estate tax planning technique. They can, however, trigger costly GST tax consequences. Any well-drafted will addresses what happens if a particular beneficiary dies. For example, if you bequeath your valuable antique gun collection to your son, your will might say that if your son is not then living, or if he disclaims the bequest (files legal documents stating that he does not wish to receive the gun collection), the gun collection will be given to his son (i.e., your grandson). This type of flexible drafting is important. Obviously, if your son has died, you want to address where assets should be distributed. But it means more. What if your son is alive and well, but for other reasons does not wish to own the particular bequest. For example, he could be in the midst of a divorce or lawsuit and not wish to expose the gun collection to creditors. He could then disclaim the bequest. This requires filing papers in the local probate or surrogates court. The result is that your will is interpreted as if he died before you. In this case, the gun collection would be given to your grand-son. This disclaimer, while accomplishing important asset protection or personal goals, may have inadvertently triggered the GST tax: the gun collection now passes to your grandson, a skip person.

HOW TO MINIMIZE THE GST TAX IMPACT ON YOUR TRUST

Several basic GST planning techniques can help you avoid the harsh tax results.

Annual per Donee Gift Tax Exclusion

You can still give up to $10,000 (indexed for inflation, $11,000 in 2002) per year to any person, including every grandchild, without triggering the GST tax. If your spouse joins you in the gift, you can give $20,000 per person per year. Thus, over a period of years, you can transfer substantial assets to your grandchildren with no GST tax cost. Again, however, the GST can be quite tricky. The requirements to qualify a gift to a trust for a grandchild or other skip person for the annual $11,000 GST exclusion are more stringent than the requirements discussed in Chapter 10 to qualify for the annual $11,000 gift tax annual exclusion for outright gifts.

Although the $11,000 annual exclusion is available for the GST tax, the requirements are stricter then those applicable to the gift tax. For gifts to a trust to qualify for the GST tax annual exclusion, several requirements must be met. During the life of the grandchild (or other skip person) who is beneficiary of the trust, payments cannot be made to any other person. Thus, the commonly used sprinkle power (the trustee has discretion to pay income and principal to anyone from a listed group of beneficiaries) will not be acceptable. This is why a single or pot trust for grandchildren will not qualify. You have to have separate trusts for each grandchild. This requirement does not, however, prevent the trustee from accumulating income in any given year rather than distributing it.

An additional requirement is that if the beneficiary dies during the term of the trust, the trust assets must be taxable in the beneficiary's (e.g., your grandchild's) estate. This requirement can prevent gifts to a typical grandchild's education trust from qualifying. For example, assume that the trust provided that assets were to be held until the grandchild attained the age of 35 whereupon the assets would be distributed to the grandchild; if the grandchild died before the trust ended, the trust assets would be held in trust for the grandchild's children. This type of trust won't qualify for the annual $11,000 GST tax exclusion because the assets would not be included in the grandchild's estate. One solution is to give the grandchild a general power of appointment (see earlier discussion and sample clause). In some cases, you may prefer the certainty of control over where the assets will be distributed. If this is the case (hence the grandchild is not given a general power of appointment), you should be certain to review the tax rules that determine when the IRS will automatically allocate the GST exemption (i.e., a portion of your $1 million GST exclusion) to that trust to be sure that you are getting the result you want.

CAUTION: The 2001 Tax Act has further complicated the process of determining when the GST exemption should be allocated to a trust. In many situations, the tax rules will assume you've allocated GST exemption to a particular trust even if you didn't want it to be allocated. Your GST exemption will be allocated automatically to direct skips and to certain indirect skips which are made to a GST trust. This is a complex term which you have to review with your tax adviser when engaging in this type of planning. Be sure to review gift tax return filing requirements with your accountant.

EXAMPLE: Grandmother has one child, a divorced daughter with two children (i.e., her grandchildren). Grandmother gives $30,000 in corporate bonds to a trust for the benefit of her daughter and two grandchildren. She may have a GST tax problem depending on the terms of the trust. If the grandmother transfers $30,000 to the trust, each beneficiary should have a Crummey demand power in order for Grandmother to qualify for the annual gift tax exclusion on the entire transfer. After the demand power lapses (which occurs if the child and grandchildren don't use it), the trustee can make distributions to the daughter and grandchildren. Where the trustee has sprinkle power between generations, there is a potential GST tax problem. Even without such a power, if distributions will skip a generation when the interests of the middle generation (i.e., the daughter) terminates (e.g., the daughter's death, or upon her reaching age 35 when the trust instrument requires a distribution to the grandchildren), a GST tax will be triggered. A better approach to avoid technical GST tax problems would be to have a separate trust for each beneficiary.

Where a husband and wife elect to split their gift, the GST is deemed to have been made one-half by each. Thus, if the wealthy spouse gives assets to grandchildren, a portion of the nonwealthy spouse's GST tax $1 million exemption can be allocated as well.

Transfers for Educational and Medical Benefits

You can give unlimited amounts of money to pay for a grandchild's (or other skip person's) education or medical benefits. With a large family and the high cost of quality medical care and education, large amounts can be transferred for the benefit of later generations with no GST tax implications. This planning opportunity should be considered before the expense, and problems, of setting up grandchildren's trusts are incurred.

This exclusion for medical and tuition payments can be used to protect distributions from trusts from the GST tax. For example, assume that you set up a bypass trust under your will permitting distributions to your spouse and descendants under a sprinkle power. A distribution to a grandchild could trigger GST tax. Instead, the trustee could make distributions to your spouse and children without limit and for the benefit of the grandchildren (i.e., skip persons) by paying for qualifying medical and tuition payments. This approach could provide for maximum flexibility without triggering GST tax.

GST Exemption

The primary protection from the GST is a one-time exclusion (similar to the use of the one-time gift and estate tax unified credit). You may give up to $1 million to your grandchildren with no GST tax cost. As noted previously, this amount is indexed for inflation for 2002 and 2003 and in 2004 through 2009 is the same as the estate tax exclusion in the table in Chapter 10. While this exemption can eliminate the GST tax for most taxpayers, it does not mean that taxpayers should not concern themselves with the GST tax. Ignoring the GST tax can still be costly. Most importantly, as illustrated in the example at the beginning of this chapter with the physician seeking to protect assets, GST planning affects planning that is not primarily GST tax motivated.

The GST exemption must be irrevocably allocated to any property transfers you make. This allocation is generally made on your gift tax return. Your executor may also allocate your GST exemption following your death (to the extent you didn't use it while you were alive). Many taxpayers plan to take maximum advantage of this exemption by setting up multiple trusts under their wills and granting their executors the authority to make certain decisions as to how these trusts will be funded, and how much GST tax exemption is to be allocated.

Once a portion or all of your GST tax exemption is allocated to a particular property transfer (e.g., to a trust), the protection of that allocation will continue to stay with the property (trust). Thus, if your GST tax exemption is allocated to property given to a QTIP marital trust, that trust will remain protected from your GST tax in future years.

EXAMPLE: You set up a domestic asset protection dynasty trust in Alaska for the benefit of yourself and all of your descendants. You give $450,000 of assets to the Alaska trust. You have your accountant file a gift tax return allocating $450,000 of GST tax exemption (unless the automatic allocation rules do so for you) to the gift (i.e., dollar for dollar). The $450,000 and the dynasty trust all remain fully GST tax exempt. The allocation of your exclusion effectively protects the trust and assets in it from GST tax.

To understand the use of your GST exemption, another bit of jargon must be introduced, the *inclusion ratio*. The GST tax exemption percentage (the inclusion ratio) is established when you make a GST gift to a trust and allocate some portion of your GST exemption.

The inclusion ratio is: [1—the applicable fraction]. The applicable fraction, where you make the gift to a trust, is determined as follows:

$$\frac{\text{Amount of GST exemption allocated to trust}}{\text{Value of property transferred to the trust}}$$

The numerator is the amount of your GST tax exemption allocated to the particular transfer. The denominator is the value of the property involved, reduced by any charitable contribution deduction and any federal or state estate or death taxes.

EXAMPLE: In the above example, when you set up your dynasty trust, you transferred by gift $450,000 to the trust. You also allocated (or the tax laws did for you automatically) $450,000 of your GST exemption to the transfer and trust. The applicable fraction for that example is $450,000/$450,000 or 1. The inclusion ratio is 1–1, or zero.

Why is the inclusion ratio so significant? An example will illustrate.

EXAMPLE: Assume that you set up a $1 million trust fund for your grandchildren and great-grandchildren. You allocate $1 million of your GST tax exemption to the trust. The assets of the trust appreciate to $10 million before being distributed in a taxable termination to your great-grandchildren on the death of the last of your grandchildren. None of the $10 million of trust property distributed to your great-grandchildren is subject to the GST tax. This is because the applicable fraction is 1, and the inclusion ratio, zero. The applicable fraction is 1 because you allocated $1 million GST exemption to $1 million in assets. Had you instead only allocated $500,000 of GST exemption to the $1 million in assets, the inclusion ratio would be 50 percent and $5 million [50% inclusion ratio × $10 million of assets subject to a taxable termination] would be subject to GST tax.

The simple answer to addressing most trust GST planning is to allocate a sufficient portion of your GST tax exemption to the trust to equal the value of all assets given to the trust. This decision as to how much of your exemption should be allocated is extremely complicated. If you allocate any portion of your GST tax exemption to a trust, that portion of the exemption is considered used, whether or not a GST tax is ever incurred. So, if you make the allocation, and no GST tax is ever possible, you will have used, and possibly wasted, that portion of your exemption. For example, assume that you allocate your $1 million GST exemption to a $1 million trust for the benefit of your child and grandchildren. However, the entire trust is exhausted making distributions to your child. Because no GST would have ever been triggered, the GST tax exemption was wasted. It may have been better to allocate the GST tax exemption to a trust solely for the benefit of your grandchildren.

GST tax exemption can be wasted in other ways. If the trust in the previous example declined from the $1 million initial gift value to only $600,000 (rather than growing to $10 million as illustrated), you would have wasted $400,000 of your exemption. Thus, in addition to the potential use of trust funds, you should also analyze all the investment and other relevant factors and estimate the likelihood of the trust incurring a GST tax. If it appears likely that the trust will incur a GST tax, then you may wish to wager some of your exemption on the trust. If the likelihood of a GST tax appears small, you might instead choose to preserve your GST tax exemption for other planning opportunities.

CAUTION: If you decide to preserve GST tax exemption instead of using it to protect gifts to a trust, you may have to have your accountant file a gift tax return advising the IRS that you do not wish to have GST tax exemption allocated to the particular gift. If you don't inform the IRS, the tax laws may, in the year 2000 and later, automatically apply your exclusion for you.

EXAMPLE: Grandpa has one son, who has two children. Assume Grandpa transferred $100,000 in trust with income to his son for life and the remainder to the two grandchildren on the son's death. Assume that Grandpa didn't allocate any of his GST tax exemption on the gift tax return. When the son dies, the trust property is worth $500,000. The inclusion ratio is 100 percent. The IRS will collect a $250,000 GST tax at the flat 50 percent rate (2002). On other hand, had Grandpa allocated $100,000 of his GST tax exemption against the $100,000 transfer to the trust when he first made the gift, the inclusion ratio would be zero. Thus, the entire $500,000 would pass free of the onerous GST tax. Assume Grandpa makes the same gift, however, he allocates $50,000 of his exemption against the transfer. The inclusion ratio is 50 percent. Therefore, if a GST tax is imposed, it will be imposed at 50 percent of the usual rate because 50 percent of the trust is exempt. Thus, on the death of the son, the GST tax would only be $125,000 [50% GST tax rate × $500,000 × 50% inclusion ratio].

Comprehensive GST Planning Example

With proper planning over time, a substantial amount of net worth can be transferred to grandchildren without any GST.

EXAMPLE: You have four children and nine grandchildren. You and your spouse set up separate trusts for each of your grandchildren, each properly structured so that $11,000 annual gifts will qualify for both the gift and GST tax annual exclusions. You and your spouse give, combined, $22,000 per year to each grandchild's trust. This amounts to $198,000 per year. Over a 10-year period (not even counting the earnings which would have made the trust balances grow substantially), you will have given away $1,980,000 to your grandchildren. This, of course, is in addition to any amounts you could have given to each of your children and their spouses (which could have amounted to an additional $1,760,000 over the same 10 years). Finally, in each of your wills, you and your spouse can provide for the maximum GST-exempt trusts to benefit all your descendants (children as well). The two trusts will total, after the last of you and your spouse dies, $3 million (in 2004 each of you and your spouse can give up to $1.5 million to a GST trust). Thus, over a 10-year period, you have transferred $4.98 million to trusts for your grandchildren. Planning, however, is essential.

If additional estate tax planning techniques are used in making the gifts in the preceding example to the trusts for your grandchildren, the amounts transferred can be increased substantially beyond what the above example indicates. For example, if stock in a closely held business, or interests in a family limited partnership (FLP), or limited liability company (LLC) rather than cash is given to the grandchildren's trusts, the gifts may qualify for lack of marketability and minority interest discounts that can enable the transfer of more economic value than the equivalent cash amount. These discounts may be available if you transfer a noncontrolling interest in an entity such that the rights of the recipient (e.g., a dynasty trust) are severely restricted. If the appropriate aggregate discount is 30 percent, then each $10,000 gift in 2001 would be equivalent to a $14,286 gift [$14,286 − (30% × $14,286 = $4,286) = $10,000]. The $1.8 million of aggregate gifts could constitute $2,571,000 of gifts [$2,571,000 − (30% × $2,571,000 = 771,000) = $1,800,000]. Without even considering any growth in the value of the stock given, more than $2.5 million has been transferred without incidence of GST.

CAUTION: Exercise great care in undertaking gifts of minority interests in businesses. Be certain to obtain a proper appraisal and have your tax adviser review the various gift tax valuation rules, including some complex rules under Chapter 14 of the Internal Revenue Code. These rules can, for example, cause restrictions in a FLP partnership agreement to be ignored when the value of the limited partnership interests given to the trust is determined if the restrictions in the partnership agreement are more onerous then the default provisions under your state's limited partnership law.

TAX ALLOCATION CLAUSES AND THE GST TAX

When planning for the GST tax, your attorney should also consider the tax allocation clause in your will or trust. Taxes should often be paid out of (i.e., should be allocated against) the assets creating the GST tax, and not simply against the residuary estate. While ideally you may wish to allocate GST tax against the portion of your estate that does not qualify for the GST (i.e., to avoid wasting any of your GST tax exemption), this is not always appropriate. From a fairness prospective, the person receiving the assets causing the tax problem should generally pay the tax. From a tax perspective, having the GST tax (if any is due) paid from property other than the generation skipping trust can create additional GST tax problems.

If your will is silent, the law may result in the GST tax being paid by the beneficiary receiving the particular property subject to the GST tax. In the case of a trust, the trustee is to pay the GST tax out of trust property where there is a taxable termination or a direct skip from the trust. Where the donor makes a gift which is a direct skip, the donor pays the tax. In such instances, the payment of the gift tax is deemed to be an additional gift.

TRUSTS AND THE GST TAX

GST planning can affect many types of trusts and the tax planning for those trusts. The use of a trust in estate and gift tax planning becomes more complex where the beneficiaries are, or could include, grandchildren (or other skip persons) instead of children (or other nonskip persons). The following situations summarize a few GST planning considerations for several types of trusts. The planning ideas discussed in the preceding section, however, can be applied to a host of other trust planning situations as well.

Marital Trust (Qualified Terminable Interest Property Trust)

A marital trust can also be allocated your $1 million GST tax exemption. A marital, or qualified terminal interest property (QTIP) trust (see Chapter 14), would provide your surviving spouse the right to all of the income, at least annually, from the trust for life. These mandatory income payments, as well as any principal invasions, will reduce (waste) the GST tax exemption amount allocated to this trust. In a very large estate, it is preferable that principal not be invaded unless absolutely necessary in order to preserve the benefits of your GST tax exemption.

Bypass/Marital Trust Combination after 2002

The amount of GST tax exemption, in the years 2003 through and including 2009, will exactly equal the amount of estate tax exclusion. Planning to take maximum advantage of both your estate tax exclusion and GST tax exemption is simplified considerably, compared to prior law (see below), because all you will need to do is fund a bypass trust for purposes of safeguarding your estate tax exclusion and GST tax exemption since one trust will be able to be funded with the same amount qualifying for each benefit.

Bypass/Marital Trust Combination Prior to 2003

Although the 2001 Tax Act has changed the manner in which GST planning in a typical will can be handled, tens of thousands of trusts are already in place that are based on the planning structure required under prior law. Therefore, many trustees and beneficiaries need to understand how pre-2003 law affected this planning. The complication under prior law is that prior to 2003 (and really prior to 2002), the GST tax exemption exceeded the maximum estate tax exclusion. The result was that you had to use several trusts in combination to preserve the maximum advantage of both of these tax benefits.

A common GST planning approach had been to establish two GST trusts to which the then $1 million (indexed for inflation) GST tax exemption was allocated. The first trust would be equal to the amount of the unused estate tax exclusion. Your executor would then allocate a similar amount of your GST exemption to your bypass trust. This transfer would not trigger any estate tax because of the estate tax exclusion. The assets in this trust would be protected forever from your GST tax because of the allocation of the GST exemption amount in a manner to assure a zero inclusion rate. A second trust could be provided under your will to absorb the remaining GST tax exemption amount. This trust would be a QTIP or marital trust, which would avoid any estate tax because of the unlimited marital deduction. Finally, this plan would probably be completed with a third QTIP or marital trust for any remaining assets. The reason to have two QTIP or marital trusts is that one of the trusts would be GST tax exempt and the other would be entirely subject to GST tax. The GST tax exempt trust would be the last to be touched for principal invasion. The non-GST exempt marital trust would be spent down first. While the GST exempt trust would waste some GST (e.g., by the requirement of paying income to your surviving spouse), it will waste less by virtue of the trustees' first spending down the other marital trust.

PLANNING FOR THE GENERATION SKIPPING TRANSFER TAX

EXAMPLE: The GST tax exemption can be allocated by your trustee (or executor if the transfer is under your will). It can first be allocated to each spouse's bypass trust. The trust will therefore have an inclusion ratio of zero and not trigger any GST tax, ever. This means that the entire trust is GST exempt since all of the assets transferred to it are covered by the GST exclusion. Securities most likely to appreciate should be allocated to this trust since it will not be included in the estate of the second spouse to die. A Q-TIP trust to which the remainder of the GST is allocated and any remaining assets could be distributed outright to the spouse (and avoid a second QTIP trust). This plan avoided any GST tax and took maximum advantage of the estate tax exclusion.

Planning for the use of the GST tax exemption when marital trusts are used presents an important, but somewhat confusing, planning opportunity. Assume the husband dies and his will establishes a QTIP trust for his surviving wife. On her death, the trust assets pass to the children. Generally, the surviving spouse (the wife in this scenario) who is benefiting from the QTIP trust would be considered the person transferring the trust assets to the children following her death. The husband who died first, and whose will established the QTIP trust, would not generally be considered the transferor of the QTIP property. Thus, only the wife's GST tax exemption can be allocated against this trust. The problem this creates is that the husband's GST tax exemption could be lost. The solution to this is a special tax election that treats the husband as the transferor of the assets in the QTIP trust for GST tax purposes. This election permits the husband to allocate his GST tax exemption against the trust. This election, which can be made by the executor of the husband's estate (or by the husband if it is a gift made during his lifetime) for an income-only marital trust, is known as a *reverse QTIP election*.

Children's Trust

Where a single trust is established for both a child and a grandchild, and the child dies, the death of the child could trigger a "taxable termination" as a result of the transfer of the trust corpus to the grandchild as the sole remaining beneficiary. Thus, the GST tax would be due. In many situations, it is advisable when setting up trusts for grandchildren to which you will make large gift transfers, to set up a separate trust for each grandchild. Alternatively, the trust assets can be included in the child's estate to avoid GST tax, as illustrated in an earlier example.

Grandchildren's Trusts

To take maximum advantage of the GST tax exemption, some trusts may be established solely for the benefit of grandchildren and other skip persons, while other trusts will be established solely for nonskip persons (e.g., children). The allocation of your GST exemption will be an important planning consideration. It will also be vital to address this allocation with the accountant completing your gift tax return for the gift. Alternatively, try a Section 529 College Savings Plan.

EXAMPLE: Where there is no surviving spouse, the plan is somewhat different. Thus, on the death of the second spouse, there is no need for a QTIP or bypass trust. On the death of the second spouse, that spouse's residuary estate can be dealt with in different ways, depending on the facts. Assume that the second spouse is survived by several children. Then one approach is put the remaining estate into a trust. All of the income from the trust could be distributed to the children and the remaining assets can eventually be distributed to the grandchildren. This trust can be divided into two parts—one exempt from GST and one not. Distributions of income to the children during their lifetimes should first be made out of the portion that is not exempt from GST so as to preserve the maximum GST tax-free portion for the grandchildren.

Insurance Trusts

Insurance trusts can be affected by GST planning. Should you allocate a portion of your GST exemption to gifts to the insurance trust? Since insurance offers one of the best methods of leveraging GST tax exemption, an insurance trust intended to skip wealth to future generations is a powerful estate planning tool. You may have to allocate your GST tax exemption on a timely filed gift tax return or the automatic allocation rules may do this for you, depending on the terms of the trust. A bigger issue with having GST tax exemption allocated to an insurance trust is that only about 2 percent of term insurance policies ever pay a death benefit. If your insurance trust holds term insurance, is it worth having valuable GST tax exemption allocated?

Charitable Trusts

Charities are not considered skip persons for GST tax purposes. They are automatically deemed to be of the same generation as the donor, grantor or other transferor. Thus, no GST tax is due on charitable gifts. This, unfortunately, does not mean that any transfers or trusts with charitable beneficiaries can always ignore the GST tax.

When planning a charitable lead trust, the choice of using a charitable lead unitrust (CLUT) or a charitable lead annuity trust (CLAT) may depend on whether grandchildren will be the ultimate beneficiaries (see Chapter 16). A special rule applies where a charitable lead annuity trust is used and the ultimate beneficiaries are grandchildren. The GST tax exemption cannot be allocated when the trust is formed. This is to prevent an excessive leveraging of the GST exemption. When the CLAT is formed, the value of the gift for transfer tax purposes is reduced substantially to reflect the fact that a charity will receive an intervening interest before the grandchildren. Instead, the GST tax exemption is allocated when the charity's interest ends. Since a major goal of CLAT planning is to grow the value of the trust principal, this will exacerbate the GST planning since the later allocation of GST tax exemption may not be sufficient to give the trust an inclusion ratio of zero.

Grantor Retained Annuity Trusts (GRATs)

A GRAT is intended to discount for gift tax purposes the value of assets given as a gift. This is accomplished by the donor retaining an interest in the trust, via an annuity payment, for the term of the trust (see Chapter 21). At the end of the term of years, the assets of the trust pass to the beneficiaries named. However, if the grantor/donor dies before the trust term ends, the assets of the trust are included in the donor's estate. This period of time is called an *estate tax inclusion period*, or ETIP. For GST purposes, the GST exemption cannot be allocated until this ETIP ends. This is at the termination of the trust, when the property is valued fully (i.e., without the discount the donor realized for gift tax purposes). Thus, just as for the charitable lead annuity trust described previously, the ability to leverage your GST exemption amount using this technique is quite limited. Consider a sale to a defective grantor trust (IDIT) as an alternative.

CONCLUSION

GST tax considerations affect a myriad of trusts and planning situations, even for many people who don't view themselves as super wealthy. It is important to carefully plan any trust or significant gift transaction to avoid, or at least defer or minimize, the GST tax impact. With proper planning, substantial assets can often be transferred with no GST tax burden and a range of other non-GST benefits can be achieved (such as with the dynasty trust).

12 HOW TRUSTS AND BENEFICIARIES ARE TAXED

The manner in which trusts are taxed for income tax purposes is extremely complicated. This chapter highlights several of the important principles of trust taxation, but most details are beyond the scope of this book. In all events, to properly plan and understand the uses of trusts, it is essential to consult with an experienced tax accountant for guidance.

Understanding the basics of trust income tax rules will enable you to better select beneficiaries for your trust. For example, because beneficiaries can be taxed on trust income when distributions are made to them, it may be advantageous to name children as beneficiaries of many trusts (e.g., a bypass trust) in addition to your surviving spouse. Trust income tax planning will help you plan the investment strategy of your trust. It will also make you sensitive to how different investment strategies can affect the different beneficiaries and the tax consequences of all beneficiaries.

THRESHOLD ISSUE—IS THE TRUST A SEPARATE TAX ENTITY?

The threshold issue in determining how your trust will be taxed is to determine if the trust income is to be reported on your income tax return (i.e., a grantor trust), or on its own income tax return—a separate tax return for the trust. If the trust is characterized as a grantor trust, the income tax consequences are generally the same as any other income you earn. If the trust is to be taxed as a separate entity, it will file its own income tax return, make its own tax elections, pay its own tax, and so forth. Trust income taxation is similar in some respects to income taxation of an individual. Many of the differences between individual and trust income taxation are explained next.

GRANTOR TRUSTS ARE NOT TAXED AS SEPARATE ENTITIES

If your trust is treated as a grantor trust, then all income and deductions of the trust are reported on your own tax return (if you were the grantor setting up the trust). The trust is disregarded as a taxable entity (it is not disregarded as a legal entity). This is not necessarily a negative situation. In many cases, your advisers will have you structure a trust in a manner that intentionally causes it to be taxed as a grantor trust. For example, if a grantor trust makes charitable contributions, you would claim the contributions as itemized deductions on your personal income tax return. The deductions would be subject to the same limitations as any other charitable contributions reported by an individual taxpayer. This might be done intentionally when you structure a charitable lead trust (CLT) as a grantor trust to secure an income tax deduction for charitable contributions. If the trust was not a grantor trust, you would not obtain the charitable contribution deduction. Grantor trust status may also be intended if you form an irrevocable grantor trust and then sell assets to that trust on an installment basis as a means of removing the future appreciation of those assets from your estate (an IDIT). Grantor trust status in such a situation assures that no capital gains will be realized on the sale.

Some grantor trusts must obtain a tax identification number, although the IRS does not generally require a tax identification number for revocable living trusts (see below). Most grantor trusts don't file an actual income tax return. You should consult with your accountant; however, some accountants like to file a "skeleton" return even if not required, to list the trust name and tax identification number, and attach a statement advising the IRS of where the trust income was reported. In some instances, the tax regulations may require that a tax return be filed.

See Chapter 4 for a discussion of what makes a trust taxable as a grantor trust.

Which Trusts Are Grantor Trusts?

Many different types of trusts are classified as grantor trusts. The following is a review of some of them:

- *QPRT.* If you establish a qualified personal residence trust (QPRT), you will want to assure that it is a grantor trust (see Chapter 22). If the QPRT is a grantor trust, you will continue to be able to deduct property taxes, mortgage interest, qualify for a tax exclusion on gain if the house is sold, and otherwise have the benefits of home ownership. In the past, this type of trust was generally treated as a grantor trust because of a right given to the grantor to substitute property of equal value for trust assets. Now, the trust may be planned to assure that the grantor has more than a 5 percent reversionary interest. This means that there is more than a 5 percent probability of the trust assets being distributed back to the grantor setting up the trust as a result of his or her dying before the trust term ends.

EXAMPLE: You establish a QPRT to remove the value of your house from your estate at a discounted cost. The trust term is 12 years. If you die before the 12 years elapses, the house is distributed back to your estate. Based on your age and life expectancy, if there is more than a 5 percent chance of this occurring, the trust is a grantor trust.

- *Revocable living trust.* These trusts are formed for nontax reasons; classification as a grantor trust makes matters simpler. There is no intent to remove assets from your estate with a living trust, or to form a separate entity to file tax returns. The objective is to use this type of trust for probate avoidance and management of assets. If you retain the right to revoke, terminate, alter, or amend a trust, you will be taxed on the income from the trust. When forming a revocable living trust, you will retain total control to modify the trust, and it will be characterized as a grantor trust.

  There are important advantages to the fact that a revocable living trust remains taxable to you as a grantor trust. This tax status can permit you to transfer, for example, your interests in your home to a revocable trust. When the home is sold, the special tax exclusion rules on the gain on the sale of a personal residence continue to be available.

- *GRAT.* If you establish a grantor retained annuity trust (GRAT) to leverage large gifts to reduce gift tax cost, the annuity payment you receive will assure that these trusts are grantor trusts (see Chapter 20).

- *Child's trust.* If you establish a trust to hold assets for your child and remove those assets from your estate, it could still be a grantor trust for income tax purposes. Taxpayers have designed children's trusts to be taxed, for income tax purposes, as grantor trusts. This can be tricky, because they must assure that the trust is not pulled back into their estates for estate tax purposes. If this can be done, the taxpayer/parent could pay income tax on the child's trust's earnings. This serves as another way of transferring value to the child's trust without any additional gift tax. If the trust income is used to discharge your legal obligation, such as the education of your minor child, the trust income could be taxable to you. See the discussion of children's trusts in Chapter 16.

- *Insurance trust.* Many insurance trusts are classified as grantor trusts (at least in part) because if income of the trust can be used to pay for insurance premiums on policies on the grantor's life, the trust is classified as a grantor trust. This is why insurance trusts, before the insured's death, often do not own any significant assets other than the insurance policies and a nominal cash balance.

Special Tax Filing Rules for Revocable Living Trusts

Although revocable living trusts are very popular, you may not be familiar with the tax filing requirements. They can generally be handled in one of three ways, but in all cases, trust income is reported on your personal tax return, Form 1040.

Alternative 1

This is the simplest and most common approach. File a trust tax return, Form 1041, and include the following type of statement: "The John Taxpayer Revocable Living Trust is a grantor trust. The income is taxable to the grantor, John Taxpayer, whose Social Security Number is 123-45-6789 and who resides at 123 Main Street, Any Town, USA. All income, deductions and credits are reported on the grantor's Form 1040."

The trust tax return, with the statement, is then filed together with your individual income tax return.

Alternative 2

The trustee (you) must give anyone paying the trust dividends, interest, or other income or gains during the year the following information: your name, address, and Social Security number. If this is done, then you as trustee are not required to file a trust tax return, Form 1041, with the IRS.

If you are not both the trustee and the grantor, then the trustee must provide you with a statement including:

- All items of income, deduction, and credit of the trust.
- Identities of the payors of each item of income.
- The information necessary to compute the grantor's taxable income.
- A statement that the above items must be included on the grantor's income tax return.

The grantor is required under this method to provide the trustee with a completed Form W-9, "Request for Taxpayer Identification Number and Certification."

Alternative 3

The trustee must furnish to all payors of income and proceeds during the tax year the following information:

- Trust's name.
- Trust's taxpayer identification number.
- Trust's address.

The trustee must file with the IRS the appropriate Form 1099s reporting each type of income and each item of gross proceeds paid to the trust during the tax year, showing the trust as payor and showing the grantor, you, as the payee.

If the trustee is not the same person as the grantor, then the trustee must provide to the grantor a statement that includes the following information for each taxable year:

- All items of income, deduction, and credit of the trust.
- The information necessary to compute the grantor's taxable income.
- A statement that the above items must be included in the grantor's income.

By furnishing this statement, the trustee satisfies the obligation to furnish statements to recipients with respect to Forms 1099 filed by the trustee.

TRUSTS REPORTING INCOME ON THEIR OWN TAX RETURNS

Generally, when a trust is required to report its income on its own tax return, it will be taxed in a manner that is similar to the way in which an individual taxpayer, like yourself, is taxed. The gross income of a trust is generally determined in the same manner as the gross income of an individual is determined. Then several modifications, discussed next, are made.

A trust is generally required to report its income and deductions using a calendar year. A trust, like any taxpayer, must use a method of accounting that clearly reflects its income. Trust income determined under the trust's accounting methods, includes all income received by the trust during the tax year, including income accumulated in the trust, income that is to be distributed currently by the trustee to the beneficiaries, and income which, in the trustee's discretion, may be either distributed to the beneficiaries or accumulated. The IRS has held that where a trustee waives or refunds trustee fees and commissions, that this amount should also be treated as income to the trust.

One of the most important concepts of trust taxation is that a trust is generally treated as a conduit (like a partnership). The trust only pays tax on income that it accumulates. If the trust distributes income to its beneficiaries, the trust will be treated as a conduit for tax purposes, passing the income through to the beneficiaries. This result is achieved by giving the trust a tax deduction for the income actually distributed (or required to be distributed) to the beneficiary. This deduction is based on a *distributable net income*, or DNI, calculation, explained later in this section.

A trust, however, is not a perfect conduit, since several items are affected by special trust tax rules. For example, all losses do not generally pass through the trust to the beneficiaries until the year in which the trust terminates. Capital losses are not deducted in the calculation of a trust's distributable net income. Thus, where a trust has a capital loss (e.g., from selling stock) but no capital gain, the loss is not passed through the trust to be reported on the beneficiaries income tax returns. Capital losses, however, can be offset against capital gains of the trust.

Deductions and Losses Available to Trusts

Trusts are entitled to certain tax deductions in calculating their income. Generally, trusts are allowed the same tax deductions and credits as are individual taxpayers. Trusts are not, however, permitted to claim the standard deduction to which individual taxpayers are entitled. The 2 percent floor on miscellaneous itemized deductions applicable to individuals is similarly applicable to trusts. A number of trust expenses may be subject to this limitation, including tax return preparation fees, safe deposit box rentals, legal and accounting fees, investment counsel fees, and so forth.

A trust must make special calculations to determine its adjusted gross income. For example, the expenses paid or incurred to administer the trust, and distribution deductions are deductible in arriving at adjusted gross income.

EXAMPLE: A trust has $10,000 of adjusted gross income (AGI). It incurs $1,000 of expenses that are chargeable against income and that are subject to the 2 percent floor rule. The first $200 of these expenses are therefore not deductible [$10,000 × 2%]. Trust income is therefore $9,200 [$10,000 − ($1,000 − $200)].

The special reduction of itemized deductions that individual taxpayers are required to make does not apply to trusts. This is the so called *stealth tax* which is scheduled to be phased out as a result of the 2001 Tax Act.

A trust is permitted to deduct expenses that are ordinary necessary business expenses incurred in its business, expenses incurred in the production of income, and expenses to determine its tax liability. Where a trust owns a house occupied personally by a beneficiary, the trust will generally not deduct maintenance and similar costs. Instead, these personal type expenses will be treated as a distribution to that particular beneficiary. Reasonable amounts incurred for trustee fees are deductible. The deductions, however, are only allowed for items that are obligations of the trust. For example, where a beneficiary pays a trustee fee instead of the trust, no deduction is allowed to either the beneficiary or the trust.

A trust is not permitted to claim any deductions for the expenses allocable to tax-exempt income. The rationale for this is that if the trust is not taxed on the income, it should not be able to deduct expenses incurred to generate that income.

EXAMPLE: A trust earns the following income:

Ordinary stock dividends	$12,400
Tax-exempt bond interest	4,500
Total income	$16,900

The trust incurs the following expenses:

Office expenses	1,000
Account fee—brokerage firm holding tax-exempt bonds	250

The expenses allocable to the tax-exempt income and which are not deductible by the trust are comprised of two components. The $250 account fee relates solely to the tax-exempt bonds and is therefore not deductible in its entirety. The office expense fee, it is assumed, was incurred in earning all income and in managing all assets. So this amount can be allocated ratably between the ordinary stock dividends and the tax-exempt bond interest, as follows:

$$\frac{\$4,500 \text{ Tax-exempt bond interest}}{\$16,900 \text{ Total income}} \times 1,000 \text{ Office expense} = \$266$$

Thus, $266 of the office expenses is not deductible. The total expenses which relate to the tax-exempt income and which are not deductible are $516 [$250 + $266].

Trusts can claim depreciation deductions, but they may have to allocate the deduction between the beneficiaries and the trust based on the allocation of trust income. Bad debt deductions, net operating losses, and casualty losses are also permitted, but may not all pass through to the beneficiary in each tax year.

Charitable contribution deductions are permitted for amounts paid to recognized charitable organizations under the terms of the trust. The rules for trusts are more generous then those for individuals. Individual taxpayers are only permitted deductions for contributions up to certain percentages of their income. These rules do not apply to trusts. The contributions, however, must be made in a manner that is consistent with the terms of the trust agreement and must be paid out of trust income (not principal).

Trusts, like individual and certain other taxpayers, are subject to the complicated passive loss rules that can limit the ability to deduct losses from rental real estate and other passive investments. The passive loss limitations are applied to beneficiaries on the passive income or deductions distributed to them, and to the trust on the passive income or deductions which it does not distribute.

Special Deductions for Trusts

There are several special deductions to which trusts are entitled and which differ from those available to individual taxpayers as described earlier.

Classifying the Trust as Simple or Complex

Every trust is entitled to an exemption deduction. Simple trusts are entitled to an exemption of $300, complex trusts $100. To determine the exemption available to a trust, you must first classify the trust as a simple or complex trust.

A simple trust is one that is required by the trust agreement to distribute all of its income currently, make no distributions other than of current income, and which has no provision for charitable contributions. The fact that the trustee may not distribute all of the income as required will not affect the characterization of the trust. The fact that capital gains must be allocated to principal rather than income, under applicable state law or the trust provisions, will also not affect the characterization of the trust as a simple trust. Any trust not characterized as a simple trust under the above rules is characterized as a complex trust. A complex trust includes any trust not required to pay out all of its income currently.

The rules for complex trusts are more difficult because complex trusts may accumulate income (i.e., when a trust doesn't pay out all of its income currently, that portion is accumulated, or kept by the trust for distribution in later years). Where income is accumulated, then some portion of the distributions in any year may be made from principal amounts. This can be principal from the original assets given to the trust, or from accumulations in prior years.

Distributable Net Income Deduction for Trusts

The most important deduction available to many trusts is the deduction for distributions to beneficiaries. This deduction is the key to avoiding double taxation of the same income by both the trust and its beneficiary. It is also the basis of a trust being characterized as a conduit for income tax purposes. To understand these rules, you must understand a tax concept unique to the taxation of trusts: distributable net income, or DNI.

DNI accomplishes three purposes: (1) It determines the maximum amount that a beneficiary of the trust will be taxed on in any year; (2) it determines the maximum amount that can be deducted by a trust for distributions which the trust makes to beneficiaries in any year; and (3) it provides for the character (e.g., tax-exempt income or nontax exempt income) of the income that the trust passes to a beneficiary.

In the simplest terms, DNI is roughly equivalent to the trust's taxable income (rather than its income determined under trust accounting concepts), though there are modifications and adjustments. The rules for DNI are different for simple and complex trusts (not that the rules are simple for "simple" trusts). These differences, which are very important, are explained in general terms next.

The trust's deduction for distributions is limited to its DNI. DNI also limits the amount taxable to the beneficiary. Also, the DNI concept preserves the character (e.g., capital gain) of income distributed by the trust to a beneficiary.

Calculating DNI—General Rules.   DNI is generally calculated by start-ing with a trust's taxable income and modifying it as follows:

1. Any deduction claimed for distributions to beneficiaries is added back.
2. The personal exemption is added back.
3. Tax-exempt interest, less deductions allocated to it (e.g., fees incurred to buy or manage tax-exempt bonds), is added back.
4. Capital gains which are allocated to the principal of the trust and which are not paid or required to be distributed to a beneficiary, are subtracted.
5. Capital losses which aren't used to offset capital gains are subtracted.

Special rules apply to foreign trusts, but are not addressed in this book.

DNI Deduction for Simple Trusts.   A simple trust is generally entitled to deduct the lesser of DNI or the amount of income required to be distrib-uted currently to the beneficiaries of the trust. For a simple trust, the DNI deduction is available even if the actual distribution is made after the close of the tax year.

EXAMPLE: You're the only beneficiary of a simple trust that is required to dis-tribute all of its income each year. The trust is entitled to a $300 exemption amount.

The trust had the following income and expenses:

Dividends and interest (ordinary income)	$13,556
Expenses relating to ordinary income	2,350
Capital gain (allocable to principal)	4,500
Expenses relating to capital gain income	1,250

You would receive a current distribution of $11,206 [$13,556 of ordinary income – $2,350 of expenses relating to ordinary income].

The trust's DNI is $9,956 [$13,556 ordinary income – $2,350 expenses relating to ordinary income – $1,250 expenses relating to capital gain income]. Note that cap-ital gains are not included in the calculation of DNI since the trust document re-quires that they be allocated to the principal of the trust and that they not be treated as income.

The amount which you, as beneficiary, would have to report on your tax return for the year is limited to the $9,956 of the trust's DNI.

The trust would receive a tax deduction for the amount actually distributed to you. Thus, the trust's taxable income would be:

Dividends and interest (ordinary income)	$13,556
Capital gain (allocable to principal)	+ 4,500
Total trust income	$18,056
Expenses relating to ordinary income	− 2,350
Expenses relating to capital gain income	− 1,250
Exemption amount (simple trust)	− 300
Deduction for distribution to beneficiary	−11,206
Trust's taxable income	$ 2,950

DNI Deduction for Complex Trusts.   Two different categories of trust distributions must be considered. The first category is distributions of current income of the trust that is required to be distributed to the beneficiaries in that year. This is similar to the concepts discussed earlier for simple trusts. The beneficiaries are taxed on this first category of income to the extent of DNI.

The second category of distributions includes all amounts, other than those included in the first category, which are paid, credited, or required to be distributed by the trust to its beneficiaries. Beneficiaries are only taxed on these second category amounts if the distributions in the first category do not exhaust all of the trust's DNI for that year.

A complex trust may deduct the amount of income that is required to be distributed during the year, whether paid out of income or principal, to the extent that it was actually paid. If different types of income are distributed, the deduction available to the trust for the distribution is allocated in the same proportion each type of income bears to the total DNI, unless state law or the trust instrument provide for a different allocation method. Rules for allocating the different deductions and classes of income to the amounts received by the beneficiary are also provided.

For a complex trust, the trustee can elect on an annual basis to treat any distribution made to a beneficiary within the first 65 days after year end, to be treated as if made in the prior year. If the trustee makes this election to include in income the amount paid within 65 days following the close of the tax year, the beneficiary must include income in the earlier year in conformity with the trustee's election. If the amount of income required to be distributed exceeds the allocable share of DNI, the beneficiary includes a proportionate amount in income.

Special Rules When You Have Several Trusts

Because each trust does have some income taxable at the lowest tax rates, and has its own exemption amount, there can be a tax advantage to forming multiple trusts so the income of each can be taxed in the lowest trust income tax bracket. To prevent abuse of the tax benefits of using multiple trusts, the tax laws provide that in certain situations, multiple trusts will be treated as a single trust. This will occur where (1) the trusts have substantially the same grantors and beneficiaries and (2) a principal purpose of having multiple trusts is tax avoidance. A husband and wife are treated as the same beneficiary for purposes of determining whether the grantors are the same.

Trust Tax Return Filing Requirements

The trustee must file a federal income tax return, Form 1041, if the trust has gross income of $600 or more. For many of the trusts described in this book, the trust will be considered to be a separate taxpayer for federal income tax purposes, and then have to file its own tax return. A major exception to this is for a trust characterized as a grantor trust for income tax purposes (discussed previously).

Estimated Tax Returns

Many trusts are also required to file estimated tax returns, similar to individual taxpayers. An important exception is provided for certain trusts that are primarily responsible for paying the debts, taxes, and expenses of a decedent; these are exempt for two years from the requirement to pay estimated taxes. Where a trust does make estimated tax payments, if the payments exceed its tax liability, the trustee can elect to give the benefit of these excess tax payments to the beneficiaries. To do this, the trustee should attach Form 1041-T, Transmittal of Estimated Taxes Credited to Beneficiaries, to the trust's tax return.

Income Tax Planning for Trusts

If the income of the trust is reported in part by the trust and in part by the beneficiary, there may be some benefit gained from taking advantage of the lower tax brackets of each. Lower income tax brackets occur because the income tax rate is graduated: the more income, the higher the rate at which it is taxed. If the trust will be taxed at a higher income tax rate than the beneficiary, consider directing (or at least permitting) the trustee to make distributions of income to the beneficiary. This is a potential income tax advantage of using a pot or sprinkle trust which gives the trustee the flexibility to distribute income (and often principal) to any of a named group of beneficiaries. A dynasty trust is an example of this.

If the beneficiaries are children subject to the *kiddie tax*, the income distributed to the child/beneficiary (a child under 14 years of age) will be taxed at the parents' higher tax rate (see Chapter 16).

Another planning technique used in past years has also been substantially curtailed. Trusts chose to use tax years ending on January 31 of each year to defer the amount of income to be reported by the beneficiaries. However, with the exception of certain charitable trusts, this is generally no longer possible.

Where a trustee wishes to distribute income to avoid the high trust income tax rates, he may be concerned about the beneficiary having access to cash. An alternative, if the trust agreement permits, is to consider distributing property. In some instances, a property distribution can carry out to the beneficiary some of the taxable income that would have otherwise been taxed at a high rate to the trust. Also, if the type of property is carefully selected it may be possible to distribute property that is not as liquid as cash so as to discourage a beneficiary from making undesired expenditures.

EXAMPLE: A beneficiary receives a distribution of stock from a trust worth $35,400. The trust's tax basis in the stock was $23,000. Assuming that the trustee does not make a special election to recognize gain or loss on the distribution, the beneficiary's tax basis in the stock will also be $23,000. The distribution will be considered to carry out to the beneficiary income (DNI) to the extent of the lesser of the adjusted basis in the property or the fair value of the property. In this case, $23,000 would be considered to be distributed.

Another planning consideration for trusts, if income cannot be distributed to a lower-taxed beneficiary, is to restructure the investment portfolio of the trust to favor tax-exempt securities, growth stocks, and other investments that do not produce ordinary income taxed currently at the highest tax rates.

CAUTION: Trustees must be careful in pursuing these types of strategies. First, be certain that the trust agreement authorizes the trading necessary and permits the types of investments that will achieve the intended tax results. Consider the different tax and economic consequences to the beneficiaries. The results may not be obvious. For example, many trust agreements provide how income, dividends, gain, loss, and so forth should be divided between income and principal. If the trust agreement is silent, you will have to consult local law. For many trusts, the income beneficiary may differ from the beneficiary who ultimately will receive all of the trust property (the remainder beneficiary). A substantial change in investment posture to reduce income could favor a remainder beneficiary at the expense of the current income beneficiary and expose the trustee to claims. Consider your liability as a trustee in light of both state law and the provisions of the trust agreement. Could you be challenged legally for violating your fiduciary responsibility as trustee of you invest all of the trust's assets in municipal bonds?

HOW NONGRANTOR TRUSTS ARE TAXED ON PROPERTY SALES AND DISTRIBUTIONS

Gain or loss for a trust or a beneficiary is calculated in a manner similar to the way you calculate gain or loss for your personal tax return. The starting point is your investment in the property sold (tax basis). But, as with so many trust tax calculations, there are exceptions and modifications. For trusts, the calculation of tax basis depends on how the property was acquired and the nature of the property sold. If the trustee acquired the property as a gift, the trust uses the grantor's adjusted tax basis for calculating any gain.

EXAMPLE: Grandparent (grantor of the trust) gives stock which cost him $70,000 and which is worth $95,000 (yes, Virginia, some people still have appreciated stock!) to a trust for the benefit of Grandchild (the beneficiary of the trust). The trust's tax basis in the stock, assuming no gift tax is paid by Grandparent on the making of the gift, is $70,000.

The calculation of adjusted tax basis becomes more complicated when the donor/grantor incurs a gift tax as a result of making the gift. If gift tax is paid (e.g., the gift was more than the annual exclusion of $11,000 and the donor had previously used up his $1 million gift exclusion), the trust's adjusted tax basis in the property is increased by the amount of gift tax paid.

EXAMPLE: Assume that in the previous example, Grandparent pays $20,000 of gift tax to make the gift of the stock to the trust for Grandchild. The trust's tax basis in the stock is increased to $90,000 [$70,000 + $20,000].

The amount by which the adjusted tax basis in the property can be increased as a result of the gift tax paid by the donor/grantor is subject to a cap. The gift tax paid can only increase tax basis to the extent that it is attributable to the appreciation in the property given to the trust. This is the excess of the fair market value of the property as of the date of the gift over the grantor's adjusted tax basis in the property.

EXAMPLE: Assume that in the previous example, Grandparent incurred a gift tax in 2001 at a 50 percent rate. The gift tax incurred on making the gift to the trust would be $37,500 [($95,000 – $20,000 annual exclusion for both grandparents) × 50%]. However, if the full gift tax were added to the Grandparent's (i.e., the donor's) tax basis, the trust's tax basis would be $107,500 [$70,000 + $37,500]. This amount exceeds the fair value of the property, so the basis to the trust is limited to the $95,000 fair market value of the property.

TIP: The general rule for capital gains is that they are allocated to the principal of the trust and are not considered part of current income for trust accounting purposes (this is different from income tax calculations). Thus, they will be taxable to the trust at the trust's tax rates. It can be advantageous in some situations to include a provision in the trust document permitting the trustee to allocate certain capital gains to income, rather than principal. This could enable the trustee to distribute the capital gains to beneficiaries, who may be taxed at a lower tax rate than the trust. This is because the lowest tax rates are phased out at very low income levels for trusts—at amounts of income that are much lower than those at which the low tax brackets for individuals are phased out.

Unfortunately, the story doesn't end with the above rules and calculations because if the trust sold the property at a loss, the loss deduction could be larger than the IRS would want. So again, a special rule applies. If a trust sells an asset at a loss, the trust's adjusted tax basis (investment) is the lower of: (1) the donor/grantor's adjusted tax basis in the property; or (2) the fair market value of the property at the time of the gift to the trust.

EXAMPLE: Assume that in the previous example, the trustee of the Grandchild's trust sold the stock four years later for $50,000. Since the property was sold at a loss, the amount of tax loss for the trust is $20,000 [$50,000 sales price − $70,000 tax basis of grantor]. This is the lower of: (1) the $70,000 tax basis of the Grandparent; or (2) the $95,000 fair market value of the property at the date of the transfer. This prevents the trust getting a deduction for the amount of the gift tax paid by Grandparent on the gift of the stock to the trust.

Where property is received by a trust from an estate (i.e., under a will), the trust's tax basis is the fair market value of the property in the estate. This is the fair market value on the date of death, or at a date six months after the date of death if the estate elected to value all assets at that date (the alternate valuation date). If the estate tax is repealed in 2010, as planned under the 2001 Tax Act, and carryover basis rules apply, the tax basis to the trust will be based on those rules. In most cases, the tax basis will be the fair value at death because of the basis adjustments permitted to a decedent ($1.3 million generally, and $3 million on transfers to a spouse). Since these rules are so new, are not scheduled to be implemented for many years, and may be changed before then, it is tough to speculate how they will apply now.

Where do you find the information for these calculations? Hopefully, the trustee has maintained the proper records. If the records are not readily available, consider any of the following:

- If a gift tax return was filed by the grantor or other person giving property to the trust (donor), a copy of the gift tax return should provide the necessary information. If the trustee, the donor, and the accountants for the trust and donor do not have copies, the IRS may be able to provide one upon request. It is also important to determine whether a gift tax was paid when the gifts were made to the trust. For example, if the gifts qualified for the unlimited marital deduction (there's no gift tax on transfers to your spouse), or if the amount given to your trust was within the remaining $1,000,000 lifetime maximum gift tax exclusion of the donor, then no gift tax cost may have been paid on the transaction of setting up your trust.
- If you can't find the gift tax return filed when the gifts were made to the trust, it may be impossible to correctly determine the adjusted tax basis for the property. In such cases, you can request that the IRS, if possible, obtain the basis information from the donor (or from the last owner of the property given to the trust), or any other person who possesses the relevant information. If the IRS can't obtain the data,

then you may be able to assume that the tax basis is the fair value of the property when the property was acquired by the donor or last preceding owner.

- If the property was transferred to the trust under someone's will, the adjusted tax basis of the assets transferred from the estate to the trust will generally be the fair market value of the assets as of the date of death. The best approach is to obtain a copy of the decedent's federal estate tax return. If no federal estate tax return was filed, a state inheritance or other tax return may have been filed.

Tax Consequences of Property Distributed from a Trust to a Beneficiary

General Tax Rules on Property Distributions

Generally, no gain or loss is recognized on a transfer of property from a trust to a beneficiary under the terms of the trust instrument.

EXAMPLE: You set up a trust for your child. The trustee is required by the trust agreement to distribute half of the trust assets to your child at age 30. When the child reaches age 30, the trust is worth $400,000. The trustee, rather than sell stocks and other investments, distributes half of the value of the trust in the form of property (i.e., not cash), a rental house worth $150,000, and $50,000 of stock, to your child.

There are, as you would by now expect, several exceptions. If the distribution is of appreciated property distributed in satisfaction of the beneficiary's right to receive a specific dollar (pecuniary) amount, or where the distribution is of specific property other than the property which is required to be distributed, a gain may be recognized.

EXAMPLE: Grandparent transfers various assets to a trust for the benefit of several grandchildren. When each grandchild reaches age 35, he or she is to receive $35,000. When the first grandchild reaches age 35, the trustee transfers stock with a tax basis of $24,000 and a fair market value of $35,000. The trust must report a gain of $11,000 [$35,000 – $24,000].

A trust must recognize taxable gain or loss when a cash bequest is satisfied by distribution of other property.

When a stated percentage of the principal of a trust is distributed to a beneficiary before the termination of a trust, it is not considered to be a satisfaction of an obligation of the trust for a definite amount of cash or equivalent value in property. The transaction is simply treated as a partial distribution of a share of the trust principal. Therefore no sale or exchange is deemed to have occurred, and therefore no gain or loss can be recognized.

The beneficiary's tax basis will be the same as the tax basis of the trust. Any gain or loss is thus deferred until the beneficiary sells the property.

EXAMPLE: Beneficiary receives a distribution of stock from a trust worth $35,400. The trust's tax basis in the stock was $23,000. Assuming that the trustee does not make an election under Code Section 643(e) to recognize gain or loss on the distribution, Beneficiary's tax basis in the stock will also be $23,000. The distribution will also be considered to carry out to the beneficiary DNI to the extent of the lesser of the adjusted basis in the property ($23,000) or the fair value of the property ($35,400). In this case, DNI of $23,000 would be considered to be distributed. The tax consequences of DNI were explained earlier.

Distributions of property, such as stocks, bonds, or other trust assets (in tax jargon, these are called "distributions in kind") are also subject to the above rule. The amount of income to be recognized by the beneficiary depends on whether the trustee chooses to apply the special tax rule to recognize income on the distribution of the property. The result of this would be to treat the property as if it had been sold for its fair market value at the date it was distributed. If the trustee chooses to have this special rule (tax election) apply, similar treatment must be given to all distributions made by the trust during the entire tax year. The trustee can't choose to make the election for some property, but not for other property.

If this election is made, the beneficiary's basis in the distributed property is the trust's adjusted tax basis prior to the distribution, increased (or decreased) by the gain (loss) recognized by the trust. Thus, the tax basis to the beneficiary becomes the fair market value of the property on the distribution.

EXAMPLE: Your trust purchased stock in XYZ, Inc. years ago for $1,000. The stock is now worth $5,000. If the trust distributes the stock to you, your tax basis in the stock is $1,000, the same as the trust's. Thus, if you sell the stock, you would realize the gain. Your tax basis will be stepped-up, or increased, to the $5,000 fair value of the stock, only if the trustee makes a special election to recognize the $4,000 of gain in the trust. If the trustee makes this election, the trust will receive a deduction for a distribution to you of the $5,000 value. When should a trustee consider making an election to pay a tax? When the tax cost to the trust of reporting the gain on the property distributed would be less than the tax cost to the beneficiary. This could occur, for example, that the trust had capital losses from other stock sales that could offset the gain.

TAXATION OF TRUST BENEFICIARIES

A beneficiary of a simple trust is taxed on the income required to be distributed, whether or not it is actually distributed during the tax year. The income, however, cannot exceed distributable net income (DNI). If the income distributed exceeds DNI, then each class of income is allocated so that only a proportionate amount is included. Each item of income retains the same character as it did to the trust, unless state law or the trust instrument requires a different allocation.

A beneficiary of a complex trust must include in his own income his share of trust income required to be distributed, whether or not the income is actually distributed. Also, amounts paid, or credited, during the year to the beneficiary must be included in income.

If the trustee chooses (i.e., makes the tax election) to deduct from trust income amounts paid to a beneficiary within 65 days following the close of the tax year (i.e., paid by mid-March), the beneficiary must include that income in the earlier year to be consistent with the trustee's decision.

If the amount of income required to be distributed exceeds the beneficiary's share of DNI, the beneficiary includes a proportionate amount in income.

If the trust has more than one beneficiary, and is to be administered in distinct shares for each beneficiary (it is one trust but the trustee in effect keeps separate accounting records for each beneficiary as if each beneficiary had a separate trust), then such separate share treatment is required to be followed for purposes of calculating DNI.

Trusts must also calculate alternative minimum tax (AMT). AMT is in effect a second tax calculation all individuals and trusts must make. The intended purpose of the AMT was to assure that wealthy taxpayers were not able to reduce their income too much using special tax breaks. Unfortunately, the AMT has expanded well beyond its intended purpose and basically represents a potential tax trap for millions of taxpayers, including trusts. This is referred to as distributable net alternative minimum taxable income. This concept is so complex that you must take two aspirin and then discuss it with your accountant.

How Different Types of Trust Income Are Allocated to the Beneficiaries

There is another important concept of basic trust taxation that must be understood to properly work with trusts. Trusts are generally treated like a conduit—passing taxable income and deductions to their beneficiaries.

EXAMPLE: A simple trust distributes all of its income currently in equal amounts to Jane and Tom. The trust earns a total of $6,000 during the year, with no expenses. $3,000 is distributed to each of Jane and Tom. However, the analysis cannot stop here. Of the $6,000 of income earned by the trust, $2,000 was interest on tax-exempt bonds, and $4,000 was interest on CDs. Jane and Tom should each be allocated $1,000 of tax-exempt income and $2,000 of ordinary income to comprise each of their $3,000 shares. If not, each of them would have very different tax results even though they were equal beneficiaries.

There can be advantages, however, in allocating different types of income to different beneficiaries. For example, if one beneficiary is in a low tax bracket, and another beneficiary is in a high tax bracket, it could be advantageous to allocate taxable income to the low-bracket beneficiary, and tax-exempt income to the high-bracket beneficiary. For example, the kiddie tax (see Chapter 16) could make it advantageous to allocate tax exempt income to a child beneficiary under age 14, while older children who are beneficiaries would receive allocations of taxable income.

As is usually the case, there is a cost and restriction on obtaining any tax advantage. The trust document must specifically make the desired allocation. This makes it difficult to achieve the optimal tax result because you will have to anticipate events when you first sign the trust, not a simple task. Further, there must be an economic effect independent of the income tax benefits of the allocation for the IRS to recognize it.

EXAMPLE: Assume, in the previous example, that Jane was allocated the entire $2,000 of tax-exempt income. Jane would thus receive $2,000 of tax-exempt income, and $1,000 of taxable income. Tom would receive $3,000 of taxable ordinary income. The trust agreement must provide for this in advance. What if the trust agreement provides that when the tax-exempt and nontax-exempt bonds are sold, the gain is divided equally between Jane and Tom. This would make it appear that the only consequence of allocating tax-exempt income to Jane was the income tax benefit. The IRS would probably not accept such an allocation. If, however, any gain or loss on the tax-exempt bonds was allocated 100 percent to Jane, and she was allocated only a third of the gain or loss on the other bonds, then Jane would bear the economic risks and rewards of the tax-exempt income allocated to her and the allocation may be accepted.

How Is a Beneficiary Taxed on the Receipt of Income Accumulated by a Trust?

Trustees will often not distribute all of a trust's income in the year it is earned. The beneficiary may not need the income or the trust agreement may not require it (or may even prohibit such a distribution). What happens, from an income tax perspective, when the trust doesn't distribute income and instead accumulates it?

CAUTION: Whether a trust may accumulate income to be taxed at a lower bracket, or alternatively if the trust may distribute income to the beneficiaries to be taxed at their lower tax brackets, will depend on the authority given to the trustee under the trust agreement. When you are having a lawyer prepare a new trust, weigh the pros and cons of leaving the trustee substantial flexibility to distribute or accumulate funds. A sprinkle power can give the trustee the right to distribute income or principal to any one or more of several named beneficiaries based on need or other criteria. Providing the trustee the flexibility of a sprinkle power may also enable the trustee to distribute income to the beneficiaries in the lowest tax brackets.

There are important nontax reasons to accumulate income. Where the current beneficiary does not need the money, and the remainder beneficiary will likely need the money, the trustee may choose to hold income rather than distribute it, assuming the trust agreement gives him or her the power to do so.

EXAMPLE: You set up a trust for the benefit of your spouse. On your spouse's death, the income and eventually the principal of the trust will go to your child. Your spouse is the current beneficiary. Your child is called the remainder beneficiary. Since your spouse has substantial income, you authorize your trustee, in the trust agreement, to distribute income to your spouse if necessary. You do not, however, require distribution. This could be a bypass trust described in Chapter 10 rather than a QTIP/marital trust described in Chapter 14. Your spouse does exceptionally well in the stock market and has no need for any income from the trust. Rather than expose the income to your spouse's creditors, especially when there is no need for the money, your trustee saves the money for future distribution to your child.

The accumulation of income, however, can later trigger a complex tax on accumulated distributions. How and when income that is accumulated by the trustee in one year, and distributed in a later year, is taxed is quite complex. The answer is found in a confusing set of rules that apply when income accumulated by the trustee in one year, is distributed to a beneficiary in a later year (in tax jargon, an "accumulation distribution"). The tax rules which apply to accumulation distributions are called *throw-back rules*. The idea is to tax the trust's income as if it had been paid to the beneficiary in the year it was earned, rather then held by the trust. This result is estimated by "throwing-back" the income to the beneficiary's tax return for the year in which the income was earned by the trust and in which it could have been distributed. There are several modifications and assumptions that the tax laws contain which distort this process in order to make the required calculations.

Fortunately (for you, not your trust accountant), these rules have been repealed the throw-back tax rules for domestic trusts. Now, these complex rules will only apply to foreign trusts and domestic trusts which are taxed as foreign trusts.

NOTE: This tax break and simplification is academic because the income tax rates that apply to trusts are so compressed that there is generally little benefit in trying to accumulate income in a trust to avoid the beneficiaries' paying higher income tax rates on distributions.

CONCLUSION

The tax rules for how a trust and beneficiary are taxed are extremely complicated. However, the benefits of using trusts to properly protect you, your family, your privacy, and your assets should not be deterred by this complexity since the benefits of using trusts will often outweigh the costs of complying with the trust tax rules. This complexity, though, makes it essential to retain specialized professional accountants or tax advisers.

Part Three

TRUSTS FOR DIFFERENT PEOPLE AND ORGANIZATIONS

13 TRUSTS FOR YOURSELF

The reasons to set up a trust for yourself are many of the same reasons you would set up a trust for others. These include providing for management of your assets in the event that you need assistance or are disabled, protection of your assets from creditors, avoiding ancillary probate (probate in states other than the one in which you permanently reside), avoiding probate entirely, saving taxes, and so forth. With or without gift and estate tax benefits, there remain a myriad of reasons to set up and use trusts.

EXAMPLE: You set up a living (inter-vivos) revocable trust for yourself, naming yourself as the trustee during your life and prior to your disability. On your disability or death, a major bank will serve as co-trustee with the eldest of your children (the remaining children named in age order to serve if their older siblings cannot). In the event of disability, you will have the professional management and investment expertise of the institution. You will also have objectivity, to be assured that your money will be used to protect you. This can be important in case Junior prefers not to spend your trust money on your care so he can increase his inheritance and get that Ferrari. On your death, the first $1 million of your assets (as of 2002) held in your living trust are transferred to a bypass trust for the benefit of your surviving spouse (see Chapter 14). Where the combined estate of you and your spouse is in excess of $1 million this approach can reduce, and perhaps eliminate, any federal estate tax. However, these tax benefits do not require you to use a living trust. They can be provided under a will. But a will cannot provide the assurance of objective management of your assets while you are alive, avoid probate, and achieve other benefits.

There are many types of trusts that you may consider setting up for your own benefit. This chapter will focus on one—the revocable living (sometimes called loving) trust.

NOTE: For a very detailed analysis of living trusts, sample trust and related forms, and how to use living trusts as a foundation for your overall financial, estate, and related planning, see Shenkman, *The Complete Living Trust Program* (John Wiley & Sons, Inc.). For a free annotated sample living trust, visit the Web site: www.laweasy.com.

OTHER TRUSTS YOU MIGHT SET UP FOR YOURSELF

There are many different types of trusts you might consider setting up which can also benefit you. These include:

- *Qualified personal residence trust* (QPRT) to which you transfer your home. While the primary benefits of this type of trust are to assure designated heirs receiving your house and obtaining gift tax benefits, you also benefit. For the years the trust lasts, you are the sole beneficiary who can use the house, or benefit from the proceeds (via an annuity payment) if the house is sold and the proceeds not reinvested. This type of trust should also make your house a more difficult asset for creditors to reach.
- *Grantor retained annuity trust* (GRAT) provides for tax leverage to transfer assets to your heirs. It can also provide for management of your assets, assure you a periodic cash flow, and should safeguard assets from your claimants.
- *Charitable remainder trust* (CRT), similar to a GRAT, can provide you with a periodic cash flow for life or a term of years, and a substantial capital gains tax savings as well.
- *Charitable lead trust* (CLT) can be used to fund your charitable gifts while the trust is in existence by your designation, through an arrangement known as a *donor advised fund*, which charities will benefit each year from the required charitable payment.
- *Asset protection trusts* (APT) can safeguard your assets while preserving some access for you to trust assets in the event you need funds. These trusts can also provide for professional management and investment of trust monies.

REVOCABLE LIVING TRUSTS

A revocable inter-vivos trust (sometime called a *living trust* or *loving trust*) is one of the most talked about estate planning techniques. While it can be a very useful financial and estate planning tool, much of the talk is hype. Living trusts, in the appropriate circumstances, can be an ideal tool to accomplish many essential planning goals. In inappropriate circumstances, they can be an unnecessary waste of time and money and create some unnecessary hassles and complications in managing your affairs. In the worst-case scenarios, you may use (or unfortunately, be "sold") a revocable living trust when another technique would have been more appropriate. The results could be disastrous.

Whatever your final decision about whether to use a living trust, it should be made with full awareness of all of the benefits and costs of setting up a living trust.

EXAMPLE: Assume you live in Vermont and have a rental vacation property in Pennsylvania. A living trust will avoid probate for the Pennsylvania property. However, a living trust will not facilitate making gifts of interests in that property to reduce your estate tax cost. A limited liability company (LLC) can achieve these two goals. Using a living trust instead of an LLC would be less than ideal. But it gets worse. If you use a living trust to avoid ancillary probate and are sued for more than your insurance coverage by an injured tenant (or your policy has an exception for the incident involved), your entire estate could be jeopardized. If instead you transferred the property to an LLC, you would have limited your liability to just the property. Your home and other assets would be safe. The incorrect use of a living trust instead of the appropriate technique or plan could be disastrous.

CAUTION: The most important point to remember is that no single estate planning step can be relied on to solve all your problems, or to solve everyone's problems. Whatever the hot item of the day, whether it's a living (loving) trust, a second-to-die insurance policy, a charitable remainder trust, or any other technique, no single step can possibly address all of your needs. The only approach to use, no matter how much money you have, or how simple your situation may be, is a comprehensive estate, financial, insurance, and tax plan. Nothing less will provide you with the comfort that you have best addressed all of the possible needs of you and your loved ones.

What Is a Revocable Living Trust?

A living trust is a trust that you set up during your lifetime. You retain complete control over the assets in the trust while you are alive and prior to your becoming disabled. For tax purposes, the trust is generally ignored and all income and deductions are reported on your own tax return (see Chapter 12). If you become disabled or infirm, a successor trustee takes over managing your assets (although it can be preferable to have that successor trustee serve as a co-trustee before you become disabled to facilitate the transition).

On your death, provisions that serve the same purpose as a will apply to govern the disposition of your assets. Since there is no current tax benefit of setting up a living trust, the format used can be quite flexible so it is adaptable to meet a broad range of personal objectives.

A couple of examples can illustrate common situations when a living trust is likely to be an appropriate planning tool for you.

EXAMPLE: You're a widower age 78 and have few family other than your children and minor grandchildren. They all live several hundred miles away. A living trust is likely to make sense unless the other facts and circumstances are very persuasive against using such a trust. Considering the age and scarcity of those who can help in a financial emergency, the use of a living trust may be ideal to provide protection against disability. If you have no fully trusted people to name as successor trustees, you could name an institution to serve as a co-trustee with friends or family members. The institution is subject to substantial regulatory scrutiny and safeguards and thus gives comfort that your assets will be looked after for your benefit. Institutions will not generally serve as agents under a durable power of attorney, so a living trust may be necessary.

EXAMPLE: You're in your mid-70s and have a substantial estate. Other than your house and some bank accounts, your entire estate is comprised of a diversified securities portfolio located in three major brokerage firms. A living trust to avoid probate (considering the size of your estate), and to provide for disability is almost certain to be the appropriate decision. Even for probate avoidance alone, a living trust is almost assuredly going to be the desired option. The estate is substantial and the assets are easy to transfer to the trust's name—simply advise your broker of what is necessary. The living trust, however, won't solve your tax problem.

Is a Living Trust Really Better Than Probate? Sometimes

A living trust is primarily touted for its use as a method of avoiding probate. Probate is not necessarily the evil and excessively expensive process many people fear, although it sometimes can be. A living trust is not necessarily the simple and inexpensive document many people expect (certainly not when it's done properly).

Cost of Setting Up a Living Trust

To set up a living trust, you must retain a lawyer to prepare a comprehensive plan and, based on that plan, a trust document. The trust document, if properly written, is not as simple as most sales pitches would have you believe. The plan and trust should be tailored to address your personal goals and objectives, the estate tax (if any), and other needs. Be certain that the attorney coordinates the tax allocation clause in your will with the tax clause in the trust.

The trust document, however, is only the first step. You should generally arrange to transfer many of your assets to the trust. For real estate, you will need to execute a deed, and depending where you live, complete various tax and other forms. If the property has a mortgage, you will have to review the mortgage for a due-on-sale clause and most likely notify your bank. Insurance policies on real estate and art will have to be changed to the name of the trust to be effective. The title insurance company that insured any real estate you want to transfer to the living trust should be asked whether a new policy in the name of the trust is required. Personal property will require a bill of sale to be transferred. These steps can be time consuming, can require the assistance of an attorney, and can create additional fees and charges, none of which would have to be incurred if you didn't set up the living trust. Bank accounts should often be retitled into the name of your trust (see Chapter 3). A separate tax identification number might be advisable as well.

Quick Access to Cash May Be Easier with a Living Trust

Unless your family has sufficient assets of their own to sustain them during the probate process (or at least until interim distributions can be made), a funded living trust can (but won't always) prove to be a simpler and quicker method for getting needed cash and other assets to your heirs. To achieve this benefit, your trust will need to hold assets before your death so it can quickly distribute them without further legal actions (e.g., the successor trustee taking over).

*Living Trust Costs Are Incurred Now; Probate Costs Are
Incurred in the Future*

If all of these steps are actually cheaper than probate costs, it still doesn't mean that setting up a living trust is the low-cost option. Remember, the costs of setting up your living trust will be incurred now, whereas the probate costs may not be incurred for 10, 20, or more years.

Other estate planning documents are needed whether or not you have a living trust.

Will

Using a living trust is not a substitute for a will. A will is often necessary to designate a guardian for minor children. You need a will because there is no assurance that every asset of yours will be owned by your living trust at your death. This could occur because of the improper or incomplete transfer of assets, acquisitions for which there was inadequate time to complete a transfer to your trust, assets that could not be assigned, and finally assets that you may not be aware of (e.g., a winning lottery ticket).

Your will should not be the typical simple pourover will many people use. This type of will provides that all assets under the will are simply to be transferred to (poured over into) your living trust. A complete will is necessary to authorize your executor to take the actions that might be necessary if circumstances change. Your pourover will should provide for how your estate assets should be distributed if your living trust is invalid or unable to accept property. Your will should include a full range of powers and other rights given to your executor. If you're concerned enough to minimize legal and other problems by having a living trust, you should be concerned enough to insist on a comprehensive will and living trust.

By using a living trust, you won't eliminate the cost of a will; in fact, you've increased your legal costs by needing two documents where one may have sufficed. And the two documents have to be coordinated, so that the will used with a living trust is actually more complex (when done right) than a will used alone.

Living Will and Health Care Proxy

These documents are essential to address medical decisions if you are incapacitated. You need these whether or not you also have a living trust. However, the living trust used with these documents can provide an even greater level of protection and perhaps minimize the likelihood of a *guardianship* proceeding (having someone approved by a court to take care of your personal decisions).

Power of Attorney

This designates a person as your agent to handle legal, tax, and financial matters if you are disabled. You should have one even if you have a living trust. It should be coordinated with the living trust to facilitate your agent's transferring assets to the living trust if you are disabled.

Living Trusts Don't Avoid Legal Challenges, They May Exacerbate Them

You can have the mental awareness (testamentary capacity) necessary to sign a will, but still lack the required legal capacity to sign a living trust. A trust is a contract so you must have the comprehension, understanding, and state of mind required to create a binding legal contract. The standard that has been accepted by the law to sign a will has intentionally been made easier to enable people *in extremis* to sign wills. The standard for signing a will merely requires you to be aware of your descendants, the extent of your assets, and the fact that you are signing a document to bequeath those assets to the persons you name.

If you are disabled or infirm, you may be legally incapable of signing a contract, but still have sufficient capacity to sign a will. If this is the case, a will and not a living trust should be used.

Confidentiality and a Living Trust

A living trust can enable you to minimize (not avoid) the risk of having your assets and wishes disclosed to the public. Your will is a public document once probated, and anybody may go see it. If your will contains a pourover provision and is probated, the probate process may require that your living trust be recorded in the public record in a manner similar to the will. If a living trust is challenged by a wanna-be beneficiary, the trust might easily wind up in court records, which are open to the public. Thus, in some cases, there may be little additional secrecy offered by the use of a living trust. That doesn't mean not to use one, just recognize the limitations of what you might achieve.

NOTE: If you have a relationship with a nonmarried partner who your family members may not approve of, the use of a living trust may be helpful in minimizing scrutiny, interference, and potential challenge. Your revocable living trust may have a degree of confidentiality that a will does not. If you transfer only a portion of your assets into the trust, retaining the remaining assets in your estate, family members adverse to your relationship may not even realize that a trust governing some portion of your estate exists. This can be an effective planning technique.

Legal Fees after Death

When a person with a living trust dies, the assets in that trust must still be transferred to the designated beneficiaries. Additional trusts may have to be set up (e.g., the bypass trust for tax benefits, trusts for minor children, or a dynasty trust). Thus, whether assets pass through probate or under a living trust, steps will still have to be taken to transfer those assets. Where the property is real estate, stocks, or other assets, the paperwork may not be that different. Also, it is often possible to probate an estate for far less in legal costs than many popular books and articles in financial publications indicate. Numbers like 5 percent to 10 percent plus of total assets are often suggested as typical costs and fees for probating an estate. In many instances, this is a gross exaggeration. The size of the estate often has little to do with the work necessary. The nature of the assets, cooperation of family members, and organization of necessary financial and personal records are important factors in determining the legal work involved. Also, the particular probate court that will handle the estate can be have a significant effect on the overall cost of probate. Many probate (surrogate) courts are extremely efficient, helpful, and professional. This can drastically reduce the cost and time delays involved.

Last, and perhaps most important, if your estate is taxable, a federal estate tax return will have to be filed. Using a living trust does nothing to reduce the costs of making this filing, and will probably do little to change the tax amount.

Executor and Trustee Commissions

State law provides for a maximum amount that can generally be charged by persons serving as executors under your will and trustees under your trust. Often family or friends are willing to serve as executor or trustee for no fee. The real best choice here depends on your personal situation.

Reducing Probate Expenses

If probate worries you, inexpensive and simple steps can be taken to avoid it. You can own assets jointly, use beneficiary designations to distribute assets without probate (e.g., IRAs and insurance—even many brokerage firms will let you designate a beneficiary for your brokerage account to avoid probate). Real estate, bank accounts, bonds and other assets can be owned as joint tenants with the right of survivorship to pass those assets directly.

If the costs associated with probate concern you, you can take steps to address those as well. Carefully maintain complete financial and legal records to save on professional fees later. When a lawyer or accountant is hired to handle your probate matter, insist on detailed bills itemizing all steps taken. Obtain estimates in advance and request regular billing and quick notification if actual costs exceed any budgeted costs. Don't be shy about questioning a bill, retainer agreement, or budget that doesn't makes sense. While the incidence of abuse is hopefully rare, when it occurs it can be financially devastating.

Making the Best Choice if You Are Disabled

In some instances, particularly if you're young, healthy, and concerned about the management of your assets in case you are disabled, the cost of a living trust to provide for disability may be excessive when compared to the use of a durable power of attorney, which is simple and very inexpensive to complete.

However, for older or infirm taxpayers, a revocable living trust may help avoid the need for a guardianship proceeding in the event of disability and thus could well be worth the cost in excess of a durable power of attorney. A living trust can provide far more detailed provisions and contingency plans for dealing with disability than does the typical durable power of attorney. It can include details on your care, that you want the best medical care regardless of the cost, the type of facilities you should reside in, and so on.

A Living Trust Does Not Avoid Estate Taxes

The only estate tax benefit from a living trust is where the other planning techniques and trusts discussed in this book are incorporated into a living trust. The use of a living trust itself does not provide any tax benefit.

EXAMPLE: You establish a living trust that helps you avoid probate on your $2 million estate entirely. On your death, your living trust provides that your entire $2 million estate passes outright to your spouse and on her later death, to your children. Although you've avoided probate, your living trust will do absolutely nothing to save estate taxes for your family. Under current law, a $2 million estate will trigger estate tax until 2006, when the exclusion is scheduled to increase to that level.

EXAMPLE: Assume the same facts as the previous example, except your living trust provides that the first $1 million of your assets will be transferred to a bypass trust to benefit your wife, without ever being taxed in her estate (see Chapter 14). On your wife's later death, her $1 million estate is protected by the exclusion of $1 million (2002) and passes free of tax to the children. By protecting your exclusion, and using your wife's exclusion as well, the estate tax is avoided through the provisions in your living trust. Your living trust, however, hasn't provided you any benefit that a will couldn't have provided.

Outright Gifts or Irrevocable Trusts May Be Better Options Than Either a Living Trust or a Will for Certain Assets

Probate and a will, or a living trust and avoiding probate, are not the only choices. Again, a thorough review of all estate, financial, insurance, and other goals is essential. If your estate is large enough, it may be better to give away certain assets as gifts to your adult children (to remove them from your estate) rather than transferring them into a living trust that won't remove them from your estate.

EXAMPLE: Your estate is valued at over $3 million. $1.5 million of your estate is stock in a closely held business. If the value of the stock exceeds 35 percent of your adjusted gross estate, your estate will qualify for favorable estate tax deferral provisions. These can permit your estate to pay out any estate tax on an installment basis over a period of about 14 years. This can be a tremendous benefit and perhaps minimize the need for expensive insurance coverage. However, for your estate to qualify, the stock must exceed the percentage threshold of 35 percent. If you merely transfer your assets to a living trust, this valuable estate tax deferral will not be available. Alternatively, if you gave away nonbusiness assets to your adult children, or transferred nonbusiness assets to trusts for the benefit of your family (including a dynasty trust of which you remain a beneficiary), your estate could qualify for this favorable tax benefit. If you have five married children, each with four of their own children, you and your spouse could each give away $300,000 in 2001 using your $10,000 annual gift exclusions. If your family is smaller, the same gifts could be completed on a tax-free basis over a several year period. In this situation, limiting your decision to probate versus living will could miss an important point, reducing the potential federal estate tax cost.

Four Stages in the Life of Your Living Trust: How Does a Living Trust Work?

The best way to understand how a living trust works is to review the four states in the lifecycle of a typical revocable living trust.

Phase 1: Formation

After a complete review of your tax, estate, financial, and personal goal and status, a comprehensive plan should be formulated. Where a revocable living trust is an appropriate component of this plan, you should retain a lawyer to draft the trust. The trust should be signed, witnessed, and notarized. Copies of the trust should be given to any professionals you have hired and your family. Assets should then be transferred to your trust (see Chapter 3).

Phase 2: Management

Manage the assets in your trusts as if they were your own, with one twist—transactions affecting trust assets will be completed in the name of the trust. You will sign trust checks and buy stock in your trust's name.

Phase 3: What if You Become Disabled?

If you become disabled, your successor trustees (or co-trustees) will take over the management of your trust assets. Your agent, acting under your durable power of attorney, may transfer to your living trust any assets you own outside the trust.

Your living trust should contain detailed provisions stating how and who should take over. The trust should make it clear how it is determined that you are disabled so that your successor trustees can know when to take over. It should also indicate that if you recover you can take back control of your financial management.

An important part of the disability provisions of your living trust is detailed instructions as to how you should be cared for in the event of disability. Many of the "form" trusts simply do not provide this type of personalized detail. Do you want to avoid being placed in a nursing home as long as possible? Do you have preferences for the type of health care facility which you should be placed in if it becomes absolutely necessary? If geographic preferences are important to you during your life, you should specify in your living trust that in the event of your disability you would wish to be placed in a facility that is located in a certain part of the country (perhaps near your family). If religious preferences are important, you may wish to specify that the health care facility be near a church, mosque, or synagogue so that you could attend services, or that the facility meet your religious dietary requirements. Do not assume that your trustees will know your preferences. Specifying such details may be vital, depending on who the trustees are. This detail can also enable your trustees to respond to a challenge by your heirs as to the appropriateness of the decisions and expenditures that they make.

Phase 4: After Your Death

On death, your trust becomes irrevocable and your successor trustees will carry out your wishes (e.g., funding a bypass trust). Any assets that were not already transferred to your trust (either by you when you formed the trust, at a later date by you, or by your agent under your durable power of attorney after your disability) can be transferred under what is known as a *pourover will*. The key provision of this will provides that any assets that you may have owned at your death which were not already in your trust, should be transferred (or poured over) into your trust. Many different types of trusts described throughout this book can all be incorporated into your living trust.

CONCLUSION

Living trusts are an important and flexible estate and financial planning tool. The benefits they can provide are substantial for some people, but not all. Your living trust should be completed as part of an overall financial and estate plan, including a durable power of attorney, a living will/health care proxy, and a pourover will.

14 TRUSTS FOR YOUR SPOUSE

Many of the trusts described in this book can be used in some manner to benefit your spouse. These include:

- *Charitable remainder trust* (CRT)—you can contribute appreciated property to a charitable trust in exchange for an annuity for the joint lives of you and your spouse.
- *Irrevocable life insurance trust*—this is one of the most common trusts used to benefit a spouse. The trust holds insurance on your life to benefit your spouse (and children or other heirs if you wish). This trust protects the insurance proceeds from whoever your spouse might marry after your death, from creditors and claimants and, if applicable, from estate tax.
- *Revocable living trust* (RLT)—a common tool used to protect the designated person in the event of illness and disability. You can also benefit your spouse under your revocable living trust by including a bypass or marital (QTIP) trust under your living trust for your spouse's benefit.

When planning for trusts to benefit your spouse, you should first develop an overall estate plan since it is the aggregate benefit and integration of all planning that is important. If your spouse is the sole beneficiary of an insurance trust with a $2 million insurance policy on your life, you may be less concerned about providing for her under other trusts you form.

The focus of this chapter will be on those trusts uniquely and specifically intended for spouses. In most cases, the focus of a spousal trust (and the factor that distinguishes a spousal trust from other trusts) is qualification for the unlimited estate and gift tax marital deduction. This deduction permits you to transfer unlimited assets to your spouse without any tax cost, if the applicable requirements are met.

When the term *spouse* is used in this chapter, it refers solely to a person whose relationship under local law is that of a marital partner. A nonmarital partner will not qualify for these tax benefits (see Chapter 15).

An important point must be considered when planning for marital deductions and marital deduction trusts. The use of a marital deduction is not a tax savings; it is a tax deferral. Thus, while the marital deduction remains a cornerstone of planning for married couples, it should not be relied upon to the exclusion of estate tax reduction planning techniques (e.g., CRTs, QPRTs, and the like).

GIFT TAX MARITAL DEDUCTION

Gift tax planning for spousal trusts can be quite important. It may be advantageous to establish an inter-vivos (i.e., set up while you are alive, rather than under your will) marital (QTIP or QDOT) trust.

For Spouses Generally

An unlimited gift tax marital deduction is available for direct gifts to your spouse. In addition, the gift can be made in trust if the trust meets the requirements of a QTIP or QDOT. Why would you wish to establish and fund a marital trust while you are still alive? If your spouse has few assets, he or she will not be able to fund a bypass trust under a will, thus wasting the $1 million (2002) exclusion to which he or she is entitled. If you make a gift while you are alive to a marital trust for the benefit of your spouse, there will be no current gift tax cost as a result of your qualifying the gift for the unlimited gift tax marital deduction. On your wife's later death, the $1 million marital trust would be included in her estate and used to fund a bypass trust to safeguard her estate tax exclusion amount. Thus, this trust could pass to your children (or other heirs designated in the marital trust you formed) without any estate tax. This will ultimately save your family a great deal in federal estate taxes. In addition, assets taxed in your spouse's estate will receive a step-up in basis to the fair value on death (at least until 2010 when the estate tax is to be repealed and carryover basis becomes law).

Why use a marital trust instead of simply giving the $1 million to your wife? Perhaps the children who are your intended future beneficiaries are from a different marriage and you want to assure that they ultimately receive the assets. Your wife might be a professional concerned about malpractice; a marital trust can provide for her financial well-being while protecting the assets in the trust from her malpractice claimants. For larger estates, a marital trust can help fractionalize ownership of assets so that the value of those assets can be reduced for tax purposes.

For Noncitizen Spouses

The gift tax rules applicable where your spouse is not a citizen present a trap to your trust planning. The unlimited marital deduction is not available for a gift to a noncitizen spouse. However, a gift of up to $100,000 per year can be made to a noncitizen spouse without incurring a gift tax. The mechanism for this is to provide that the annual per donee gift tax exclusion is increased from $10,000 (indexed) to $100,000 indexed. In 2002 the indexed figures are $11,000 and $110,000 respectively. This provision is quite valuable in that substantial assets can be transferred to the noncitizen spouse during your life. However, this restriction must be carefully considered in setting up any trusts for the benefit of your spouse.

ESTATE TAX MARITAL DEDUCTION

When planning to use the unlimited marital deduction, review with your estate planner the pros and cons of deferring estate tax. In some instances, it may be advantageous to use less of the marital deduction and actually incur some tax on the death of the first spouse. This could be done, for example, to take advantage of the lower graduated estate tax brackets. However, after the 2001 Tax Act with large increases in the exclusion, and estate tax rate reductions scheduled, this benefit will be less likely.

Qualifying for Unlimited Marital Deduction

An unlimited marital deduction is available for qualifying bequests under your will to a trust for your wife. The following requirements must be met:

- The property that is intended to qualify for the marital deduction must pass from you to your surviving spouse. The property must be transferred under your will (or under your state's laws of intestacy if you died without a will), as a result of joint ownership between you and your spouse, or by a beneficiary designation (e.g., on an IRA).
- The rights and property transferred to your spouse cannot be a right that will terminate or fail as the result of the passing of time, the occurrence of an event or contingency (for example, a trust that lasts until she remarries), or the failure of an event or contingency to occur. A life estate ("my spouse shall have our home for her life") or a bequest for a term of years ("my spouse shall have my yacht for 15 years") are terminable interests and do not qualify for the marital deduction.

    The most common exception to this rule denying a marital deduction for property interests that may terminate, however, is the exception called a qualified terminable interest property, or QTIP, trust. This is the most popular marital trust. If the following requirements are met, your estate will qualify for the estate tax marital deduction on bequeathing assets to a QTIP trust for your spouse. In addition to the marital deduction, you will maintain control over the use and ultimate disposition of the property.
- No person can have the power to appoint the trust assets to any person other than your surviving spouse prior to her death.
- Income from the trust must be paid to your spouse at least annually.

- Your executor must elect to qualify the trust for the marital deduction.
- The property must pass from your estate to her trust.
- On the death of the surviving spouse, the entire value of the QTIP property is included in your surviving spouse's gross estate.

Pros and Cons of a Marital Trust

When in doubt, use the trust. Why? While a trust creates a bit more complexity and cost, it assures you control. It also provides a number of important tax benefits. Your executor can determine what portion of the trust should qualify for the marital deduction. This can enable your executor to use hindsight to preserve some of your exclusion. Your executor can also make decisions to maximize the GST tax benefit, using the benefit of hindsight.

Alternative Ways to Qualify for a Marital Deduction

There are other alternatives to qualify for an estate tax marital deduction. These are not nearly as popular as a QTIP, but perhaps worth considering.

A Life Estate Coupled with a General Power of Appointment

If your surviving spouse is given a life estate coupled with a power of appointment in the property, this qualifies for the unlimited gift or estate tax marital deduction. This requires that your surviving spouse be given the right to all of the income from the entire property (or from a specific portion of the property) for life. This income must be payable at least annually. If the property is held by a trust for the surviving spouse's benefit, she must have the right to require that any nonincome producing property be converted into income-producing property. In addition, your surviving spouse must have a general power of appointment (i.e., the power to designate where the property will be distributed on her death), exercisable by her alone, to dispose of the entire interest in the property as she chooses. This power must include the right to appoint the property to herself or her estate. No other person can have the right to appoint the property involved to any person other than your spouse.

Estate Trust

The estate trust is another method of qualifying a bequest for the unlimited estate tax marital deduction. It is another exception to the terminable interest rule, described earlier, which would otherwise prevent this deduction from qualifying for the estate tax marital deduction. This type of trust will qualify for the unlimited marital deduction for a U.S. citizen where the previously mentioned requirements for a life estate and general power of appointment are met and the income from the estate trust that is not required to be paid to the spouse at least annually can be accumulated and added to the trust. However, the estate trust must require that the accumulated income and principal be paid out at some future time to the surviving spouse, or to her estate. Thus, the spouse may receive no income from this trust, but on her later death the entire trust will be paid to her estate and distributed as she directs.

Marital and Charitable Trusts Combined

There are a number of ways you can combine marital and charitable trusts to achieve more specific goals. You could include a QTIP marital trust in your will to provide for your wife, then on her death, direct that the remaining trust assets be paid to charity. The result will be no tax in your estate as a result of the marital deduction and on your wife's later death there will be no tax in her estate as a result of the charitable contribution deduction.

PLANNING TIP: Depending on your circumstances, the QTIP with a charitable remainder can be better then using the far more popular charitable remainder trust (CRT). This is because your wife will receive all income of the QTIP trust (and even access to the principal if you wish) instead of being limited to only a specified annuity payment under the CRT.

Charitable remainder trusts (CRTs) can be combined with marital deduction planning. Your wife could be the sole noncharitable beneficiary of a charitable remainder trust. This would entitle her to a payment each month (or quarter or year) during her lifetime. The interest she has will qualify as a marital deduction and thus not be taxable (see Chapter 17).

Marital Deduction for a Spouse Who Is Not a Citizen

If your spouse is not a U.S. citizen, the unlimited estate tax marital deduction will not be available unless you make special provisions. The popular QTIP trust described earlier will not defer estate tax for a noncitizen, although there is a credit provision that can mitigate this result to some extent. The credit works as follows. If you bequeath property to your noncitizen spouse and that property transfer is subjected to the estate tax, but would not have been taxed had your wife been a citizen, a credit will be available. On the death of your spouse, her estate will receive a credit for the tax paid by your estate on the earlier transfer to her that did not qualify for the marital deduction.

The best answer, short of becoming a U.S. citizen, is usually to use a special trust for your noncitizen spouse that will qualify for the marital deduction. If you transfer assets into a qualified domestic trust (QDOT), the marital deduction will be available without limit. To qualify, a QDOT must meet the following requirements:

- *Trustees.* At least one of your trustees must be either a U.S. citizen or corporation. This requirement must be contained in the trust documents. Provisions should be made for alternate trustees to assure compliance with this requirement. For example, a final alternate should be a U.S. bank or trust company.

- *Income.* The surviving spouse must generally be entitled to all of the income from the trust, payable at least annually. This requirement is similar to the QTIP trust for a citizen spouse.

- *Regulations.* The trust must meet additional requirements prescribed by IRS regulations which are intended to assure that the trust assets will not escape U.S. taxation.

- *Election.* Your executor must make an irrevocable election on the U.S. estate tax return with respect to the trust.

Estate tax will be levied on distributions of principal (corpus) from the QDOT other than annual income distributions. This tax will be calculated as if the amount distributed had been included in your estate (i.e., the first to die is the citizen spouse). This calculation adds all prior distributions from the QDOT to your taxable estate in order to push the tax on the QDOT distributions into the highest federal estate tax bracket. A limited exception is provided for hardship distributions. In addition, a tax will be assessed on the assets left in the QDOT on the your wife's later death.

Because of the complexity involved, if your will doesn't include all the requirements, the IRS will often let you modify (reform) the trust to qualify as a QDOT.

Bypass/QTIP Two Trust Approach

A simple will generally bequeaths all of your assets to your wife on your death. The problem with this simplistic approach is that it wastes the $1 million (2002) exclusion available to your estate. The effect is to double up assets in your wife's estate possibly subjecting them to an estate tax that could otherwise be avoided. On your wife's later death, all of the family's net worth becomes taxable in her estate with only her $1 million exclusion (yours is wasted if your will leaves everything to her outright) to offset it. The better planning approach is to use a bypass trust for the first approximately $1 million of assets (see Chapter 10). If your estate exceeds this amount (which is scheduled to increase in future years), you could leave the balance to the QTIP trust as discussed earlier.

Assets transferred to your bypass trust remain free of estate tax in both your estate and your surviving wife's estate no matter how large they grow. If the $1 million grows to $5 million by the time your wife dies, it remains estate tax free.

The "Disclaimer" Option

Not sure which approach to use? Perhaps you are weighing the simplicity of giving all assets to the surviving spouse and letting the children worry about the taxes (after all, they will inherit so much anyway). If your combined family estate is close to, but under, the $1 million exclusion, you may not be convinced that the paperwork (e.g., annual trust income tax returns after the bypass trust is funded following your death) are worth it. There is another option. Instead of your will or trust forcing the funding of a bypass trust, you can bequeath assets outright (without a trust) to your wife. However, unlike the simple will, which forgoes planning, you can provide in your will the flexibility for her to decide within nine months of your death if some portion, or all, of your estate should go to the bypass trust. This mechanism gives your wife the flexibility to determine whether, or to what extent, to use a bypass trust. Following the 2001 Tax Act, this approach is even more popular. With the large scheduled increases in the exclusion, to as much as $3.5 million in 2009, flexibility to choose the amount to go into a bypass trust can be important.

How Do You Divide the Estate between the Credit/Shelter and Marital Trusts?

Once you've determined that your will or revocable living trust should take the "classic" bypass/QTIP estate planning approach, these documents must include a mechanism to divide your estate between these two trusts. There are two choices:

- *Fractional share method.* This approach divides your remaining estate into two shares and places the appropriate proportion in each trust. Your will or living trust might say: "The fiduciary shall transfer to the QTIP trust that fractional share of my residuary estate which, when added to all other assets passing to my spouse which qualify for the unlimited estate tax marital deduction, is the minimum amount necessary to reduce the federal estate tax as close as possible to zero using the unlimited estate tax marital deduction. The remaining fractional share shall be distributed to the bypass trust." Any appreciation or depreciation in assets is shared proportionately. There is no income tax cost to funding the trusts.
- *Pecuniary share.* This method transfers a specified dollar amount (as contrasted to a share as above) to one of the trusts (e.g., the bypass trust), with the balance to the QTIP trust (or outright to your wife). All appreciation or depreciation in the value of assets from the date of death through the date the trust is funded inures to the residuary trust (either trust can be the residuary depending on how your lawyer prepares the document). Thus, you could provide: "I give to the Trustee, in trust, a pecuniary sum equal to the largest amount that

will not result in any federal estate tax payable after giving effect to the exclusion to which I am entitled, as well as the state death tax credit and other credits applicable to my estate." (Note that the state death tax credit is being phased out following the 2001 Tax Act). There can be an income tax cost if the pecuniary share is funded with appreciated assets (i.e., the property increases in value after the date of your death). Many attorneys prefer this approach because it can be simpler to understand and administer.

SPOUSAL RIGHT OF ELECTION

State law gives every spouse the right to demand a specified minimum percentage of a deceased spouse's estate. If you leave your wife less, she can assert this claim and take what state law permits. These rules differ substantially between states and can be quite complex in how they determine the percentage and which of your assets are reachable. The goal of these laws is to assure a surviving spouse a minimum inheritance. These rules can be important to address when planning to transfer assets to trusts.

Under a typical state law, your surviving spouse may have the right to elect to take her "elective share" of one-third of your assets. A QTIP (marital) trust under your will counts as what your wife received in some states, but not in others. In some states, assets bequeathed to the surviving spouse in trust (e.g., a bypass or QTIP) are only partially counted toward meeting the surviving spouse's minimum inheritance.

If you may leave your wife less than required by law, consult an estate planner. A common approach is to have each of you and your wife agree to forgo (waive) your right to make this claim against the other's estate under state law.

ALIMONY TRUST

In some divorce cases, trusts are used to fund alimony payments. This can be done to minimize the contact and interaction you will have with your ex-spouse, and to give greater certainty to the receipt of alimony payments.

EXAMPLE: Tom and Jane divorce. Tom places $5 million in a trust. Jane is to receive the income for her life. On her death, the trust assets are to be distributed to their children. The trust eliminates Jane's worry over receiving alimony payments when due.

Alimony trusts face a special tax problem. If you form a trust and then use the trust money to pay an obligation of yours, all trust income will be taxed to you. You cannot use a trust to discharge your legal obligation of support without incurring a tax. There is an exception to this rule for certain alimony trusts. If you set up an alimony trust to pay income to your former spouse, and the marriage was ended by a court-issued divorce decree or a decree of separate maintenance, your spouse will be taxed on the income instead of you. This rule is flexible in that the divorce agreements (or court orders) don't have to require the formation of the trust. If you had previously formed a trust for your spouse even before the divorce, it can still qualify.

CAUTION: This special tax rule for alimony trusts is not available for payments to children.

CONCLUSION

For married couples, the use of the gift and estate tax martial deduction can be the most important planning technique to minimize the overall gift and estate tax burden on transfers to living trusts or trusts which become effective on your death. However, simply claiming the maximum martial deduction ("all my property to my spouse on my death, and vice versa") is almost never the optimal approach where you and your spouse have significant assets. Planning is imperative to avoid what could otherwise be a substantial estate tax where one spouse is not a U.S. citizen. The spouse can either become a citizen or use a special trust, called a QDOT, to defer the estate tax.

15 TRUSTS FOR NONMARRIED PARTNERS

Nonmarried couples face planning difficulties traditionally married couples do not. Tax and property laws clearly favor married couples. The result is that careful planning is essential and different.

One of the first steps many in committed nonmarital relationships should consider, before addressing trust planning, is a cohabitation (living together) agreement. This is a contract customized to your personal situation addressing any economic, estate, personal and other issues important to you and your partner. This can include inheritance rights, how living expenses will be shared, the treatment of children (if any), what happens if the relationship ends, and so on. The enforceability of this type of agreement cannot be assured, but it is a very important starting point in evaluating trust planning that is appropriate for you.

The goals for your cohabitation and trust planning may include:

- Availability of the personal residence and other specified property to the surviving partner.
- Protection in the event of illness or disability.
- Minimization of estate and gift taxes.
- Minimization of the risk your surviving partner will face from claims or lawsuits by family or others.

LEGAL PROBLEMS AFFECTING NONMARRIED PARTNERS

State laws are biased against couples living together outside of marriage. The result is that there are many problems gay, lesbian, and other nonmarried couples face, but which advance planning can mitigate.

Intestacy Laws Differ for Nonmarried Couples

If you die without a will (and haven't used a revocable living trust, joint ownership, or other estate-planning device), state intestacy laws will dictate the distribution of your property. Although these laws are different from state to state, on the death of one spouse, the surviving spouse will generally inherit a substantial portion of the estate, even without a will. If there is no spouse, then children or other blood relations will inherit. Non-married partners are not on the list. Advance planning must be done: a properly drafted will providing for distributions to your partner, tax planning, properly planned ownership (title) to assets, and trusts.

If proper planning is not implemented, it may mean devastating financial consequences to your partner. Substantial personal conflicts with any family members who did not approve of the relationship may follow.

No Spousal Right of Election Available

A surviving spouse has the right, under state law, to inherit a specified portion of a deceased spouse's estate (elect against the estate). This can permit the surviving spouse to obtain a statutory minimum amount of property even if the deceased spouse had changed his or her will to disinherit the surviving spouse. This right is generally not available to a surviving partner if the state does not recognize a the partnership as a legal marriage. So if you don't provide for your partner, the law won't do it for you.

ESTATE AND GIFT TAX DIFFERENCES FROM THE MARITAL SITUATION

Not surprisingly, the tax man views nonmarried couples differently from married ones.

Estate Tax Considerations for Nonmarried Partners

The gift and estate tax laws are generally extremely biased against non-married partners. The tax laws provide especially favorable treatment to married couples. As a result, every married couple can readily avoid any estate tax on the death of the first spouse. Any husband or wife can, on death, transfer to the surviving spouse unlimited assets without any tax cost. The concept behind the favoritism shown married couples is that they are viewed for tax purposes as a partnership, a single economic unit. All assets of the marital economic unit will be subject to the estate tax after the death of both spouses. This same principle is behind the filing of a joint income tax return by a married couple. While there is logic and equity in this concept, these same benefits are denied to any non-married couple. There is no unlimited "partner" deduction equivalent to the unlimited marital deduction even though nonmarried partners are often as much of a single economic unit as married couples. This is not because of old laws only. The 2001 Tax Act assures that if the estate tax is

TRUSTS FOR NONMARRIED PARTNERS   189

repealed and the carryover basis rules follow (assets you inherit will have the same tax basis as the decedent, assuring that a large capital gains tax will eventually be paid), the tax laws will still show tremendous favoritism to married couples.

A spouse can generally make unlimited transfers of property to the other spouse during life as gifts, or after death through intestacy or under a will. All of these transfers are free of federal and state gift and estate taxes. However, this right is not afforded to nonmarried partners. This presents substantial and costly problems to nonmarried partners. Nonmarried or married couples alike can give or bequeath up to $1 million in 2002 (the value of assets exempted from estate tax by the exclusion) to anyone they choose without any gift or estate tax cost. If your estate is not in excess of this amount, you will not face any federal estate tax problem (although there can still be significant state transfer taxes). If your estate exceeds this amount (or the exclusion which is applicable in the year you die), the federal tax cost will be substantial. You cannot transfer unlimited assets above this amount to your partner (as you could if you were married). Other tax planning steps must be taken to protect assets, to avoid tax costs, and to assure that your partner will in fact receive the assets.

Possible suggestions to address the potentially costly problem of a significant estate tax on the death of the first partner to die include:

- The partner with the most significant assets can purchase life insurance to cover the estate tax. The insurance should be owned in an irrevocable life insurance trust to remove the proceeds from the reach of creditors, and to keep the proceeds out of the taxable estate of the first nonmarried partner.
- Begin an aggressive gift program to reduce the wealthier partner's taxable estate. This can use the annual exclusion for gifts of $11,000 (indexed).
- Use the tax-oriented trust and related techniques (e.g., a grantor retained interest trust, GRIT).

Gift Tax Considerations for Nonmarried Partners

Married spouses are permitted to make unlimited transfers to each other without triggering any gift tax. For partners other than a husband and wife, the maximum amount that can be transferred in any year to any one donee (recipient) is $11,000 although unlimited amounts may be paid for tuition and medical care for any person, including a partner (if paid directly to qualifying providers). Any transfers above this amount will first be applied to reduce the $1 million exclusion, and thereafter a tax will be triggered.

As a result of these limitations, nonmarried couples should begin a gift program early. In addition, the techniques discussed in this book to discount gifts (lack of marketability discounts, limited partnerships, grantor retained interest trusts, and the like) should be used.

TAX-ORIENTED TRUSTS FOR NONMARRIED PARTNERS

A number of varieties of trusts may be used to look after nonmarried partners, and still avoid taxes.

Grantor Retained Interest Trust (GRIT)

You can transfer substantial assets to your less wealthy partner using a grantor retained interest trust (GRIT). This is similar to the GRAT discussed in Chapter 20, but somewhat more favorable since it is not subject to the same tax restrictions as a GRAT. You will receive an annuity for a specified number of years, after which your partner (or a trust for his or her benefit) will own the assets.

The GRIT is often used in tandem with other techniques to enhance tax benefits (and protection). For example, your assets are first transferred to a limited liability company (LLC) or family limited partnership (FLP). Then noncontrolling (less than 50%) equity interests are given to the GRIT. Noncontrolling interest are valued lower for gift tax purposes (20%–50% or more discounts) so that you can leverage your lifetime exclusion and transfer substantially more assets to your partner tax free. These techniques can also assure management control and keep creditors, claimants, and disapproving family members at bay.

Sale to Intentional Defective Irrevocable Grantor Trust (IDIT)

This is similar in result to the GRIT. You set up a special type of trust that is recognized for gift and estate taxes, but ignored for income taxes. You sell assets to that trust on an installment basis. If the growth of the assets is substantially more than the minimum interest rate you have to pay you will shift substantial value to your partner as beneficiary of the trust.

Charitable Trusts

You can give assets to a charitable remainder trust (CRT) from which your partner is to receive periodic payments. The value of the payments to your partner, however, will be treated as a taxable gift. You could make a gift to a charitable lead trust (CLT) which will pay a periodic amount for many years to one or more charities. You and/or your partner can designate which charities benefit. When the trust ends, your partner receives the assets. This technique can discount the value of a large gift to your partner.

Dynasty Trust

You could make transfers to, for example, an Alaska or Delaware trust of which you and your partner are both beneficiaries. Properly structured, the gift can be made at a discounted value and can assure that the growth in the assets involved will be outside of the tax system.

TRUSTS ARE A KEY PLANNING TOOL EVEN IF GIFT AND ESTATE TAXES AREN'T A CONCERN

The 2001 Tax Act has increased the amount you can transfer while you are alive without tax to $1 million. The amount you can bequeath at death will increase to $1.5 million in 2004, and more in later years (you can't double up—what you give while you are alive is subtracted from what you can give at death tax free). This will assure that many nonmarried couples will not have to pay a gift or estate tax. Even so, trust planning remains important to address many personal goals.

Revocable Living Trusts

A flexible and advantageous ownership structure for nonmarried partners is the use of a funded revocable living trust (see Chapter 13). The trust must be funded (i.e., property actually transferred to the trust) in order to obtain the benefits it offers. A revocable living trust arrangement has several advantages over other types of planning. The trust is far more flexible then joint ownership of assets. Also, the partner owning the property retains control so that if the partnership dissolves, ownership does not become an issue. As contrasted with a will, having a revocable living trust own the property avoids the probate and publicity that could invite more scrutiny, problems, and even legal challenges from the family of the deceased partner.

A revocable living trust can assist you and your partner in managing assets in the event of disability better than either a durable power of attorney or joint ownership. Be certain to detail how you and your partner should be cared for. Standard forms tend to ignore these important points.

Irrevocable Grantor Trust

The wealthier partner could transfer assets to a trust for the benefit of the less wealthy partner. If the trust is effective under state law, the transfer would be a completed gift, thus assuring that your partner would receive the assets involved on the death of the transferor partner. This could also help insulate the assets of the wealthier partner from creditors, potential malpractice claimants and others.

The irrevocable trust could, as an alternative, be structured so that it is intentionally ineffective as a property transfer for federal gift and estate tax purposes. For example, the wealthy partner could retain a general power of appointment over the trust assets (e.g., the right to designate who should receive the assets) so that the transfer would not be complete for federal gift tax purposes. This would avoid any current gift tax cost for the transfer. This approach, however, does nothing to reduce potential estate tax costs since the entire balance of the trust would be included in the estate of the partner who transfers the assets to the trust.

Special Needs Trust

If your partner is ill, a trust can be the ideal vehicle to protect him or her. Your partner could perhaps be a co-trustee with a friend, and you can name a list of friends or family members as successor trustees. This will assure that trusted and caring people selected by the two of you will be available to help if your partner's illness should become incapacitating. In some situations, it may be advisable to consider planning such a trust to qualify as a special needs trust (SNT). This is a type of trust designed to make funds available for services and needs that are not provided by state or other government-sponsored programs, thus preventing nursing homes or government agencies from demanding that trust money be used to provide care government programs would otherwise have paid for. Since the programs and rules vary significantly from state to state, consult with a specialist in the state where you live. An experienced attorney may be the most familiar with these types of programs.

Insurance Trusts

If life insurance is to be purchased to fund living expenses of your partner (to create an estate), it can also be used to pay any estate tax. The insurance should often be owned by a trust to protect insurance proceeds from creditors, provide a management structure for the insurance proceeds, and gain other benefits as discussed previously.

ADDITIONAL PLANNING FOR NONMARRIED PARTNERS

For the trust planning just mentioned to be effective, other planning is essential, including:

- As a nonmarried partner, you should also plan how to own any assets not held in trust. You can own property solely in your own name. On death, the property is then transferred under your will to your partner. Property can also be owned as joint tenants with the right of survivorship so that on your death, ownership (title) automatically transfers by operation of law (i.e., without the need for probate) to your partner. This avoids probate and is inexpensive and simple. For estate tax purposes, the full value of the property will be included in your estate unless your surviving partner can demonstrate that he or she has made a contribution to the acquisition or improvement of the property.

- You need to have a will addressing distribution of assets, appointing an executor, and perhaps dealing with guardianship issues if you have a child.

- You must have a durable power of attorney authorizing your partner to handle legal, tax, and financial matters if you become disabled.

- A living will/health care proxy is essential to address medical issues. Be certain to expressly authorize your partner to take actions since some hospitals will be loath to let a nonspouse, nonfamily member act.

CONCLUSION

Where any nonmarried couple becomes involved in trust and related planning, additional care must be exercised because of the unfairness of the tax and property laws. The need for using trusts in planning is, therefore, even more important than for married couples. Ancillary planning and tax issues differ from those affecting married couples and warrant specific attention.

16 TRUSTS FOR CHILDREN AND OTHERS

Trusts are one of the most important aspects of planning for children, grandchildren, and other heirs. The discussions will apply whether the intended beneficiary is your child, grandchild, niece, nephew, or any other minor. With the exception of the generation skipping transfer (GST) tax, which affects trusts for grandchildren and certain others (Chapter 11), the considerations for all these beneficiaries are generally similar. Trusts are as commonly used to protect children who are minors, but the trend is clearly to retain assets in trust for many years past the age of 18 or 21 to provide greater protection.

IS THERE A BETTER OPTION THAN TRUSTS?

Often trusts are the only answer. If you are preparing a will and have young children, you should include trusts to protect their inheritance. If your goal is to set aside a modest amount for a child, a custodial account which is simple and no cost, is probably better. One of the more popular uses of children's trusts had been to set aside parental funds, or gifts from grandparents, to fund college. But the 2001 Tax Act has changed this for many. Before paying for a trust for a child or grandchild's education, consider a Code Section 529 college savings plan.

Code Section 529 College Savings Plans

You can contribute to state-run college education savings programs to fund educational costs for heirs. You avoid the complexity and legal cost of a trust agreement. There will be no need to file extra annual income tax returns, as there is with a trust. Money saved in these programs can be used to pay for tuition, room and board, and similar expenses. These plans can be set up for family members including sons, daughters, grandchildren, brothers, sisters, nephews, nieces, certain in-laws, and spouses.

You can give more in one year to a Section 529 college savings plan than to a child's education trust, which is limited to the annual gift tax exclusion of $10,000 (indexed $11,000 in 2002). With a Section 529 plan, you can elect to treat contributions as if made over a five-year period, so you can give up to $50,000 in one year. A married couple can thus fund $110,000 free of gift, estate, and GST tax in a single year. Grandparents and parents undertaking education planning should give consideration to this.

Many states have plans to assist investors and families in taking advantage of these benefits. The investment allocation models (the portion of the assets invested in stocks, bonds, and other investments) of the various plans, the flexibility of investment options, and other factors can vary from state to state.

The earnings on the Section 529 college savings plan assets will never be subject to income tax so long as used for higher education expenses. This is a tremendous benefit that far outweighs a child's trust in most cases.

In most cases, if your goal is saving for education, you will be better off with a Section 529 college savings plan than a trust unless there is already sufficient money in the Section 529 plan to cover college or you wish to make gifts of interests in a family business and want to retain control of the business interests.

Custodial Accounts: Uniform Gifts (Transfers) to Minors Act

Custodial or UGMA/UTMA (Uniform Gift/Transfers to Minors Act) accounts are popular. They are simple and have no cost, but also inflexible and don't generally protect money long enough. If the amounts involved are too small to warrant a trust, consider this approach first. These laws, different in each state, provide that a designated person acts as custodian for the minor's assets in the account until the minor reaches a specified age. Just open a brokerage account or bank account and tell your broker or bank officer that you want the account name to reflect that the gift is being made under the Uniform Gifts (or Transfers) to Minors Act with your name as guardian. You can then administer the account for the child's benefit. When the child reaches the age of majority, the child can take control of the assets.

UGMA/UTMA accounts have many drawbacks that make trusts preferable if the cost is not excessive in comparison to the assets being saved. The assets in an UGMA/UTMA account are the child's and you as custodian can only use the property as permitted by state law, for the benefit of the child. Trusts are often more flexible. If you give assets to a minor in a custodial account and serve as custodian, on your death all the assets in the account will be taxable in your estate. A minor owning assets in an UGMA account can, after reaching age 14, petition the court to have an accounting of the money.

To designate a successor trustee under an UGMA account, a custodian must execute and date a written designation, and have the document witnessed. This is rarely done. Where a trust arrangement is used, one or more alternate trustees are almost always named.

Family Limited Partnerships and Limited Liability Companies Are an Alternative Option to Trusts

You can use a family limited partnership or limited liability company to control assets given to children. The advantage of these entities over a trust is that they are not irrevocable in that the agreements governing them can be modified in the future. More cautious taxpayers can actually combine the two techniques. They will transfer assets to a family limited partnership or limited liability company, and then form trusts for the benefit of their children to own the limited partnership interests or the limited liability company membership interests. This approach, while more complex, affords even greater protection and tax planning possibilities (by permitting lack of marketability discounts and other techniques).

TRUSTS CAN BE THE BEST OPTION FOR CHILDREN AND OTHER HEIRS

Because children (of many ages!) have important financial needs for their education and care, and often lack the maturity to manage their assets, the use of trusts is often ideal. The need to provide for management of assets, and to protect the children from themselves, a potential divorce, or creditors, makes trusts the ideal approach to providing for your children and other heirs.

The desire to help your children, reinforced by the high gift, estate, and generation skipping transfer tax rates, often provides a strong impetus to make gifts to take maximum advantage of the annual $10,000 exclusion. If larger transfers are contemplated to minimize estate taxes (e.g., gifts of interests in a family limited partnership), a trust offers a second layer of control and protection for those interests.

Children's Trusts Raise Tax Issues

Gifts to a child's trust raise complex tax issues:

- To qualify for the annual $11,000 exclusion (and preserve your lifetime gift exclusion), the gift to the trust must meet a technical requirement of being a "gift of a present interest." This can be done through the use of what is called a *Crummey power* (Chapter 10), or using a special trust known by the Internal Revenue Code Section creating it—a *2503(c) trust,* discussed shortly.
- If you are a trustee and trust funds could be used to meet your legal obligation to support the child, the income earned by the trust may be taxed to you instead of the trust.
- Trust income tax rates are compressed so that trust income reaches the highest tax rates at modest amounts of earnings. Thus, investments

have to be carefully planned. Often this will include growth oriented stocks, mutual funds managed to minimize current taxable income, and tax-exempt bonds.

- Consider the kiddie tax, which taxes the net unearned income of a child who has not reached the age of 14 at the parents' tax rate. The kiddie tax will apply to distributions from a trust to the child. The trustee of a child's trust will have to weigh the benefits of retaining income in the trust and subjecting it to trust tax rates, versus distributing the income to the child so that the kiddie tax may apply.

TYPES OF TRUSTS FOR MINORS

Almost any trust in this book can be used to benefit a minor child. Children are often discretionary beneficiaries of a bypass trust under your will (they cannot be beneficiaries of a marital trust). They are almost always included in insurance trusts as beneficiaries. Children are typically the *remainder beneficiaries* (those who receive assets after a preceding beneficiary's interests end) of charitable lead trusts and qualified personal residence trusts. The trusts discussed next, in contrast, are specifically designed for child beneficiaries. These trusts all endeavor to qualify gifts you make to your child's trust for the annual $10,000 (indexed $11,000 in 2002) gift tax exclusion.

PLANNING TIP: If your estate is substantially below the increased estate and gift tax exclusions enacted as part of the 2001 Tax Act, you may be able to reasonably ignore all the complexities involved in qualifying gifts to a child's trust for the annual gift tax exclusion. This will simplify trust planning, but won't obviate the need for trusts for your child. All the nontax benefits and goals remain.

Income Only Trust (Section 2503(b) Trust)

An income-only minor's trust will qualify for the annual gift tax exclusion under Code Section 2503(b). This trust must distribute all income annually to your child or other beneficiary. This will permit you to make a gift of up to $11,000 per year and qualify for the annual gift tax exclusion. The child will then be taxed on all of the income earned by the trust. Where the child is under 14, the kiddie tax will apply. The income can be distributed to a Uniform Gift to Minors Act trust without jeopardizing the benefits of the annual exclusion. The assets of in the trust will have to be income producing. Because most parents want control over distributions, this trust is not popular.

Right to Withdraw under Crummey Power

A typical child's trust accumulates income and makes distributions in the trustee's discretion, such as for college, and then at ages 25, 30, and 35; in each of these age-based distributions, one-third of the principal is distributed. Such a trust is often planned as a Crummey power trust. This technique gives you flexibility in planning trust distributions while qualifying for the annual exclusion. A gift to this type of trust will qualify for the annual exclusion up to the amount which the child can withdraw each year from the trust. The annual demand power gives the child the right to demand a distribution up to the amount of the annual gift. If the child doesn't exercise this right (which they almost never do), the money remains in the trust.

There are a host of complications to this type of planning. These should be reviewed carefully with the attorney assisting you with estate planning.

Special Trust for Children under Age 21 (Section 2503(c) Trust)

With this trust, you can transfer $11,000 per year to a trust, the trust can accumulate the income, and you can still qualify for the annual gift tax exclusion. To qualify, the trust must be set up to benefit a minor child. The trustee must have the ability to use the income for the benefit of the minor child without restriction. The trust assets must be invested in income-producing assets (stocks, bonds, and CDs, not raw land). If the child dies prior to age 21, the trust assets must be distributed to the child's estate, or in a manner that the child designates. When the child reaches age 21, the trust must be distributed to the child. This latter requirement is the reason that this trust is not commonly used. Most custodial accounts can hold assets to age 21. The primary reason many parents opt for trusts is to protect and manage the income until a later age. If all of the principal must be distributed at age 21, the primary benefit of using a trust is defeated.

There is no requirement that the child actually take the assets at age 21, merely that the child have the right to do so. Thus, the child can be given the right to require that the assets of the trust be distributed when he or she reaches age 21, but may voluntarily choose not to elect to take the money. This option, however, does not compare favorably to the Crummey power arrangement. If a child who is beneficiary of a Crummey power trust exercises the right to take the money (something the parent will probably not intend to be done), the most the child can take is often $11,000. Contrast this with a Code Section 2503(c) trust. At age 21, the child legally can demand the entire trust! Is this a risk worth taking?

For income tax purposes, the trust will pay income tax on income it does not distribute and the child will pay income tax on income distributed to him or her.

Trusts for Grandchildren

If you plan significant gifts to grandchildren, consideration should be given to establishing trusts for their benefit. When forming grandchildren's trusts, the income and gift tax issues and options discussed for children's trusts apply. The same decisions must be made to qualify for the annual gift tax exclusion. However, when planning grandchildren's trusts, an additional layer of complexity must be addressed: the generation skipping transfer (GST) tax.

Gifts which qualify for the annual $11,000 per year gift tax exclusion can also avoid GST tax only if additional planning is done. The requirements to qualify for the GST annual tax exclusion are more restrictive. Generally, the grandchild-beneficiary should be the only beneficiary of the trust. Further, if the grandchild-beneficiary should die before the trust ends, the assets of the trust must be included in the grandchild's estate. This can be done by actually distributing the trust assets to the grandchild's estate, or alternatively by giving the grandchild a general power of appointment to appoint the trust to anyone. Many grandparents are not comfortable with these options. They can instead elect to allocate a portion of their GST tax lifetime exclusion to the trust each year.

Trusts for Special Children

Where a child has special needs as a result of a handicap or illness, trusts represent the most important tools to protect the child. This is because a trust arrangement can provide for the care of your child for many years into the future, even when you are no longer able to assist. These trusts, however, raise several unique issues that must be addressed.

CAUTION: When planning for the special child, trusts are only one component of your plan. It is very important to sign durable powers of attorney so that in the event of your disability, monies can be applied for the benefit of your child. Your durable power of attorney can even include a provision authorizing expenditures on behalf of your special child. Such a provision can take the same form as the provisions for the trusts described in this section. Also, pay careful attention to the provisions of your will, which should also include special needs trust (SNT) language.

There is a complex patchwork of government programs that can provide benefits for a special child. Thus, the difficult goals for many families are to preserve wealth for the family unit as a whole without undue depletion to meet the needs of the special child, to maximize the availability of public and other program resources available to the special child, and to assure that the special child's needs are met.

These goals are not simple to meet. They can often be contradictory. The laws and various entitlement programs are not only complex, but they can change frequently. The use of several different types of trusts may be helpful to protect the family with a special child:

- *Life insurance trust.* The purchase of life insurance held by an insurance trust (Chapter 20) can provide a safety net to assure a minimum level of support for the special child and other family members, while avoiding estate tax.

- *Special needs trust (SNT)*. These trusts can be set up under your will to hold assets for the benefit of the special child. These trusts restrict distributions to safeguard the assets for the special child's needs that government and other programs don't provide for. If the trustee is simply given discretion to apply trust income and principal for the support of the special child, the income and assets of the trust will similarly be considered available to pay for shelter and medical care in lieu of many government benefits that may have been available otherwise. If instead the trustee has discretion to apply income or principal to meet special needs for which government programs do not pay, the government should not be able to reach trust assets. A spendthrift provision is typically included in these trusts. The trust can clearly state that the trustee is not to make distributions which can be met from other government or charitable sources. Rather, only the gaps in those programs, and additional items for personal comfort, should be provided for.

In some cases, a more extreme provision is included that will terminate the trust and require the distribution of all of the assets in the trust to children, other than the special child, where the state or other government agency can reach the trust assets. The objective of this type of provision is to dissuade government agencies from suing the trust for reimbursements for medical care. The effectiveness of such a provision, however, is not guaranteed.

When planning any trust for a special child, each of the available government or charitable programs, and the requirements and qualifications of each, must be considered. Medicare and Social Security are two important federal programs. Social Security can provide benefits where the special child is totally disabled. Medicare provides for limited basic medical coverage. Supplemental Security Income (SSI) Medicaid, welfare, and other programs may be available as well. To qualify for these need-based programs, the income and assets of the child/recipient must be quite limited. Assuring qualification for these, and any other, need-based programs is a cornerstone of planning. The trust arrangement that you set up must not result in the child's being considered to have more income or assets than these programs permit, or the benefits will be lost. Various states have additional programs, such as cost-of-care type programs, which may also be available. These should all be reviewed with an experienced estate or financial planner. Crummey power and other techniques described previously for children's trusts generally are not appropriate.

CONSIDERATIONS WHEN DRAFTING TRUSTS FOR MINORS

Although one should give at least as much care in drafting a trust for a minor as one would give to any other trust, some factors bear special consideration.

Choosing Trustees

Carefully consider the choice of trustees and successor trustees (see Chapter 6). Should you name the same persons who are named the guardians of your children under your will? This provides complete control and avoids any conflict between the guardian's need for money for your children, and a trustee's opinion of what is appropriate to spend. Many parents prefer to separate these functions so that some checks and balances are built into the arrangement. Also, serving as a guardian requires personal skills. Serving as a trustee requires financial skills. Different people may have different skills and should be picked accordingly. A common compromise approach is to have the guardian serve as co-trustee with another person who is not the guardian. This gives the guardian some input, but prevents the guardian from having complete control.

Investment Planning

Every trust should include the investment considerations, goals, and limitations on the trustees (see Chapter 7). For minors' trusts, consideration of the tax consequences of trust taxation, taxation of distributions to the minors, and the expected needs of the minor should all be considered. For example, if the child will need help paying for private elementary school education, investment criteria will differ from those in a trust when it is expected that the monies won't be needed until graduate school. Trusts that require the distribution of income (such as a Code Section 2503(b) income only trust) will require a different approach than the trusts which do not (e.g., Crummey power trust).

Spendthrift Provision

A trust can contain a spendthrift provision to limit the rights creditors of your children may have to the assets of the trust. This is an extremely important protection for the child beneficiary.

Distribution Provisions

The trustee can be authorized to distribute income of the trust among your children and other beneficiaries based on their need or simply in the trustee's discretion (a sprinkle power). This approach can be advantageous because it is often impossible to determine what the needs of each child will be in the future and the sprinkle power provides the flexibility to make the decisions when the circumstances are known. A right for the trustee to spend the principal (not just income) can be provided for in the event of emergencies.

You must decide at what ages your children should be given the assets from the trust. A common approach is one-third of the total at ages 25, 30, and 35. The idea is to accustom the child to receiving money over a period of time so that if the child is irresponsible at the first distribution, there will be two more opportunities to learn responsibility. For older children, older ages are often used. Lifetime trusts are becoming more common.

You must determine whether you should have one trust for all of your children, or separate trusts for each child. If the beneficiaries are grandchildren, you will need separate trusts for purposes of qualifying annual $10,000 gifts for the GST gift tax exclusion (see Chapter 11). If your assets are not that substantial, you may prefer a single trust to minimize cost. Similarly, if there are substantial differences in the needs or ages of the children you may prefer a single "pot" trust to provide for all of the beneficiaries. For example, if three children are past college and the fourth child is in grade school, a pot trust may be appropriate. This can permit the trustees to use the money primarily for the youngest child who has had the least help, and has the greatest needs. However, in the event of an emergency, the money will be available for any child in need. When the youngest child completes his or her education, the trust can then be divided equally between all four children. Generally, however, where resources are adequate, its usually best to have a separate trust for each child. This avoids problems of jealousy, funding different needs of different children, and the like.

CONCLUSION

Planning for the welfare of your children, particularly minor children, or other heirs (nieces, nephews, or others) is often accomplished through the use of trusts. There are a number of different approaches that can be used. They should all be considered carefully in light of the tax, financial, and emotional background of your family. In all cases, the lengthy expected duration of the trust requires careful planning, selection of many alternate trustees, and building flexibility into the trust terms to deal with future contingencies.

17 TRUSTS FOR CHARITIES

The charitable remainder trust (CRT) and the charitable lead trust (CLT) are popular planning tools. Even if the 2001 Tax Act has you confident that gift and estate tax won't apply to you, charitable planning remains important. Nontax goals of contributing to society, teaching your children philanthropy, and controlling distributions of wealth remain important. The CRT remains important for income tax planning benefits. If you still face a significant gift or estate tax cost, CLTs are a tremendous tax planning tool. If not, it is still an excellent vehicle to defer a portion of an heir's inheritance.

CHARITABLE REMAINDER INTERESTS

If you use a charitable remainder trust (CRT), you donate property (real property, stock, business interests, and so forth) to a charity and receive a charitable contribution tax deduction in the year of the donation. The charity will only receive the full benefit of the property at some future time. For example, you can reserve an income interest in the charitable remainder trust for your life and the life of your spouse as the income beneficiaries. If this is done, the income generated from the donated property will be paid to you for your life and thereafter to your spouse (if she survives you) for her life. After the death of the latter of you and your spouse, the charity will obtain full use and benefit of the donated property.

The savings in income taxes, federal gift or estate tax, state inheritance tax, and probate and administrative costs can enable you to transfer substantial benefits to a deserving charity at a very favorable cost.

Other Benefits of CRTs

A CRT can be a tremendous estate and financial planning vehicle. The following example illustrates this.

If you have some charitable intent, but don't wish to part entirely with the benefits of your property (e.g., the income it generates) presently, a CRT may be appropriate.

EXAMPLE: Ira Investor purchased XYZ, Inc. stock in 1999 for $1 per share. The value per share is now $1,000 per share. The stock pays almost no dividends. Ira is retiring and needs more income to cover living expenses. He also wishes to diversify his XYZ, Inc. holdings because they have become such a substantial portion of his estate. However, to sell XYZ, Inc. stock would trigger a substantial capital gains tax. Ira could instead donate the stock to a CRT and receive back a monthly payment for life (and even for the life of his wife as well). The charity could sell the stock and invest in a diversified portfolio geared to generate income. The charity should not have to recognize any capital gains tax on the sale. As a result, Ira can effectively have the entire investment, undiminished by capital gains tax, working to generate his monthly income. The financial benefits are potentially tremendous. Ira should also consider other techniques like an exchange fund.

Requirements for CRTs

A number of requirements must be met for a CRT to qualify for favorable tax benefits, including:

- The CRT must be irrevocable.
- The payment made from the CRT must be for a term of years not in excess of 20 years, or for the lives of the individual beneficiaries named.
- The yearly payment percentage must be equal to at least 5 percent (5%) of the net fair market value of the trust assets.
- The CRT cannot have a payout of greater than 50 percent of the fair market value of its assets.
- The value of the remainder interest to be received by the charity, determined on the date you contribute property to the CRT, must be at least 10 percent of the value of the property.

Types of CRTs

Your CRT must make specific types of payments to you in the form of an annuity trust or unitrust payment to qualify for the tax benefits. An exception from these rules exists for gifts of a remainder interest in a personal residence or farm property.

Charitable Remainder Annuity Trust (CRAT)

A charitable remainder annuity trust (CRAT) will provide a fixed annuity to yourself, or the people you designate in the trust agreement, as the income beneficiaries. The minimum rate of return to them cannot be less than 5 percent and it must be a fixed or determinable amount. The beneficiaries' income is calculated based on the fair market value of the property transferred to the trust. Once the trust is established, no further contributions can be made to it. Where the trust income is insufficient to meet the required annual return, the principal must be invaded.

Charitable Remainder Unitrust

A charitable remainder unitrust (CRUT) provides a form of variable annuity benefit to its income beneficiaries. The minimum rate of return to the income beneficiaries must be 5 percent. This rate of return is calculated on the fair market value of the property determined on an annual basis. This requires an annual appraisal, which may be difficult to value (e.g., closely held business interests and real estate), that could be prohibitively expensive. For this reason, an annuity trust approach is likely to prove more appropriate when such assets are to be contributed. The trust may provide that if the annual income earned by the trust property is insufficient to meet the required distribution to the income beneficiaries, principal may be invaded. If principal is not required to be invaded, than the trust must provide that the deficit will be made up in later years. Once a unitrust is established, additional contributions may be made in later years under certain conditions.

The valuation of the remainder interest of the unitrust is determined under methods provided for in the Treasury regulations. The valuation considers the value of the property transferred to the trust, the age of the income beneficiary, and the pay-out rate from the trust (e.g., 5 percent or some greater figure).

Phases in the Use of a CRT

When a charitable remainder trust is used for a donation to a charity, the donor transfers property (real property in this instance, although publicly traded securities, stock in a closely held business, and other assets may also be used) to the charity. The donor then receives a charitable contribution income tax deduction in the year of the donation.

The donor reserves for the income beneficiaries an income interest in the CRUT for the beneficiaries' lives. This means that a portion of the income generated from the donated property will be paid to the donor for his life and concurrently to his spouse (when the spouse is the second beneficiary) for her life.

On the death of the donors, there will be no estate tax from the value of the life income interest retained by the donor since it is exactly offset by the estate tax charitable contribution deduction. If the only other beneficiary is the decedent's spouse, there will be no tax on the income interest passing to her as a result of the unlimited estate tax marital deduction.

The charitable remainder beneficiary only receives the full benefit of the property (i.e., the principal of the charitable remainder trust) upon the death of the last of the designated income beneficiaries.

Tax Consequences of a CRT

As discussed earlier, many different taxes may apply to any trust and a CRT is no different. We discuss some of the tax consequences next.

Income Tax Deduction on Forming a CRT

The donor of property to a charitable remainder trust is entitled to a deduction for income tax purposes. The deduction is based on the present value of the charitable remainder interest. The amount of the charitable contribution deduction is equal to the fair market value of the property at the time of the donation to the CRT, less the present value of the income interest retained by you (or you and your spouse if she is named a beneficiary). The value of the tax deduction depends on numerous factors, including the marginal tax bracket of the donor, the income interest reserved to the donor (and others), and the income level of the donor relative to the tax deduction (which will affect the applicability of the charitable contribution percentage limitations).

Gift and Estate Tax Consequences of a CRT

In addition to a current income tax deduction, you may also receive a valuable estate tax benefit as well. If you are one of the income beneficiaries of the charitable trust, the value of the trust will be included in your gross estate when you die. However, since the interest will pass to the charity, there will be an offsetting estate tax charitable contribution deduction. Thus, the value of the property donated will be effectively removed from your estate.

Similarly, upon the death of the surviving spouse, the value of the charitable remainder trust will be included in her gross estate. However, since the interest will pass to a qualified charity, there will be an offsetting estate tax charitable contribution deduction. Hence, the value of the donated property will effectively be removed from the spouse's estate as well.

How Beneficiaries Are Taxed on CRT Income

The amounts paid to a trust beneficiary under a charitable remainder trust retain the character they had in the trust. Regular trusts characterize payments based on the trust's income and other activities during the particular year. A noncharitable income beneficiary of a charitable remainder trust is taxed as a recipient of ordinary income to the extent of the trust's current and prior undistributed income. After all ordinary income is exhausted, amounts will be taxed as follows:

1. As short-term capital gain to the extent of current and past undistributed short-term capital gains.
2. As long-term capital gain to the extent of current and past undistributed long-term capital gains.
3. As other income, such as tax exempt income, to the extent of the trust's current and past undistributed income of such character.
4. As tax-free distributions of principal.

The trust will generally be exempt from tax. However, where the trust generates unrelated business taxable income (UBTI) it can be subject to tax. This can be an issue where, for example, trust assets are debt financed or stock in an active business is contributed. These rules are extremely complex and require professional assistance.

Variations and Special Techniques Using CRTs

The unique nature of charitable remainder trusts allows for the use of a number of special techniques. CRTs may also be combined with other estate-planning tools.

Combining Insurance with the Charitable Remainder Trust

The reason insurance planning is so frequently combined with charitable remainder trust planning is to replace the value of the property donated to the charity with insurance passing to the grantor's heirs. The concept is quite simple. You fund a CRT with appreciated assets and receive an income stream back. You then use some portion of the increased income stream to establish and fund an irrevocable life insurance trust for the benefit of your heirs (e.g., children). You can meet your desired charitable goals of providing for a favored cause. The income tax savings from the charitable contribution deduction provide cash flow to make gifts to an irrevocable life insurance trust, or to the heirs directly. Your investment is diversified and you receive an increased and more certain income stream. The trustee of the irrevocable life insurance trust purchases life insurance on your life (or, if you are married, second-to-die life insurance on the lives of both you and your spouse) in an amount that is sufficient to replace the value of the assets that you transferred to the charitable remainder trust. In many cases, a large amount of insurance is purchased under the presumption that the asset given to the charitable remainder trust would have grown prior to your death. On your death, the insurance proceeds are not taxable in your estate. Your heirs receive the insurance proceeds in an amount approximating the value of the assets that you had transferred to the charitable remainder trust.

EXAMPLE: Donor owns real estate worth $1 million with an adjusted cost basis of $200,000. Transferring the property to a charitable remainder trust could generate a $400,000 contribution deduction. This could provide an income tax savings of approximately $140,000. Further, the Donor will avoid approximately a $220,000 capital gain on the sale of the property. The trustee may be able to pay the Donor an annual income of $60,000. The Donor can make an annual gift, with his spouse, to their son and daughter-in-law totaling $40,000 under the annual gift tax exclusion. This money can be used to purchase life insurance on the Donor's life of $1 million, sufficient to replace the $1 million worth of real estate transferred to the charitable remainder trust. The son will receive the same $1 million on the parents' death that he would have received had the planning not been undertaken. However, had no planning been undertaken, the $1 million real estate that the son would have received may have been reduced by a 50 percent marginal estate tax. Thus, the son may actually receive more than double the result where this charitable/insurance plan is implemented.

Life insurance can be used in a somewhat different manner in planning for charitable remainder trusts as well. The charitable remainder trust techniques assume that an income stream will be paid to a life-beneficiary for some period of time. Should the sole life-beneficiary die prematurely, the family unit will have effectively been denied the benefit of the expected income stream. In the appropriate circumstances, the charitable remainder technique can be combined with a life insurance policy on the life of the income or life-beneficiary of the charitable remainder trust. Where this life-beneficiary dies prematurely, the insurance proceeds can supplement the income stream that the family unit will have lost. This could be done, for example, with a life insurance trust for the benefit of the children or spouse of the named life-beneficiary. The life insurance trust should be structured to assure that the proceeds are not included in the estate of the life-beneficiary. In some cases, an insurance arrangement providing for decreasing coverage (to approximate the decline in the loss of expected income as the life-beneficiary lives through the intended term of the trust), can be used.

CRT as a Retirement Plan: The Income Only Unitrust Option of CRT

A modified form of charitable remainder unitrust (CRUT) can be used where the income beneficiary receives what is called an "income only arrangement." In this type of CRUT, the income beneficiary would only receive the actual trust income if the income is less than the fixed percentage payment required (e.g., 5 percent of principal of the trust). This type of trust can also include a "make-up provision." In early years, actual income is less than the 5 percent required CRUT payment. In later years, when the net income of the trust exceeds the specified percentage of trust assets required to be paid (e.g., 5 percent), this excess can then be paid to the income beneficiary to make up for the shortfall in prior years. The shortfall is determined based on the difference between the amounts actually paid in prior years, and the amounts that were required to have been paid based on the fixed percentage. This concept can best be illustrated with an example.

EXAMPLE: Donor has a substantial income, is getting on in years, and wishes to provide for his favorite charity. Donor expects to retire in five years. Upon retirement, Donor expects his income to drop, leaving him in a lower tax bracket. Donor establishes an income-only charitable remainder unitrust arrangement with a make-up provision. Donor funds the trust with a $1 million initial contribution that is invested in low-dividend paying growth stocks. The unitrust percentage is set at the lowest permissible amount, 5 percent. The dividends on the stock portfolio produce a mere 0.75 percent return, or $7,500, which is paid to donor. After year five, the Donor retires. The stock portfolio, which has appreciated to $1.5 million, is liquidated and invested in high-yield bond instruments. These bonds produce a return of 8 percent, or $120,000. Donor would be entitled to 5 percent of the $1.5 million asset value based on the unitrust amount provided, or $75,000. However, as a result of the make-up provision, the Donor can be paid additional amounts in each of the remaining years of the trust to make up for the shortfall in prior, preretirement years. If the shortfall has totaled $212,500 [(5 years × $50,000) – (5 years × $7,500)], Donor will be entitled to all of the income from the income-only unitrust for a number of years to come.

Generation Skipping Transfers and Charitable Remainder Trust Planning

While the generation skipping transfer (GST) tax will not apply to charitable gifts, GST tax considerations are important where your grandchild (or another skip person) is made the life- or income-beneficiary of the charitable remainder trust (or the remainder beneficiary of a charitable lead trust, see discussion following). Where such a situation occurs, the donor must carefully plan the allocation of any of his remaining GST lifetime $1 million exemption to the trust.

Charitable Gifts and the Closely Held Corporation

Charitable remainder trusts can have special use when a key asset is stock in a closely held business. A charitable bail-out of a closely held business stock can address important planning problems for an owner of a closely held business. Stock in a closely held corporation can be difficult, or impossible, to sell. This is because any outsider will generally be very reluctant to own a minority interest in a closely held corporation. Another problem could relate to the type of corporation involved. Assume that the corporation is a C corporation (i.e., not an S corporation) and has available cash that you would like to donate to charity. However, it may not be practical to make a dividend distribution to provide the cash for such donation since a dividend distribution will result in double taxation (the corporation first pays tax on the earnings and then you pay tax again on the dividend). Another common problem scenario for a closely held business is when a parent owns stock in a closely held corporation and wishes to transfer control to a child without triggering income tax on a redemption. One possible solution for this latter scenario is called a *stock bail-out.* You can make a gift of any portion of the stock in your corporation to a charity. At some later date, the charity may, at its sole discretion, sell some of the stock that it then owns back to the corporation. This provides you with a charitable contribution deduction, for income tax purposes, for the stock donated. The charity can eventually receive a cash amount for the contribution. When the corporation redeems the stock, the interest of the children owning stock will increase. This is because the charitable bail-out/redemption of your stock will increase their relative ownership interest.

The charity cannot be obligated to sell any portion of the stock back to the corporation. Where a prearranged plan for the resale of the stock exists, it can be difficult to draw the line as to whether or not the charity was so obligated. If the charity is in fact under no legal obligation to resell the stock it receives, there is a possibility that it could sell the stock to another, vote the shares in manner which is not consistent with the donor's desires, and so on. The alternative minimum tax could reduce the value of the gift.

Combining Charitable and Marital Trusts

Another twist on the use of a charitable remainder trust is to combine a CRT with the marital trusts discussed in Chapter 14. Special rules apply if you wish to transfer property to both your spouse and a charity. These rules can permit you to take advantage of both charitable contribution deductions and the marital deduction, and thus they can provide valuable planning benefits in the appropriate circumstances. For example, assume that you transfer property to a charitable remainder trust. You and your spouse are the sole income beneficiaries. The only other beneficiary is a charitable remainder beneficiary. On your death, your estate will qualify for both a charitable contribution deduction and an estate tax marital deduction. This assures no tax as a result of any interest you had in the CRT on death.

An alternative approach to consider using is simply to establish a qualified terminable interest property (QTIP) trust for your spouse, with the remainder interest, on your spouse's death, to go to a specified charity (see Chapter 14). A QTIP trust generally permits your spouse to receive all of the income from the trust, and on her death, the trust assets go to the persons, or in this case the charity, which you designate. While this approach is simpler, there can be no income tax deduction with a QTIP with a charitable remainder, as there would be available where a charitable remainder trust is used with you and your spouse being named as income beneficiaries.

CHARITABLE LEAD TRUSTS

A charitable lead trust (CLT) is also called a front trust, because the charitable beneficiary receives its income in front of the ultimate beneficiaries' (remainder beneficiaries) receiving their share. Typically, the remainder beneficiaries are your children, although other beneficiaries can be named. Reasons for setting up a CLT include deferring and controlling when an heir receives funds, encouraging philanthropy, and reducing gift or estate tax cost. The reduction in tax cost is achieved by virtue of the fact that the remainder beneficiaries must wait to receive the property until the expiration of the charitable beneficiary's interest. The concept can be illustrated with a simple example.

EXAMPLE: You give $100,000 to a charitable trust. A designated charity will receive annual payments (usually in the form of an annuity or unitrust amount) for each year of the trust. Following the end of the trust, which will occur after the number of years you determined when setting it up (usually 10 years to 20 years, and sometimes longer), your children will receive the trust assets (this will hopefully be more than $100,000, depending on the investment results during the period the charity received payments). If the term of the charitable interest is made long enough, the value of the gift to your children can be reduced to nearly zero for purposes of the gift tax.

Comparison of CLTs and CRTs

Type of Trust	Type of Payment to Initial Beneficiary	Remainder Beneficiary
Charitable lead unitrust (CLUT)	Charity receives unitrust payment based on percentage of value of assets in trust each year.	Noncharitable beneficiaries, usually your grandchildren.
Charitable lead annuity trust (CLAT)	Charity receives an annuity payment based on a fixed percentage of the value of the assets when the trust was formed.	Noncharitable beneficiaries, usually your adult children.
Charitable remainder unitrust (CRUT)	You or other noncharitable beneficiaries receive unitrust payments based on percentage of value of assets in trust each year. A minimum 5% payout is required.	One or more charitable beneficiaries.
Charitable remainder annuity trust (CRAT)	You or other noncharitable beneficiaries receive an annuity payment based on a fixed percentage of the value of the assets when the trust was formed. A minimum 5% payout is required.	One or more charitable beneficiaries.

Variations of CLTs

Like charitable remainder trusts, charitable lead trusts are available in many variations. You can form a CLT while you are alive (*inter-vivos*) or under your will (*testamentary*).

A CLT is usually structured as a nongrantor trust. This means that the transfer of assets to the CLT is a completed transfer and CLT earnings are not taxed to you. You will not receive an income tax deduction for any charitable contributions made by the CLT during its term. If instead the CLT is structured to be a *grantor trust* (see Chapter 4), you will be taxed on the income earned by the trust (unless the income is primarily tax-exempt bond income). However, you will also qualify for deductions for the charitable contributions made by the CLT.

When a CLT May Make Sense for You

The CLT can be a valuable, and appropriate, estate planning tool where you have charitable intent, the desire to increase the eventual (but not current) net worth of family members or other designated heirs, and the goal of reducing gift and estate taxes.

Benefits of a CLT

The use of a CLT can provide numerous benefits, including:

- Appreciation on the property transferred to the CLT will ultimately pass to your beneficiaries free of any gift or estate tax.

PLANNING TIP: A CLT will have the most tax advantage where an asset is expected to have unusually large appreciation compared to the interest rates assumed in the applicable Treasury tables used in making the calculations.

- You can meet long-term charitable giving objectives. Establishing a CLT will assure annual distributions of a specified amount (where an annuity arrangement is used) to designated charities for a specified number of years.

PLANNING TIP: If you combine the CLT with a donor advised fund arrangement, you, or designated family members, can each year decide which charities will receive donations. This is a great way to involve younger family members in charitable giving.

- The duration for which a CLT lasts can be coordinated with other estate and financial planning to assure your children or other heirs the availability of assets for a long-term time horizon.

EXAMPLE: Taxpayer establishes a trust under his will to pay income annually to his child. Principal is to be paid out of the trust fund in approximately one-third equal amounts when the child attains ages 30, 35, and 40. The child is presently age 22. If Taxpayer establishes a CLT for a duration of 23 years [(40 – 22) + 5], the child will receive the assets of the CLT at age 45. This is timed to continue the five-year payment sequence with the hopes of distributing assets in stages to both protect the remaining assets as well as to minimize the potentially adverse consequences of the child receiving too much wealth at one time.

- If your charitable contributions are so large that you cannot qualify to deduct them currently as a result of the limitations on the portion of your income that can be given to charity, the use of a CLT may help avoid these restrictions.

Drawbacks to a CLT

There are drawbacks to the use of a CLT to consider:

- Tax and other benefits can only be realized if the CLT meets all applicable tax law requirements, which can be burdensome, costly, and difficult. For example, CLTs can be subject to the rules concerning self-dealing, excess business holdings, and jeopardy investments of private foundations.
- A special tax is imposed on a CLT that sells or exchanges property within two years after the property was transferred to the CLT. When

this rule applies, the CLT is taxed at your (i.e., the grantor's) income tax rate. The objective of this provision is to prevent you from gaining a tax advantage by transferring property intended for sale to a CLT to sell.

- CLTs are not tax exempt. CLTs can be liable for an income tax. A CLT only avoids taxation if the amounts paid to charity are sufficient to offset any income tax otherwise due by the CLT.
- Gifts to CLTs do not qualify for the annual exclusion.
- CLTs create complications for GST planning. GST exclusion cannot be allocated to a CLT until the charitable interest ends. Thus, if a 20-year CLAT is used the determination will be made at the end of year 20. If the CLT worked as planned, this is when the assets will be highly appreciated and the allocation the most inefficient to make. The better option is to use a CLUT since the allocation of the GST amount can be made when you set up the CLT initially.

CONCLUSION

Charitable planning with trusts can present valuable planning opportunities even if you are not particularly charitably inclined, and even if gift and estate taxes are not a major concern. The benefits can sometimes be far greater than expected. However, always obtain competent legal, tax, and insurance advice since charitable trusts are some of the most complicated types of trusts.

Part Four

TRUSTS FOR SPECIFIC TYPES OF ASSETS

18 TRUSTS TO PROTECT YOUR ASSETS

Many people think of trusts, first and foremost, as a tool to protect their assets from creditors. The same techniques can be used to protect the assets of children and incompetents.

PROTECTING ASSETS SHOULD BE AN INTEGRAL PART OF MOST ESTATE AND FINANCIAL PLANS

Anyone, at any time, can be sued for a substantial amount of money. A child slips on your porch, you are in a car accident, an employee claims harassment, and so on. Given the tremendous risks a major liability or other claim can pose, everyone should take some steps to protect assets. In most cases, basic trust planning that protects you and your loved ones from all the other issues discussed in this book will also help protect your assets. This chapter shows you how.

What, Me Worry?

Yes, you should worry. If you are a professional, you should be concerned about avoiding potential malpractice claims. If you own real estate, you must be concerned about environmental problems, tenant and visitor claims, and so forth. If you own a business, you should consider protecting assets with different risk profiles from other assets. For example, if your manufacturing plant occupies a building, the ownership of the building should be separated from the manufacturing business that likely creates different and greater risks.

EXAMPLE: You are a professional (such as a doctor, lawyer, or engineer). You are personally liable for all professional services rendered to your clients. If you are sued for malpractice and either your malpractice insurance is insufficient, or an exception to the policy denies coverage for a particular event, you will be personally liable. Insulating some of your assets to preserve them in the event of a successful malpractice challenge could be the most important estate and financial planning step you can take. Planning must be completed in advance of any problems occurring.

CAUTION: Operating as a professional corporation or a limited liability corporation (or limited liability partnership) is not guarantee of insulation from liability. Even as a shareholder of a professional corporation you will generally remain personally liable for acts of malpractice committed by you, or employees under your supervision. Thus, a professional corporation can help limit, but cannot eliminate, liability. If you have organized as a limited liability partnership (LLP), you may be relieved of professional liability due to acts of other principals, but you remain responsible for your professional malpractice and that of people operating under your supervision. You may also, depending on state law, be liable personally for contractual claims (e.g., lease liability).

Asset Protection Planning Involves Many Techniques

You've heard of the rich doctor with the foreign asset protection trusts (APTs) to address liability exposure. Well, in most cases, there is a lot of more basic planning that can be done before heading to some little-known island country. You should first exhaust all the appropriate on-shore planning. You can use a domestic asset protection trust (DAPT). You should also use techniques other than trusts to protect assets. S corporations, family limited partnerships, limited liability companies, and so forth are all integral parts of the asset protection process and often are used in combination with each other and trusts. When you consider trusts for asset protection, don't think only about APTs. Many of the trusts discussed in this book can have asset protection benefits too.

EXAMPLE: You own a securities portfolio and real estate as investments. The property is owned individually by you. You are therefore personally liable for any liability from the property because personal ownership does not give you any protection. If a tenant is injured and successfully sues for more than the amount of your insurance, you will be personally liable. Transfer your real estate to a limited liability company or limited partnership to limit your liability exposure on the real estate to the value of your equity in the particular property. You can set up an LLC or FLP to own some of your securities. This second LLC or FLP can function as a holding company that owns the real estate LLC or FLP. This will insulate your securities holdings from the claims associated with the real estate property. It is then common to have the interests in these entities (which own the properties) given to various trusts, such as a dynasty trust in Alaska, for example. This approach provides several layers of asset protection, a structure to manage assets in the event of disability, and possibly consolidation of assets to provide better investment choices. The gift, estate, and even income tax savings can be substantial.

Planning for Asset Protection

Asset protection planning is extremely complex because it is affected by so many different laws: property ownership, taxation, estate planning, debtor/creditor laws, bankruptcy, corporate law, and so on. If the transactions cross international boundaries, complexity increases because the laws of at least two countries, and any treaties or other agreements between them, must be addressed.

Transfers That Defraud Creditors Will Not Be Successful

Debtor-creditor laws of your state, federal bankruptcy laws, and other laws must be addressed. Many states have adopted some version of the Uniform Fraudulent Transfers Act. If you transfer property with the intent to defraud your creditors, or which the law deems to be, the transfers will not be successful. A transfer of assets to hinder or delay your creditors' collecting can be voided. Further, should you find yourself in bankruptcy, your prior attempts to hinder creditors could have substantial adverse consequences. The bankruptcy judge may not permit you to discharge certain debts. Poor asset protection planning can make your situation worse than had you done nothing at all!

These rules are applied very strictly to protect creditors. Almost any transfer for which you do not receive a fair price could be suspect. Even transfers for a fair price, which occur within certain time periods before a declaration of bankruptcy or insolvency (liabilities are greater than assets) could be questioned. These transfers may be classified as "preferences" to be set aside by a court.

Several factors indicate a possible intent to defraud creditors (called badges of fraud), thus increasing the likelihood of a court setting aside the transfers:

- Transferring assets immediately before or after incurring a significant debt. You should implement your planning well before any claim or debt arises. Obtain a credit report, judgment, and lien search to prove no claims or debts existed at the time the transfers were made.
- Transferring substantially all of your assets at the same time. Always assure that you have left exposed sufficient assets and/or income to provide for your personal needs.
- Transfers of assets outside the United States. Consider an Alaska or Delaware trust.
- Transfer of assets when you are nearly insolvent. Prepare a financial statement to prove you're not.
- Transferring assets to a close relative or business associate. Consider an independent trust with an institutional trustee.

Husband or Wife: Who Should Own Assets?

Many asset protection plans are founded on the transfer of assets to your spouse's control (whether outright or in a trust controlled by your spouse). While your creditors may generally not be able to reach assets of your spouse, there are many exceptions. For example, if your spouse is a co-owner of the business involved or co-signed a note that is involved in a lawsuit, the creditors will also be able to reach your spouse's assets. Where a husband and wife own assets as tenants by the entirety, there are special privileges. This type of ownership can provide some measure of protection from creditors, depending on state law. If the creditor has a claim against only one of the spouses, assets co-owned by the other spouse cannot always be reached. This should be considered before you change the ownership of your assets to find a bypass trust (e.g., change your house from tenants by the entirety to tenants in common). Even this protection, however, is not foolproof. When the nonliable spouse dies, the creditors of the surviving spouse may be able to reach the entire asset. Transferring assets to your spouse does nothing to protect assets from claims against her. Better planning is usually possible. At minimum, consider forming a QTIP trust to hold the assets you give your spouse to provide some control and protection.

Nontrust Steps to Protect Assets from Creditors

Many different steps can be taken to protect assets against claims:

- Get adequate property and liability insurance protection including a large personal excess (umbrella) liability insurance. If you are in a car accident or someone is injured at your home, an umbrella liability insurance policy can provide substantial coverage above the limits contained in your homeowner's and auto insurance policies.
- Use FLPs, LLCs, or other entities for each business or investment asset. This can help prevent a domino affect when one asset becomes subject to a lawsuit if you observe all formalities.
- Giving away an asset is perhaps the best way to protect it (if fraudulent conveyance rules can be avoided). However, you must not need the income and value of the asset to do so. If you can't forgo any benefits from the assets to be given away, use a domestic asset protection trust in Alaska or Delaware. You can remain a beneficiary but theoretically your creditors and claimants won't be able to get at the assets. Be cautious, however, these laws are relatively new and unproven.

Ancillary Asset Protection Considerations

When evaluating any asset protection technique, review the impact of the following issues:

- Asset protection steps are not always consistent with tax, personal, and other goals. If you give away or tie-up your assets, you could forgo the ability to fund a bypass trust on your death.
- There can be substantial transfer and other costs involved.
- If assets are transferred to children or grandchildren to remove them from the reach of your future creditors, gift, estate, and generation skipping transfer taxes could all be due.
- Transferring assets to your spouse to avoid creditors may subject you to greater risk in the event of a divorce. Although many states have equitable distribution laws which state that the manner in which property is

owned should not determine how it is divided, these laws cannot assure that there will be no negative consequences. Equitable distribution laws seek to equitably divide assets, without regard to whose name the assets are in. However, even if the end result may be the same whether you keep your assets or transfer them to your spouse to avoid your potential creditors, the transfer could still have an important affect on the dynamics of the divorce process. If your spouse has substantial assets, it may be far easier for your spouse to raise money for legal and other fees to fight the divorce. You might be forced to rely on checking overdrafts and home equity loans to fund living costs until the marital assets you gave to your spouse are reallocated in a settlement.

How Can Trusts Be Used to Protect Assets?

Trusts can be an important tool in your asset protection planning. Many trusts that you might consider using to meet tax, financial, personal, or other goals can have important asset protection benefits as well. For example:

- *Defective trusts.* These trusts will be irrevocable and hence provide asset protection benefits, while being treated as incomplete gifts for income tax purposes to avoid income tax implications. This is tricky, since the power retained should not be so significant that it is construed as a general power of appointment which could give you the right to appoint assets to your estate—or your creditors.

- *Child's trusts.* These trusts have strong nonasset protection motives of saving for your child and protecting valuable assets from the whims of a young child. Assets saved in your name for your child can be given to a trust instead to protect them.

- *QTIP (inter-vivos) trusts for your spouse.* You can form a marital trust for your spouse during your lifetime. The trust can qualify for the unlimited gift tax marital deduction if your spouse receives all of the income annually and certain other requirements discussed in Chapter 14 are met. This is an alternative to giving assets outright to your spouse to avoid your creditors, and thereby losing control and putting those assets at risk by your spouse's creditors, too.

- *Grantor retained annuity trusts.* GRATs are used primarily to achieve tax savings when making large gifts. They can also provide a measure of asset protection for the principal. However, a court may permit a creditor to reach the annual payments you receive from the trust.

- *Life insurance trust.* Insurance proceeds are often substantial and should be protected. If held in a trust, the beneficiaries can be benefited while limiting the rights of their creditors to reach the proceeds. Also, there is a measure of protection afforded to insurance as an asset under some states' laws.

Include a "Spendthrift" Provision in the Trust

When asset protection is a motive for a trust, include a spendthrift provision to prevent the beneficiary from assigning any part of his or her interest in the trust to third parties before it is received. There are two important exceptions to the protection afforded by a spendthrift provision. Many state laws permit creditors who have provided necessities (e.g., food, shelter, and medical care) to a beneficiary of the trust to reach assets of the trust for payment. Also, as you might expect, the courts have held that the IRS can reach the assets of a spendthrift trust to satisfy a federal tax lien.

Trustees' Rights and Powers

When planning the use of trusts to shield assets, carefully consider the persons named as trustees (independent), and the powers and rights given to the trustees (limited to you). If you are the grantor setting up and transferring assets to the trust, and you seek to protect your assets from creditors, you should preferably not have any right to the trust's assets. If you can reach the trust assets for your own benefit, in most states your creditors will be able to do so as well. The exception to this is if the trust is formed in a state whose laws are specifically designed to permit this, such as Alaska or Delaware. Foreign-based asset protection trusts may be a stronger, albeit more costly and complex, alternative. These trusts can achieve what may not be possible under U.S. law because the trusts are intentionally based in countries whose laws are less favorable to creditors and thus permit this type of planning.

Using Domestic Trusts in Asset Protection Planning

Several states (Alaska and Delaware are the most popular) have revised their state laws to entice you to form a trust within their jurisdiction. These changes can affect several important aspects of trust planning, including:

- The rule against perpetuities has been eliminated. This law prevented trusts for lasting more than a certain number of years. Now you can create trusts to last forever (*dynasty trusts*). This is important to asset protection and tax planning. If the trust can continue forever, that's a long time for creditors to wait.
- State tax savings for trusts can enhance earnings over a long period.
- Debtor protection laws can enable you to be a beneficiary of a trust you establish (*self-funded*) while still protecting trust assets from creditors. This is a major incentive for creating these trusts, although the laws are still new and unproven. These rules are generally less aggressive than those that apply in the countries in which foreign asset protection trusts are set up. The statute of limitations and fraudulent conveyance rules are much stricter. If you're running

from a known or imminent problem, these domestic asset protection trusts won't work.

Domestic asset protection trusts have a number of important advantages over their foreign counterparts. They are established with U.S. institutions, subject to a host of federal and state regulations to assure their safety and integrity. They are based in the United States, which remains the safest capital haven in the world. The risk of political insurrection jeopardizing your assets is essentially zero. The documents, laws, and personnel all speak and think in a familiar manner.

USING FOREIGN TRUSTS IN ASSET PROTECTION PLANNING

A *foreign situs trust* (FST) is also known by other names, including *asset protection trust* (APT), *international offshore estate planning trust* (IOEPT), or simply a foreign trust. Foreign trusts are often the first thing that comes to mind when the phrase "asset protection planning" is heard. Foreign trusts can provide asset protection planning benefits, but the limitations, costs, complexities, and risks of using these trusts should be addressed before proceeding. Finally, foreign trusts—like any other single tool—are never the entire answer to your asset protection concerns. They should be used as only part of an overall program that includes other appropriate asset protection techniques. The foreign trust can provide a means to protect the assets of people who have a high net worth willing to incur the expense and difficulties.

Benefits of a Foreign Trust

There are several potential benefits that can be afforded to investors using a foreign trust:

- Where the foreign trust is established as an irrevocable trust, you (as grantor) may have no authority to terminate the trust or direct the distribution of its assets. Thus, if a judgment creditor is successful in a U.S. court, the court may not succeed in ordering you to turn over trust assets to the creditor. However, many foreign trusts are set up as revocable trusts so that you can avoid the U.S. excise and gift taxes which may otherwise be due on a transfer of assets to such a trust.
- The country where you locate your foreign trust will have laws favorable to your protection. (After all, that's why you chose that country.) For example, the statue of limitations for filing claims may be shorter so that a creditor must make his or her claim before the time period ends or he would be prohibited from pursuing the assets. Further, the statute of limitations may begin to run at the actual time of the transfer, which can be much earlier than the time of claim. Thus, in many

instances, the statute of limitations will have already expired by the time the creditor obtains a judgment.

- Foreign law may preclude a fraudulent conveyance challenge by a creditor who was not known to be a creditor at the time of your transferring assets to the foreign trust.

- Assets held in a foreign trusts may be more difficult to discover, identify, and seize then assets held in a domestic trust.

- If a creditor seeks to pursue a claim against you in the foreign country in which your trust is based, he may have to establish your personal liability again under the laws of that foreign country.

- Foreign jurisdictions may not recognize U.S. judgments. Therefore, a new case may have to be brought.

- The foreign trust can be a good vehicle for global investing since foreign jurisdictions often are subject to less stringent securities regulation than in the United States. As a result, investment products available to overseas investors are not always available to United States-based investors. This can be a legitimate and important non-asset protection motive for establishing a foreign trust.

- The secrecy laws of foreign jurisdictions may provide more privacy than domestic trusts can offer.

Foreign Trust Combined with Family Limited Partnership

The foreign trust may be structured with both a family limited partnership (FLP) or limited liability company (LLC) and a trust created in a foreign jurisdiction. You could form an S corporation controlled by you. An FLP could then be formed as a limited partnership with the S corporation serving as the general partner. You could retain substantial control through controlling the S corporation general partner. A trust is then created in a foreign country and the limited partnership interests are transferred to the trustees of that foreign trust. Alternatively, you could sell the limited partnership interests to the foreign trust in exchange for installment notes, or a private annuity. The bulk of the value of the assets would then be owned by the limited partnership interests held by the foreign trust.

In some cases, where this limited partnership structure is used, you do not have to transfer the limited partnership's assets offshore initially. Instead, the assets, such as a securities account, could remain in the United States and be transferred offshore by the trustee if and when a lawsuit is threatened.

Other Options for Structuring Foreign Trusts

In some instances, the investments are made through a corporation organized in a tax haven country, all of the stock of that corporation is owned by the trust. The advantage of the use of a corporation is that the corporation can be organized in a country with favorable tax and creditor protection laws which differs from the country in which the trustee is based or in which the trust is organized. This may serve as yet another hurdle for a potential claimant to surmount.

Which Foreign Country Should You Use?

Review the following matters with your attorney in deciding which foreign country to use as the location of your foreign trust: the political, economic, and social stability of the jurisdiction; the jurisdiction's reputation in the world business community; whether language barriers exist; whether the jurisdiction has modern telecommunications facilities; whether the jurisdiction offers adequate legal, accounting, and financial services; the jurisdiction's income, gift, and estate taxes (there should be no significant taxes); the standard of proof that a creditor must meet in attempting to show fraudulent intent on the part of the transferor; the extent to which a transferor may retain a benefit in, and control over, a foreign trust without exposing the trust to the transferor's creditors; the importance of the grantor's solvency following transfers to the foreign trust; the duration and starting date of the statute of limitations pertaining to a particular action; the particular jurisdiction's recognition of the holdings of a U.S. court in a particular case; whether the jurisdiction's trust law is favorable, well-defined, and protective; the recognition to be given to judgments and orders of foreign courts that affect a foreign trust, its trustees, and its assets.

PROTECTING ASSETS FROM MEDICAID

For many older people, the threat of paying long-term nursing home care poses the greatest threat to their financial independence and for the potential destruction of any savings or inheritance they had hoped to pass to their children. How to finance extended health care costs is a major obstacle. There are three basic options for paying for such care: private funding, private long-term care insurance, or governmental programs. Private funding is not feasible for many senior citizens. Only the wealthy can afford to pay the tremendous costs of long-term health care and still retain assets for personal luxuries and leave an inheritance for their children or other heirs (and often they should consider long-term care insurance or other planning as well). Spending away your remaining assets is not a desirable option for most seniors. Private insurance is available, but for many people, it is inadequate or unaffordable. The remaining option is to rely on state and federal programs such as Medicaid.

Medicaid is not the only governmental aid program to be considered in your planning, although it is the primary long-term nursing home care program. Many senior citizens may qualify for the Supplemental Social Security Income (SSI) Program. States often provide supplements in addition to the monthly SSI benefit. Medicare is a federally funded program to provide money for hospital and medical costs. Since the programs can differ considerably from state to state, and change over time, be certain to discuss these issues with an elder-law expert in your state.

Qualifying for Medicaid to Meet Long-Term Care Expenses

To qualify for Medicaid, you will have to divest yourself of most of your assets, except for the very limited amount of assets that your state's laws permit you to retain. To a great degree, this is tantamount to voluntary impoverishment. The only exception is the ability to retain certain assets that are not counted in the tests for determining Medicaid eligibility. Trusts can play an important role in this process. To understand the role of trusts in this type of planning, however, an overview of some general concepts is necessary.

To qualify for Medicaid, you must meet several general types of requirements. Since the states have discretion to apply more lenient or restrictive requirements, it is important to consider applicable state laws. You must be a citizen or resident of the United States, and possibly a permanent resident of the state in which you are applying for coverage; be over age 65 or disabled; meet a resource test that your financial resources, or assets, do not exceed certain amounts; and have income less than a certain level.

The key to understanding planning with Medicaid qualifying trusts is the definitions of assets and income. To qualify for Medicaid, you must spend down or divest yourself of assets until your net worth reaches the permitted levels. Assets that are counted can include all property owned in either your name or your spouse's name, certain property in joint name, and certain property transferred for less than a fair price within a certain number of months (it can range from 30 to 60) before you seek Medicaid. Certain transfers of exempt assets (also called *inaccessible resources*), such at the transfer of your home to your spouse or a disabled child, among others, may not be considered. A few other items are also considered to be exempt assets under many state laws and are therefore not counted in determining whether you exceed the assets you are entitled to retain and still qualify for Medicaid. These permissible assets may include, in addition to your home, a car of limited value, some amount of personal effects, a burial plot, a wedding band, and a few other nominal assets. A critical factor is determining which assets are not to be counted. Transfers that you can prove were made for fair consideration, or which were for purposes other than trying to qualify for Medicaid, may not be considered. These exceptions vary from state to state and should be carefully evaluated. Whether other assets should be considered is more difficult to ascertain. For example, will assets owned by a trust for your benefit be counted? These laws are changing rapidly and you must consult with an elder-law specialist in your state.

Only a modest amount of income can be retained, with the balance going to fund your medical care. Income that is counted in determining whether you meet the Medicaid requirements is called *available income.* This available income can include certain income of your spouse as well as your own income. It is generally income that can be used to meet your basic needs. Some courts have held, however, that only income of a spouse or parents can be deemed countable for any person attempting to qualify for Medicaid.

How Can You Protect Your Assets and Still Qualify for Medicaid?

There are several approaches that you can use to protect your limited resources. Use nonexempt assets to invest in assets which are considered inaccessible or exempt resources (i.e., invest stocks—which are nonexempt assets—into an exempt resource, such as your home, which is not applied toward medical bills), make gifts to children, or transfer assets to a Medicaid qualifying trust. These gifts and transfers, however, must consider complex look-back and other rules.

Risks and Uncertainties Abound

The entire Medicaid planning process is complicated by the interplay of extremely confusing federal, state, and other rules. Further, these rules are changing at a rather rapid pace. Therefore, before completing any attempt at a Medicaid qualifying trust, be certain to consult with an attorney who is an expert in elder law. Divesting yourself of most of your assets can also be a dangerous plan. Once you have divested yourself of assets, you have no ability to reclaim control or use those assets. Situations change. The beneficiaries of your largesse may decide to be less generous with you than you expected, or even less generous than they had promised. These risks are real and asset divesture should not be undertaken without very careful consideration.

Medicaid Qualifying Trusts

Medicaid qualifying trusts are irrevocable trusts which try, similar to the asset protection trusts described in the preceding section, to shield assets from claimants, only in this case the claims relate to medical care and health care facilities. These trusts are subject to some of the same uncertainties and risks to which other trusts are subject, and also to several problems peculiar to Medicaid planning. Medicaid trusts are even more difficult to plan for than asset protection trusts in that the assets of both spouses can be considered in the calculations of Medicaid eligibility.

If not properly structured, the assets of the Medicaid qualifying trust could be reached to pay for medical and nursing home bills. On the other hand, where the trust is properly structured to avoid Medicaid liability, you could lose substantial control over assets.

230 TRUSTS FOR SPECIFIC TYPES OF ASSETS

The use of trusts, as compared to gifts, offers important advantages. If you make a gift, you lose complete control over the assets given away. Further, the assets could be subject to creditors or the terms of a divorce of the recipient. Where you transfer the assets to a trust, however, the trust instrument provides some control over the authorized uses of the assets and can insulate the assets from the creditors or divorce of an individual recipient.

Some of the different approaches to a Medicaid qualifying trust include having a relative set up an irrevocable trust for your benefit that can provide only for luxuries, and not for necessities. The hope is that this type of restriction will prevent the attachment of trust assets to pay for necessities that Medicare would otherwise cover.

When you give assets to a Medicaid trust, the understanding is that for some period of time, say 60 months, trust assets will be used to pay for your nursing home or other health care needs. You can purchase long-term care insurance to cover costs for this 60-month period. Following this period, the transferred assets should be safe, your long-term care coverage lapses (as planned, to minimize the cost of the coverage) and you can be provided for by state or other programs.

Another approach is to have a third party set up a sprinkle trust. This is a trust over which the trustee has the authority to sprinkle income to any of the named beneficiaries (one of which will be you) in the trustee's sole discretion. Where the distribution of any money is solely within the absolute control of an independent trustee, the state will hopefully be unable to attach trust assets to pay for your medical and nursing home care. Further, in these types of trusts, language is often included giving, or directing, the trustee to refuse demands by governmental agencies for funds. A statement, or even a restriction, may be included prohibiting the use of trust income or principal for any expenditure for which the state would otherwise provide coverage. These trusts should obviously contain spendthrift clauses.

CONCLUSION

Setting up trusts to protect assets can provide numerous advantages. Great care, however, must be exercised in preparing the trust document to meet your specific objectives, transferring assets to your trust, and then operating it with the proper formality.

19 LIFE INSURANCE TRUSTS

This chapter discusses trusts pertaining to life insurance. As alluded to earlier, life insurance trusts can be an important part of an estate plan.

WHY IS A LIFE INSURANCE TRUST SO IMPORTANT?

The importance of a life insurance trust arises from many factors. Some of these have been mentioned earlier, but these factors are discussed in detail in this chapter.

Insurance Is Not Tax-Free without Use of an Insurance Trust

Life insurance trusts are one of the most important trusts. The dollar amounts of even small insurance policies are generally so large that the economic and investment management that a trust can offer make sense even if you will never pay an estate tax. Insurance trusts are too often overlooked because people erroneously assume that life insurance is tax free. It is not. Life insurance is taxable in your estate if you owned the policy. Even if life insurance escapes taxation on your death because it is paid to your spouse, it only escapes estate taxation as a result of the unlimited marital deduction, not because insurance is tax free. On the later death of your spouse, 50 percent of the insurance proceeds remaining could be paid in estate tax (to the extent the proceeds and your other assets exceed the estate tax exclusion).

Life insurance trusts can avoid estate taxes and safeguard your loved ones' financial future. Even people of modest means could often benefit from an insurance trust.

EXAMPLE: Mr. and Mrs. Youngcouple have negligible net worth. They own a home that is fully mortgaged. They have two children. Because of their limited resources and great needs (i.e., the two children), Mr. and Mrs. Youngcouple each purchase $1.5 million term life insurance policies. Because of their young ages, the premiums are very inexpensive. If both Mr. and Mrs. Youngcouple are killed in an automobile accident, their children may have to pay nearly $1 million in estate taxes!

Although almost any trust can own insurance policies and receive insurance proceeds, life insurance trusts are formed with the intent of owning only insurance policies on your life, or even the life of another person, such as your spouse.

NOTE: If you buy second-to-die (also called survivor's) insurance to pay estate tax, you will need an insurance trust. But you don't have to be rich to need an insurance trust. A young family with children, and a very modest estate, needs substantial insurance to protect against the death of a breadwinner. That insurance could trigger a huge estate tax and make the government your biggest beneficiary. Your surviving spouse, endeavoring to cope with your loss, dealing with a family alone, and other pressures, could be particularly susceptible to hustlers selling inappropriate investments. An insurance trust is the answer.

Typical Use of a Second-to-Die Insurance Trust

Perhaps one of the most common uses of an irrevocable insurance trust is to hold second to die or survivor's insurance. In a typical estate plan, here is how this technique works. Assume that your estate is worth $4.2 million. The proper use of credit shelter trusts in the wills signed by you and your spouse (and retitling of assets to be certain those trusts are funded) can remove $2 million (2002) from your combined estates, leaving a $2.2 million taxable estate. Assuming a 50 percent estate tax bracket, a $1 million second-to-die (survivor's) insurance policy is purchased by the insurance trust. On the death of the last of you or your spouse, the insurance proceeds are paid to the trust. The trustee can then invest the proceeds and use them to care for your heirs, to purchase assets from your estate, or to loan your estate the money to pay the tax. Your heirs will inherit the equivalent of almost your entire $4.2 million estate.

PROVISIONS TO INCLUDE IN AN INSURANCE TRUST

In addition to the common provisions addressing trustees, trustee powers, distributions, and so on, there a few special provisions to address in an insurance trust, including:

- Powers to deal with the insured's estate. This could enable your trustee to purchase assets from your estate to provide cash needed to pay estate taxes. If your estate includes valuable property, the trust could use insurance proceeds to purchase these nonliquid assets, thus providing your estate with cash to pay expenses and estate taxes.
- If you die within three years of transferring the insurance to your trust, the insurance proceeds will be included in your taxable estate. There is a backup approach that can salvage an estate tax benefit. If you are married, transfers to your spouse can qualify for the unlimited marital tax deduction. Thus, your life insurance trust can provide

that if the insurance is to be included in your estate as a result of your dying within three years of making the transfer, the trust will be converted into a trust that qualifies for the marital deduction.

WHAT STEPS ARE NECESSARY TO IMPLEMENT A LIFE INSURANCE TRUST?

Setting up a life insurance trust is complicated. Let's take it step by step.

Step 1: Evaluate Your Needs

Evaluate your insurance, estate tax, and living expense needs and determine the appropriate amount and type of insurance you want. Investigate the quality and soundness of the insurance company. If you are buying several million dollars of coverage, consider splitting your policy between a few insurance companies to diversify the risk of company failure. Make the decision whom to appoint as your trustees, who should benefit from the insurance proceeds, and so on.

Step 2: Complete the Trust Document

Have your lawyer prepare your insurance trust and sign it. Be sure the trustees also sign.

Step 3: Applications

Have the trustees complete and sign (in their capacity as trustees) all applications and forms from your insurance agent. You should take any required medical examinations to qualify for the insurance desired. Provide your insurance agent with a copy of the insurance trust so that your agent will have the correct name of the trust and trustees.

Step 4: Obtain a Tax Identification Number

Obtain a federal tax identification number by filing Form SS-4 with the IRS or calling them to obtain the number by telephone/facsimile. Calling tends to be much faster.

Step 5: The Trust Buys Insurance; Transfer Insurance to the Trust

If the trust is to purchase insurance, it can do so once formed. If you are planning to transfer existing insurance policies to the trust, contact your insurance agent and request a written estimate of the value of the insurance policies being transferred, the balance of any loans outstanding, the amount of the policy that can be borrowed against. Your insurance agent should be able to provide you with a calculation of the value of the insurance given, in accordance with the prescribed IRS formula. The value of the policies is important so you can plan to avoid any gift tax cost on making the transfer. To remove the death benefit of an insurance policy you own from your estate, you must effectively transfer all economic benefits and incidence of ownership in the policy.

Step 6: Open a Bank Account

Your trustee should take a signed copy of your trust agreement and your tax identification number to a bank and open a trust bank account. Deposit a nominal amount to get the account started, or a larger amount in the event that your trustee will have to pay an insurance premium.

Step 7: Follow Crummey Power Requirements

Your insurance trust will probably include an annual, noncumulative, demand or Crummey power to qualify your gifts to the trust for the annual $11,000 gift tax exclusion. Once a gift is received, the trustees should send the beneficiaries Crummey notices and be sure that the beneficiaries sign and return them for the trustee to hold.

Step 8: Pay the Premiums

Your trustee can pay the insurance premium and accept the policy. If existing policies are being transferred, the necessary steps discussed in the following section should be addressed.

PROBLEMS IN IMPLEMENTING AN IRREVOCABLE LIFE INSURANCE TRUST (ILIT)

Not so long ago, insurance companies were viewed by the public as pillars of stability. Not only does this view no longer hold, but be wary of the professional who recommends a specific product without having done the appropriate due diligence. Perhaps, the best approach for addressing this problem is for you and your financial planner or insurance consultant to make the final selection.

Where an existing insurance policy is transferred by the insured to an ILIT, the insured must survive for three years following the transfer or the death benefit of the policy will be included in your estate.

A problem that can occur when transferring an existing policy to an insurance trust is that the value of the policy may exceed the annual exclusion amounts (see discussion following). The value of a life insurance policy is determined under prescribed Treasury regulation guidelines. Where a permanent insurance product has cash surrender value, the interpolated terminal reserve value is used. For term insurance, the value is generally only the unexpired premium. In some instances, it may be feasible, the insurance contract permitting, to address this problem by having the insured borrow some portion of the cash value of the policy to reduce the value of the policy for gift tax purposes on its transfer to the trust. However, this raises the issue of transferring a policy subject to a loan to a trust. In some instances, the tax costs could weigh against this approach.

Transfer all "incidences of ownership" of a policy to remove it from your estate. Anything less may leave you with a tax problem.

EXAMPLE: You transferred an insurance policy to your spouse five years before death. However, you retained the right to borrow against the policy in the event of a business emergency. This single right could result in the inclusion of the entire policy proceeds in your estate. This is because all incidences of ownership must be surrendered more than three years prior to death.

An incidence of ownership means the right to borrow the cash value, change the name of the beneficiary, assign the policy to another person, borrow against the policy, and so forth. To eliminate all incidences of ownership, and remove the proceeds of an insurance policy from your estate, you must assign the policy a new owner and surrender every power over the policy and all of the benefits the policy can provide. You must irrevocably give up all these rights. The following rights could be deemed incidences of ownership that could taint the planning: the right to change or designate a beneficiary or contingent beneficiary of the policy; the power to prevent a change in beneficiary by withholding consent; the option to repurchase insurance from an assignee in some instances; other reversionary interests that have a value, immediately before the decedent's death, which exceeded 5 percent of the value of the policy. Incidents of ownership can flow indirectly, such as through a controlled corporation.

These rules can be violated in less than obvious situations. For example, if your insurance trust is legally obligated to pay taxes, debts, or other charges against your estate, the entire proceeds would be included in your estate. This is why, contrary to what most taxpayers believe (i.e., that the money in the insurance trust will directly pay their estate tax), the insurance trust can have no legal obligation to pay the tax on your estate, nor can it pay that tax. Rather, the insurance trust could loan money at an arm's-length rate to the decedent's estate to pay the tax. Alternatively, the insurance trust can purchase assets at an arm's-length fair market value from your estate infusing cash to pay the tax.

You should generally not serve as trustee of a trust owning insurance on your life. However, if you are named a trustee of a testamentary trust that owns life insurance on your life through no action of your own and the powers cannot be exercised for your benefit, the proceeds of the policy may not be included in your estate.

You will probably transfer cash to your insurance trust at least annually so the trustee can pay expenses, essentially the insurance premium. These transfers, and the transfer of any existing insurance policy (to the extent of its value), constitute gifts. Unless those gifts qualify for the gift tax annual exclusion, you will use up a portion of your lifetime exclusion. Once you have depleted your credit, a gift tax will be currently due. The availability of the gift tax annual exclusion for gifts to your insurance trust is generally determined by the availability of a Crummey power.

If your insurance trust is created for the benefit of your grandchildren, you must be concerned about the generation transfer skipping (GST) tax. To the extent that the GST tax exemption is allocated on your annual gift tax return, or automatically by the IRS, to cover gifts you made to an insurance trust for grandchildren, the trust fund could be permanently exempt from GST tax.

CONCLUSION

Irrevocable life insurance trusts (ILITs) are a key estate planning document for many people, not just the very wealthy. The tremendous benefits of these trusts should not be overlooked.

PLANNING TIP: To see a sample annotated life insurance trust, see the Web site www.laweasy.com.

---

20 TRUSTS FOR SECURITIES

One of the most common forms of assets is stocks, bonds, and other securities. Many different types of trusts can hold these assets, depending on your circumstances and goals.

TRUSTS TO HOLD SECURITIES USUALLY COMBINED WITH FLPS OR LLCS

For many of these trusts, a common planning technique is to first transfer securities to a family limited partnership (FLP) or limited liability company (LLC) and then transfer equity interests in the FLP or LLC to the trusts. This two-tier approach gives greater control (you can be a general partner of the FLP or manager of the LLC), better asset protection planning (a claimant has to pierce the entity as well as the trust) and better tax benefits (the value of a noncontrolling—less than 50 percent—interest in the FLP or LLC is typically valued at 20 to 50 percent lower than the value of the underlying assets).

TRUSTS TYPICALLY USED WITH SECURITIES

- *Revocable living trust (RLT).* These are commonly used by the elderly to hold many—if not all—assets to avoid probate and provide management in the event of illness or disability. If securities are a major asset, they too would be transferred to your revocable trust.
- *Asset protection trust (APT).* Securities are frequently transferred to a domestic or foreign asset protection trusts in order to protect the assets from creditors, malpractice claimants, and others. When asset protection is a goal, the use of FLPs and LLCs, as well as ancillary techniques, are usually used as well. (See Chapter 18.)
- *Charitable remainder trust (CRT).* A charitable remainder trust can provide a tax-advantaged method of diversifying highly appreciated securities, avoiding all capital gains taxes, and providing you a periodic payment for years (or for your life, or your life and your spouse's

life). These types of trusts are typically funded with appreciated securities. (See Chapter 17.)

- *Grantor retained annuity trust (GRAT).* This type of trust is used to maximize the gift tax benefits on large gifts. Securities are commonly used as gifts to GRATs, but typically are combined with an FLP or LLC to discount the value of the securities so given. (See Chapter 21.)

- *Charitable lead trust (CLT).* CLTs can be used to reduce the gift tax cost on large gifts to a charitable beneficiary prior to family or other heirs receiving assets. These types of trusts are often funded with securities. (See Chapter 17.)

- *Child's or grandchild's trust.* Parents and grandparents commonly set up trusts for children and grandchildren. These are often funded with cash, via check, or by the transfer of securities.

CONCLUSION

There are a host of different types of trusts that can be used to plan for securities you own. This chapter listed many of these different types of trusts.

21 TRUSTS FOR BUSINESS ASSETS

Trusts have long been used with business assets. For example, a common planning technique for many family businesses is to have trusts for children own passive business assets (e.g., costly equipment, real estate, and intangible property rights such as a trade name) that are then licensed or leased to the business. This approach has frequently been used to assure children not active in the business some economic benefits from the family business. It also serves to separate, for liability and creditor protection, passive business assets from the active operation of the business itself.

Tax-oriented trusts can also be used to remove equity in closely held business interests from your estate.

When planning for any trusts to hold business assets, be certain to review with your tax adviser the consequences of the trust planning on your estate's ability to qualify for the estate tax deferral provisions under Code Section 6166. These provisions can enable an estate, which consists of at least 35 percent closely held business interests, to defer paying estate taxes for about 14 years. If gifts to trusts reduce your ownership of closely held business below this 35 percent threshold, this valuable tax benefit could be lost. These rules were liberalized by the 2001 Tax Act.

When planning for any closely held business, income tax, business succession planning, and legal planning must all be integrated with your trust planning. The legal documents for the business (a shareholders' agreement for a corporation, a partnership agreement for a partnership, or an operating agreement for a limited liability company) must be coordinated with your trust planning.

QUALIFIED SUBCHAPTER S CORPORATION TRUSTS (QSST)

S corporations are one of the most common forms for owning small and closely held businesses. Although limited liability companies (LLCs) are becoming the entity of choice, the vast majority of closely held businesses continue to be S corporations because of the tax cost of changing.

S corporations have been popular because they offered the protection of limited liability that any properly formed and run corporation offered its owners, and they generally could avoid any tax at the corporate level. This is because all of the income (and loss) of an S corporation is taxed to its shareholders.

Careful consideration must be given to the special rules that apply to trusts owning such stock.

Requirements to Qualify as an S Corporation

For a corporation to qualify for these valuable benefits, it must meet a number of requirements, including: it cannot have more than 75 shareholders (the number was once 35), it must file the required election statement with the IRS (and possibly with state tax authorities), and it can have only one class of stock. In addition, the types of persons who can be shareholders is quite limited. Corporations and nonresident aliens (non-U.S. citizens) cannot be shareholders. Only trusts that meet very specific requirements can qualify to own stock in an S corporation. These requirements are the focus of the following discussion since it is essential to your trust planning for business interests.

What Trusts Can Own S Corporation Stock

Several different types of trusts can qualify to own S corporation stock: qualified subchapter S trust (QSST), electing small business trusts (ESBTs), and grantor trusts.

Electing Small Business Trusts

A trust that meets the requirements for electing small business trusts (ESBTs) can be a shareholder of an S corporation. For a trust to qualify, all of its beneficiaries must be individuals or estates (i.e., partnerships, corporations, and other entities cannot be beneficiaries). Certain charities can be contingent remainderpersons (i.e., the beneficiaries who receive trust income or assets if all prior beneficiaries die or cease to qualify as beneficiaries). ESBTs can provide greater flexibility than the QSSTs described next in that they can have many current income beneficiaries. This means several different people can receive income each year from the trust. QSSTs require a separate trust for each beneficiary.

QSSTs Can Qualify to Own S Corporation Stock

The most common approach to a trust owning stock in an S corporation is for the trust to qualify as a qualified subchapter S trust, or QSST. This can enable many types of trusts, if the necessary QSST provisions are included in the trust document, to own S corporation stock.

EXAMPLE: Father owns 55 percent of a mortgage servicing corporation that is organized as an S corporation. He decides that it is time to start transferring stock to his children to reduce his potential federal estate taxes. He sets up a qualified S corporation trust for each of his minor children. He joins with his spouse to jointly give $20,000 in value (based on an appraisal of the corporation) of stock to each child's trust. This approach enables him to control the use of the assets for the benefit of each child, and the stock could be insulated from both his creditors and the child's creditors.

To obtain the benefits illustrated in the previous example, the trust owning the stock must meet a number of strict requirements. If any of these requirements are not met, the trust will generally cease being a QSST on the date any requirement is no longer met. This can, in turn, jeopardize the corporation's favored tax status as an S corporation. Many types of trusts can include the QSST language and qualify:

- The qualified terminable interest property marital trust (QTIP) can qualify as a QSST so that you can bequeath S corporation stock to your spouse in trust. (See Chapter 14.)
- The typical Crummey power trust established for the benefit of minor children may not qualify for QSST treatment without modification to include the required QSST language. If the language is included, these trusts can own S corporation stock. (See Chapter 16.)

PLANNING TIP: If your child's trust doesn't include the required QSST language, talk to your tax adviser about how the Crummey power may convert the trust into a grantor trust to the child thus qualifying to hold S corporation stock.

- Some charitable remainder trusts may qualify as QSSTs prior to the death of the individual income beneficiary. They cannot qualify after the death of the income beneficiary since a charitable organization cannot qualify as an S corporation shareholder. For example, the unitrust and annuity trust amounts required to be distributed to comply with charitable trust laws may be less than the actual income that would have to be distributed to comply with QSST rules. (See Chapter 17.)

Requirements for a Trust to Qualify as a QSST

Election.   The income beneficiary (such as your child) must elect to be taxed as the owner of the S corporation stock for income tax purposes. This is because the income beneficiary will be taxed on his or her share of the income from the S corporation. The election must be made within 2½ months of the trust's becoming a shareholder, or within 2½ months of the beginning of the first tax year of the S corporation. If this election is not made, the S corporation's election may not be valid. The IRS has, in some situations, reinstated the S corporation's election where it deemed the failure to comply to be inadvertent.

Tax Reporting. The single beneficiary of the QSST trust will be treated as if he owns the portion of the trust that consists of stock in the S corporation. The effect of the election is to treat the beneficiary as the deemed owner of the S corporation stock. This means that the S corporation's income allocable to the shares of stock owned by the QSST will flow directly to the beneficiary as if he were the shareholder.

Required Income Distributions. During the life of the current income beneficiary, the trust's income must be distributed to one beneficiary. This beneficiary must be a person who is qualified to be a shareholder of an S corporation (a nonresident alien cannot qualify). This means the trustee cannot have the power to sprinkle trust income among different beneficiaries. If the trust holds assets other than stock in an S corporation, this requirement need only be applied to the income generated by the S corporation stock owned by the trust.

EXAMPLE: Father sets up a trust for the benefit of his minor child, Junior. Father makes gifts of two assets to the trust: (1) 10 Shares of stock in XYZ Company, Inc., an S corporation, and (2) a Certificate of Deposit. The S corporation pays a dividend of $2,450 per share. The Certificate of Deposit pays $530 of interest. The trust agreement should require the distribution of the $2,450 S corporation dividend. However, the trust agreement could provide for a different treatment of the $530 of interest.

To determine the "income" that must be distributed, the fiduciary accounting income as calculated under the provisions of the trust agreement is used.

EXAMPLE: Assume a trust earns $100,000 of income from an S corporation, realizes a $25,000 capital gain on the sale of stock, and pays a $6,000 fee for the trustee's commission. Assume that the trust agreement requires that ordinary income be treated as income, but capital gains from the sale of assets be treated as principal (called "corpus"). If local law or the trust agreement require that the trust commission be charged against principal, the accounting income for the trust will be $100,000 (the $25,000 capital gain, less the $6,000 commission, is added to the principal of the trust). For tax purposes the trust's income is $94,000 ($100,000 – $6,000) since the trustee commission may be deductible. Accounting income of $100,000 would have to be distributed, or required by the trust agreement to be distributed (see Chapter 12). The beneficiary, however, would be treated as taxed on the capital gains if they related to the S corporation stock. This could be capital gains realized by the S corporation and passed through to its shareholders, as well as capital gains realized by the trust on the sale of some of its S corporation stock.

The distribution requirement will not necessarily destroy the trust's status as a QSST where the trust requires that all income be distributed, but the trustee simply fails to do so. Where the trust agreement does not require that all income be distributed, it is sufficient that local law requires it.

Beneficiaries.   There can be only one beneficiary.

Distribution on Termination.   If the trust ends during the current income beneficiary's life, the trust assets must all be distributed to the current income beneficiary.

If the trust was not properly formed, it may be possible for the trust agreement to be corrected (reformed) by a court or by the consent of the beneficiaries, to meet this requirement.

Grantor Trusts Owning S Corporation Stock

Grantor trusts may qualify to own stock in an S corporation. For example, if you set up a trust and retain certain reversionary rights, the trust income is fully taxable to you. An example is the living trust described in Chapter 13. For a discussion of other types of grantor trusts, see Chapter 4. Not all grantor trusts will qualify to hold S corporation stock. Therefore, have your estate planner carefully review any trust agreement before transferring S corporation stock to that trust.

Trusts That Cannot Own S Corporation Stock

Many common trusts cannot own stock in an S corporation. If stock in an S corporation is transferred to a nonqualifying trust, the S corporation could lose its favorable tax status as an S corporation. This means it could be taxed as a C corporation with income subject to corporate taxes and then individual taxes—a double tax bite which an S corporation generally avoids. The typical bypass trust used in many estate plans (Chapter 10) can create serious problems if you owned shares in an S corporation.

GRANTOR RETAINED ANNUITY TRUSTS (GRATS)

One of the most effective trusts to use for gift and estate tax planning with business interests is a grantor retained annuity trust (GRAT). These trusts can dramatically reduce the gift tax cost of a large inter-vivos (while you are alive) gift transfer.

What Types of Assets Are Given to a GRAT

Although many different types of assets can be held in a GRAT, the most common approach is to contribute equity (ownership) interests in a closely held business into a GRAT. If other assets such as real estate or marketable securities are to be contributed, they are generally first contributed to a family limited partnership (FLP) or limited liability company (LLC). When noncontrolling interests (i.e., less than 50% of the voting interests) are contributed they are valued for gift tax purposes at a fraction of the value of the actual assets.

> **EXAMPLE:**   You transfer a $2 million securities portfolio to an LLC. The value of the LLC is $2 million. You then give 25 percent of the LLC membership interests to a GRAT. 25 percent of the underlying securities is worth $500,000. However, 25 percent of an interest in an LLC is worth considerably less because a 25 percent owner has no control over investment, distributions, or other policies. If the fair market value, less discounts for these restrictions, is $300,000, you can either give more assets to the GRAT without using more of your $1 million exclusion or give the desired amount of assets but use up less of your exclusion. The $200,000 discount above is the discount on the LLC. The GRAT itself offers another level of discount (see the next section).

The GRAT Technique Discounts Gifts Twice

A GRAT can be illustrated as follows: If you, as the donor or the grantor, give property to a trust for the benefit of your children, you would pay a gift tax on the discounted fair value of the property given to the trust. If instead the gift is structured through a GRAT, the value of an interest in the trust that is retained by you (i.e., the monthly, quarterly, or annual required payments) may be subtracted from the discounted fair value of the property given to the GRAT (the 25% LLC interests in the example) to determine the amount of the taxable gift. This reduction in the value of the gift to reflect the value of the annuity interest retained by you is only allowed if your retained interest is in the form of an qualifying annuity interest or unitrust interest (this latter interest is a GRUT, see following). If you reserved an annuity interest of, say, 6 percent for 10 years, you would be paid $18,000 year (6% × $300,000) for 10 years. This would reduce the value for tax purposes of the $300,000 LLC (remember that this represents $500,000 of securities) to, say, $200,000. You have thus achieved two layers of discounts, which needless to say, the IRS is not fond of.

Requirements for a GRAT to Work

For a GRAT to achieve the intended tax results (illustrated in the previous section), the annuity paid to you must meet the requirements of a *qualified interest*. The annuity must be either a fixed sum of money, usually defined as a percentage of the initial value of the property given to the trust (6% of the $300,000 LLC value in the previous example), or it must be a unitrust interest (a GRUT which is not the primary focus of this discussion, as explained next).

Qualification as a GRAT (or GRUT) is only required for transfers to certain family members. These rules do not apply if an uncle gives property to a trust and retains an interest, with the property passing to his niece, or you make a gift to a nonmarried partner. The requirements apply to transfers to children or other lineal descendants, such as grandchildren. For gifts to GRATs for nonfamily members, a slightly different, and somewhat more favorable technique of a GRIT (*grantor retained interest trust*) can be used.

This payment must be made in each taxable year of the trust's term, which can be any period (10 years in the previous example). This payment amount is required to be made at least annually, regardless of the amount of income actually earned by the trust. If the GRAT doesn't have enough cash flow, then interests in the assets of the GRAT (e.g., membership interests in the LLC in the previous example) can be transferred back to you.

Determining the Value of the Gift for Gift Tax Purposes on Forming Your GRAT

A number of different factors affect the value of the gift you make to your children or other heirs through a GRAT.

- The value of the property contributed to the GRAT. When marketable securities are used, the answer is generally quite simple: the fair market value of the securities given to the GRAT. If nonmarketable assets (such as real estate, an FLP or LLC owning securities, or interests in a closely held business) are given to the GRAT, an appraisal must be obtained to determine value.
- The annuity percentage selected. The higher the percentage annuity payment to be made periodically to you during the GRAT term, the lower the gift tax value. However, the reduced gift tax value comes at a cost, leakage of additional payments from the GRAT to you and hence back into your taxable estate. If the GRAT does not produce enough income to make the annual payments, principal used to fund the GRAT will be paid back to your estate.

NOTE: The earnings (total return, not current income) of the GRAT in excess of the required payments will inure to the benefit of the remainder beneficiaries without any additional gift or estate tax cost. This can provide a substantial additional benefit to the GRAT planning concept.

- The annuity term selected. The longer the period for which the annuity payments will be made by the GRAT to you, the lower the value of the gift to the remainder beneficiaries (e.g., your children) for gift tax purposes. The longer the term, the better the tax result. However, if you do not survive the specified GRAT term, the entire principal of the GRAT is pulled back into your estate. The practical result is that you may prefer to use a short (say, three- to five-year) GRAT, and when that GRAT ends, complete another GRAT.
- The frequency of the payments under the GRAT: annual, quarterly, or monthly. The more frequent the payments, the greater the value of your retained interest and the lower the value of the gift for gift tax

purposes. The frequency, however, must be weighed in light of the administrative burdens it creates.

- The applicable federal rate (interest rate determined under tax law guidelines) in effect for the month in which the GRAT is created.

The combination of these factors will determine the value of the gift upon creation of the GRAT (and hence the amount of gift tax that may be due).

What Happens When Your GRAT Ends

A GRAT will end at the earlier of your death or the end of the period of time specified in your GRAT. If you die before the GRAT ends, the assets of the GRAT are transferred back to your estate and included in your taxable estate. If you survive the term of the GRAT, when it ends the assets in the GRAT are distributed to the beneficiaries you've named in the trust, typically your children. The persons receiving the GRAT assets after the trust term ends are called *remainder beneficiaries*. In some instances, such as concerns over the trustworthiness of your remainder beneficiaries, you might have the GRAT assets held in further trusts for them, rather than distributed outright to them.

Provisions to Include in Your GRAT

A number of different provisions should be reviewed with your estate planner when discussing the trust document to be prepared to implement your GRAT:

- An annuity equal to a specified percentage of the net fair market value of the GRAT assets on the date that the GRAT is created must be paid to you. The payment should be set as a percentage so that in the event of an IRS audit resulting in the assets given to the GRAT being revalued higher, the annuity payment would automatically increase. This can protect you from incurring an unexpected gift tax cost on the audit. The percentage can fluctuate or change.
- The periodic annuity can be paid either monthly, quarterly, or annually. The frequency must be decided at the time that the GRAT document is signed.
- The annuity payment for each tax year must be paid to you no later than April 15 of the following year.
- The number of years (the fixed term) for which you will receive the annuity from the GRAT must be specified.
- If you do not survive the fixed term of the GRAT, the GRAT document should provide that the trust assets will be paid back to (and hence taxable in) your estate. An alternative with the same tax consequences is to provide that in the event you do not survive the fixed term of the

GRAT, you will have a general power of appointment to state in your will to whom the GRAT assets will be distributed.

- The GRAT must explicitly prohibit additional contributions to the GRAT. (The rules for a GRUT are different).

- The GRAT must prohibit *commutation*. Commutation is when a prepayment is made by the trust to you in order to terminate the trust at an earlier date than the fixed term established initially for the GRAT.

- The GRAT must prohibit payments to anyone other than you during the fixed term of the GRAT.

- The GRAT should state that your intention is to create a qualified annuity interest under applicable tax laws.

- The GRAT should explicitly state that it is *irrevocable* (cannot be changed once formed).

- The trust document must specify which state law will govern the GRAT.

- You should select several persons (and alternates in the event that the named persons cannot act) to act as trustees of the GRAT. You can serve as a co-trustee of your own GRAT if you wish.

Tax Consequences of a GRAT

Not surprisingly, there are a number of tax consequences to forming a GRAT. These will be discussed by tax form.

Income Tax Consequences of a GRAT

Since a GRAT is an independent entity for tax purposes you will have to obtain a tax identification number for the trust. A separate income tax return for the GRAT should not be required because it is classified as a grantor trust. Therefore, all of the income of the GRAT is reported on your personal income tax return.

Gift Tax Consequences of a GRAT

A gift tax return will be required. The gift you make to your children or other heirs through a GRAT cannot be protected by the $10,000 (as indexed $11,000 in 2002) gift tax annual exclusion. This is because the annual exclusion does not apply to a gift in a trust, such as a GRAT. The Crummey power technique (discussed in several prior chapters, including Chapter 10) cannot be used since it would conflict with the required annuity payment which must be made from the GRAT. Your gifts to a GRAT, however, can avoid current gift tax by the use of your exclusion (sufficient to exempt asset transfers of $1 million in 2002–2003, and higher in later years). In fact, many GRAT arrangements are structured intentionally to avoid exceeding your (and perhaps your spouse's) remaining exclusions.

CAUTION: You could manipulate the various options in structuring your GRAT so that your retained interest constitutes close to 100 percent of the value of the GRAT. This would mean that the remainder interest to the beneficiaries would have nearly a zero value. When you couple discounts on FLP or LLC and the additional discounts the GRAT can create, the leverage is substantial. You can give away substantial assets while utilizing relatively little of your exclusion.

Estate Tax Consequences of Creating a GRAT

If you survive the fixed term selected for the GRAT, the GRAT property should pass to the persons designated by you in the GRAT document without further estate tax consequences. However, if you do not survive the fixed term of the GRAT, a portion or all of the GRAT property will be included in your estate for estate tax purposes. If the GRAT is included in your taxable estate it may increase your estate tax. However, the increases in the exclusion made in the 2001 Tax Act may minimize or eliminate the tax. Even if the GRAT assets are included in your taxable estate, the GRAT document does not require that the assets actually be paid to your estate. Thus, your probate assets passing under your will could have to bear the tax cost created by the GRAT assets passing to the beneficiaries specified under the GRAT. Be certain to have your attorney consider the tax allocation clause in your will and address who pays the estate tax.

Generation Skipping Transfer (GST) Tax and Your GRAT

A GRAT is not an efficient technique for making gifts to later generations (skip persons) such as grandchildren (or more remote descendants). (See Chapter 11.) This is because the $1 million (2002–2003 as indexed) generation-skipping transfer (GST) tax exemption cannot be allocated to protect the assets in a GRAT until the end of the GRAT. This is disadvantageous because the assets transferred are likely to have appreciated by then. If you're looking to benefit grandchildren, a sale to a defective grantor trust, or simply gifts of discounted interests in a LLC or FLP to a trust, will be preferable approaches.

GRANTOR RETAINED UNITRUST (GRUT)

In a GRUT, the periodic payment is determined annually by multiplying a set percentage by the then-existing value of the trust's assets. This contrasts with a GRAT where the percentage is applied to the value of the assets once, on formation. GRATs or GRUTs are typically funded with assets expected to appreciate. If assets appreciate, the unitrust payment will cause the payments back to you as grantor to increase in future years. This will cause more of the trust assets to be paid back to your estate than would a GRAT. This would reduce the tax benefit and defeat the point of the tax plan. Thus, GRUTs are less commonly used.

SALE TO AN INTENTIONALLY DEFECTIVE IRREVOCABLE GRANTOR TRUST (IDIT)

This is a sale to a trust that is intentionally structured to qualify as a *grantor trust* for income tax purposes, hence the term *defective* (see Chapter 4). This is an aggressive estate planning technique that could potentially offer you substantial tax savings.

The defective grantor trust is an irrevocable trust on which you, as the grantor, pay the income tax on income earned by the trust. With nearly a 40 percent marginal income tax rate, this can be the economic equivalent of large additional transfers by you to the trust, without incidence of additional gift tax. The theoretical basis for this tax position is that the classification of a trust as a grantor trust under the tax laws makes you, the grantor, primarily responsible for the payment of the income taxes on the trust. Thus, by paying income taxes, the grantor is meeting his or her legal obligation. Not surprisingly, the IRS has taken a contrary view and has argued that your payment of trust income taxes is an additional gift to the trust. This risk should be weighed against the benefits of the additional economic benefits conferred on trust beneficiaries and in light of whether the making of additional taxable gifts is reasonably consistent with the estate planning goals of the grantor.

Note Sale Transaction

When the technique of a note sale to a defective grantor trust (IDIT) is used, the defective, or grantor trust, status of the IDIT is important. This is because, in addition to the income tax benefit described in the preceding paragraph, the intent in an IDIT transaction is for you to sell assets, on an installment basis (i.e., for a note) to the trust. If the IDIT is classified for income tax purposes as a grantor trust, you won't recognize any gain for income tax purposes on the sale. It's as if the sale has not occurred. If the IDIT were not so classified, then gain would be triggered.

You sell those assets to the IDIT which you expect to appreciate substantially after the sale (i.e., at a rate greater than the interest rate paid by the IDIT to you on the note). Since it would be anticipated that the IDIT would purchase interests in the family LLC, the discounts inherent in the valuation would leverage or boost this return.

The IDIT pays you for the property you sell it by executing an installment promissory note to you. The IDIT, as a grantor trust, is not treated as a separate entity for income tax purposes. Since the trust is not recognized as a separate taxpaying entity, when you sell assets to the trust, it is equivalent to a sale to yourself, and therefore no gain or loss is recognized for income tax purposes. Also, the trust earnings after the sale remain taxable to you for income tax purposes. Thus, when an IDIT is successfully structured as a grantor trust for income tax purposes, the income, gain and losses of the trust are reported on your personal income tax return, and not on a separate tax return filed by the trust.

When you sell assets to the trust, you receive back an interest-bearing note, with interest payments at the prevailing interest rate required by the tax laws. The note typically has a balloon payment at the end of the note term. The premise of the arrangement is that if the transaction is properly structured, the asset is valued at the face value of the note, and therefore there is no gift. If you sell $100,000 of LLC membership interests (discounted as explained above) to the IDIT for $100,000, there is no gift. Although in the typical IDIT transaction you would give some assets, say 10 percent of the value of the assets being sold to the IDIT at an earlier date so that there would be assets other than those sold to serve as collateral for the note. The objective is to imbue the transaction with commercial or arm's-length terms.

At some future date, the note should be unwound, preferably before your death. This can be accomplished by the IDIT selling the assets it owns and using a portion of the proceeds to pay off the note. Alternatively, you may repurchase the underlying assets from the IDIT for the prevailing fair market value. The payment to the IDIT should also not trigger any taxable gain to the IDIT, again because the trust is a grantor trust. In this latter scenario, when you repurchase the (hopefully) highly appreciated assets held by the IDIT, they would be included in your estate. On your death, the assets would receive a step up in tax basis and the capital gains would be permanently avoided. These multiple tax benefits are the very reason the IRS has significant incentive to attack IDIT transactions. Therefore, these transactions must be regarded as aggressive and risky. Careful planning is key.

Gift and Estate Tax Considerations

In spite of these results, the transaction can be structured to qualify as a completed gift transfer for gift and estate tax purposes.

The IDIT technique raises several gift, estate, generation skipping, and income tax issues. In addition, the technique should be compared to that of a grantor retained annuity trust (GRAT) and the tax consequences of a GRAT. The major differences are that the IDIT has greater leverage, and hence tax benefit (because of the lower interest rate used), but is not based on firm regulatory guidelines, as is a GRAT.

Generation Skipping Transfer (GST) Tax Considerations and the IDIT Transaction

An IDIT could arguably be the most valuable GST leveraging technique available. The IDIT transaction could theoretically be structured to have a gift value of $1 against which GST exemption could be allocated. Following the provisions of the 2001 Tax Act, your GST exemption may be automatically allocated to the IDIT so that you would not have to report the transaction on a gift tax return to have it GST exempt. If you intend to establish a dynasty trust, the IDIT could be protected by GST exemption and leverage transfers for your dynasty trust. A key advantage of the IDIT over the GRAT transaction is that in a GRAT, because of the payments of the annuity amount to the grantor, an *estate tax inclusion period* (ETIP) exists and therefore no GST exemption can be allocated until the termination of the GRAT. In contrast, with an IDIT transaction, there is no ETIP, so GST can be allocated at the outset. This is an extremely important and valuable leveraging technique, especially when the IDIT is purchasing assets for which substantial appreciation may occur post-purchase. The discounts on value to be achieved through the use of the family LLC will contribute to the appreciation potential over the gift tax value.

VOTING TRUSTS

A voting trust is a legal arrangement, in the form of a trust, where shareholders join together to have their stock voted (as a single block) by a designated person who is the trustee of the voting trust. A voting trust provides the trustee an irrevocable right to vote stock in a corporation for a designated period of time, 10 years being common. The trustee does not generally have the right to sell the stock, or receive the dividends paid on the stock. This is because the purpose of a voting trust is merely to vote stock. Certain shareholders may prefer not to be actively involved in business matters, and thus appreciate the opportunity to relieve themselves of voting and related burdens. Certain shareholders may wish to join together to vote their shares as a block in order to exert more influence over the corporation. Unless prohibited by the shareholders' agreement or other legal restriction, they can do so. A voting trust arrangement is not generally appropriate for use in making gifts of stock to children and grandchildren because retaining voting control through a voting trust arrangement could cause the inclusion of the stock in the parent's or grandparent's estate for estate tax purposes.

Another common situation that could benefit from the use of a voting trust arrangement is divorce. Voting trusts can provide a method to permit the ex-spouse who is active in a business to continue to control the business, while the other ex-spouse can protect his or her interest in the divorce settlement agreement by actually owning stock in the business.

EXAMPLE: Ex-Wife owns 60 percent of a design business. Ex-Husband is awarded 25 percent of the value of the business as part of the equitable distribution divorce settlement negotiations. Ex-Wife has resigned herself to transfer to Ex-Husband the amount necessary to resolve the divorce. However, if she actually transferred 25 percent of the stock to Ex-Husband, she would lose control of the business. Worse yet, she would have put a sizable portion of the stock into the hands of someone who may be adverse to the business and other shareholders. The solution could be to give Ex-Husband the 25 percent of the stock, but require that his shares be transferred to a voting trust controlled by Ex-Wife. To fully protect Ex-Husband's interests, however, he should also negotiate a shareholders' agreement that has reasonable restrictions on how much Ex-Wife and other shareholders can withdraw as salary or benefits. Without this additional protection there may be no money left in the corporation for distribution as dividends on the stock.

In one case a court refused to permit an ex-spouse to revoke a voting trust agreement. The court reasoned that since the use of the voting trust arrangement for a closely held business was bargained for at arm's length and was an integral part of the divorce settlement agreement, the ex-spouse should not be able to change it.

There are other approaches that may be used instead of a voting trust. For example, shareholders could sign a proxy giving a designated person a right to vote their shares. Alternatively, a shareholders' agreement between all of the shareholders of the corporation could provide rules for governing the corporation's operations. It could contain, for example, requirements that certain decisions be made by more than a 50 percent, or more than a 75 percent vote of the shareholders. The voting trust, however, can be a more flexible and fluid arrangement giving the trustees greater latitude to respond to unforeseen situations.

Voting trusts are a flexible and useful technique for controlling the voting interests in a closely held business without affecting the economics of the transactions. They can be used in estate planning, financial planning (e.g., where someone unable to manage their business turns control over to another person), and in divorce planning.

CHARITABLE REMAINDER TRUSTS FOR BUSINESS ASSETS

Charitable remainder trusts (CRTs) can be a tremendous tool for removing highly appreciated stock in a family business from your estate. Properly planned, a CRT can be used to "bail out" some portion of business interests in a tax advantaged manner. (See Chapter 17.)

CONCLUSION

There are many different types of trusts that can be used, depending on the circumstances and your objectives, in planning for business interests. This chapter has analyzed several of these trusts, and provided references to trusts in other chapters that can also be used in business planning. In addition to investigating tax concerns with your tax planner, be certain that the businesses' attorney and other owners have approved, to the extent required, any transaction you are contemplating.

PLANNING TIP: To see a sample annotated voting trust, visit the Web site www.laweasy.com

---

22 TRUSTS FOR REAL ESTATE

There are many different types of trusts that can be used to plan for real estate assets. The trusts used and the benefits they can provide are quite varied. This chapter provides an overview of some of these trusts. Since many of the trusts that typically hold real estate are general purpose trusts that can hold other assets as well, they have been discussed in other chapters as well. These trusts are noted and their use in owning real estate explained.

CHARITABLE REMAINDER TRUSTS

A charitable remainder trust (CRT) can be used to diversify a large investment in a real estate property while avoiding capital gains. It can be used to generate a monthly annuity and eliminate the need for ongoing management. For example, as you age, daily management of a residential rental property could grow increasingly difficult. If you give the property to a charitable remainder trust, the charity could sell the property without incurring capital gains, reinvest the proceeds, and pay you an annuity for life. The CRT is even flexible enough to permit you to donate raw land, which can be sold at a later date. The annuity payment you receive can be coordinated with the sale of the property so that the trust will not be obligated to make payments to you before it has the income or cash flow to do so. (See Chapter 17.)

GRANTOR RETAINED ANNUITY TRUSTS

Grantor retained annuity trusts (GRATs) can provide a method of transferring commercial real estate to your children or other heirs at substantially discounted gift tax costs. More commonly, a family limited partnership (FLP) or limited liability company (LLC) owning commercial real estate is used instead of giving away real estate directly. The discounts available to gifts of noncontrolling interests in an FLP or LLC owning commercial real estate are more substantial than those typically available for an FLP or LLC owning securities. This can make real estate a more favorable asset to use for a GRAT than securities. (See Chapter 21.)

REVOCABLE LIVING TRUSTS

If you own real estate in a state other than where you reside, your heirs will probably have to go through probate in that other state to transfer real estate located there following your death (ancillary probate). If you transfer the real estate to a revocable living trust, your heirs should be able to avoid this additional probate proceeding. However, if the real estate is rented, an FLP or LLC is a better approach to minimize liability risks. If the real estate is a vacation home, a qualified personal residence trust (QPRT) discussed next may be a better option. (See Chapter 13.)

LIFE INSURANCE TRUST

Since real estate is not always easily saleable, it is common for many real estate owners to purchase additional life insurance to assure liquidity and to avoid a forced sale. In many instances, the insurance trust will use the insurance proceeds to purchase the real estate from your estate. Therefore, it is important to address the possibility of the insurance trust owning real estate. (See Chapter 19.)

QUALIFIED PERSONAL RESIDENCE TRUSTS (QPRTS)

A qualified personal residence trust (QPRT) can transfer your home or vacation home to your children at a substantially discounted value. With a QPRT, you, as grantor, transfer your residence to a trust, retaining a term interest (the right to live in the house for a specified number of years), and naming family members as remainder beneficiaries. QPRTs, similar to GRATs, take advantage of the time value of money to dramatically reduce gift taxation. The idea is that because your children must wait until the trust ends, the value of the gift to them is less in current dollars.

Upon the expiration of the specified term of years, the residence is then distributed to other family members, typically your children. The residence can be retained in a further trust for those family members at such time.

The tax benefits of the QPRT include the ability to leverage the use of your exclusion and remove any appreciation in the value of your home after the gift to the QPRT from your estate.

EXAMPLE: If a residence is worth $1.2 million, a gift of the residence could trigger an immediate gift tax (since the $1.2 million gift would use up your entire $1 million (2002–2003) exclusion, and the $200,000 excess would trigger a current gift tax cost. Where the transfer is to a QPRT, none of this gift can qualify for the annual $10,000 gift tax exclusions. However, the discounting effect of the QPRT calculation can reduce the current value (for gift tax purposes) of the residence to $1 million or less (2002–2003, more in later years), thus protecting the transfer from triggering any current tax cost.

EXAMPLE: If the residence in the preceding example appreciates to $1.6 million at the end of the 10-year QPRT term, the entire appreciation of $400,000 ($1.6 million – $1.2 million) is removed from the grantor's estate.

EXAMPLE: If the discounted QPRT value of the residence at the date of the gift (which will depend on the term of the QPRT and the applicable interest rate for the month of the transaction, and your age) is $600,000, then assuming you live the 10-year term of the QPRT, you would have removed from your estate an asset valued at $1.6 million at a "cost" of using up only $600,000 or your exclusion. Thus, $1 million has been removed from your estate without any tax cost. Assuming a 50 percent estate tax bracket, the federal estate tax savings is $500,000.

A risk taken in a QPRT transaction is that if you don't survive the term of the QPRT, the residence is brought back into your estate. However, since any portion of your exclusion used in the QPRT is restored, the whole transaction (but for professional fees) is a wash. The downside should be negligible compared to the potential benefits.

For many taxpayers, yet a further advantage of the QPRT makes it even a more desirable planning tool. A QPRT can enable taxpayers to reduce the size of their taxable estate without the expenditure of investment assets they believe they need to support themselves in their retirement years.

EXAMPLE: Sam and Selma Senior have an estate which consists of $2 million of securities and a principal residence, without a mortgage, valued at $750,000. Thus, their combined estate of $2,750,000 exceeds their combined exclusions in 2002–2003 by $750,000. This could result in a substantial tax cost. If their estate appreciates, the cost would be worse. This problem, however, could be addressed with an aggressive gift program of annual gifts. They have four children (each of whom is married and has three children of his or her own, for a total of 20 beneficiaries). Thus, the Seniors could give $10,000 each to every child in 2001, spouse of child, and grandchild, without triggering any gift tax cost or use of their exclusion. This could total $400,000 ($20,000 × 20). In one year and one day, they could give away $800,000, thus eliminating any potential estate tax cost. Few elderly taxpayers would be comfortable doing this. As the age of the taxpayers declines, the expected discomfort with such large gifts would grow dramatically. The QPRT offers a better option. If the residence is given to a QPRT, the value of the house could be removed from their estate at a discounted rate. Also, all future appreciation, which could only compound their tax problem, would also be removed. The key benefit: The Seniors may achieve their goals while retaining their investment portfolio (the earnings of which they live on) intact.

Requirements to Qualify as QPRT

A number of specific requirements that must be met for a QPRT to obtain the tax benefits hoped for are discussed next.

Assets Excluding Cash

The only assets that the QPRT can hold are a residence, home insurance policies (and payments under such policies), and a modest amount of cash for upkeep.

Restrictions on Cash Held

The cash that a QPRT can hold include only the following:

- Funds to pay the QPRT's expenses. This can include any trust expenses, including but not limited to mortgage payments. Expenses that qualify are those which have already been incurred, or which can reasonably expected to be incurred in the six months following.
- Funds to pay for improvements to the residence held by the QPRT over the next six months.
- Condemnation proceeds or proceeds from insurance paid for the damage or destruction of the residence (and any earnings on those proceeds) may be held for two years from the date of the event (condemnation or destruction) if the trustee intends to reinvest the proceeds.
- Upon formation, the QPRT can also hold funds to purchase a new residence within the next three months. However, the QPRT agreement must prohibit the gift of additional funds to the trust until a contract to purchase a residence exists. Cash funds in excess of those permitted by the regulations must be distributed quarterly to the grantor, and upon the termination of the QPRT.

Residence

The property contributed to the QPRT must be a qualified residence: a principal residence, vacation home, or even a fractional interest in a principal residence. A key concept is that the residence must be available for your use as a residence. Interests in a cooperative apartment can also qualify. The IRS has permitted interests in a cooperative apartment to qualify even where the cooperative board of directors refused to give permission to the grantor to make the transfer. The definition of vacation home provides that if the personal use of the property exceeds the greater of 14 days or 10 percent of the days the property is rented, it is classified as a residence. Any particular QPRT can only hold a single residence, used by you, for the entire term of the QPRT. If the qualifying residence held by the QPRT is sold, another qualifying replacement residence must be acquired or the cash must be used to pay you an annuity, as described next.

Number of QPRTs

You cannot have interests in more than two QPRTs.

You Must Survive Trust Term

Another important characteristic of the QPRT is that you must survive the retained term of years for the residence not to be taxed in your estate. If you do not survive the term of years, then the residence is taxed in your estate at its then fair market value, thereby rendering this estate planning technique unsuccessful. This is similar to the result for a GRAT. As a result, it is generally recommended that the trust contain a provision that if you die during the term of your retained interest that the property revert to your estate. Having such a provision in the trust permits a further discount on the value of the gift ultimately going to your family members (i.e., the remainder interest). The rationale for the discount is that there is a possibility that the remainder beneficiary will never receive the property. The value of this reversion is based on your age and the IRS specified actuarial tables.

QPRT Distribution Requirements

During the term of the QPRT, the trust agreement must prohibit the trustees from making income or principal distributions to any person other than you. The only exception is that on termination of the trust, distributions can be made to the remainder beneficiaries. Income earned by the QPRT must be distributed to you at least annually.

QAT in Event of Trust Failure

The trust agreement must also require that in the event that the QPRT fails to qualify as a QPRT, the corpus (assets of the trust) will be distributed in one of two prescribed manners. This requirement further highlights the underlying purpose of a QPRT—namely to hold a residence. One of the options available in this instance for the QPRT to be converted into a trust in which you have a qualified annuity interest, or a qualified annuity trust (QAT). This is an annuity payment similar to the GRAT.

Tax Planning and QPRTs

A primary benefit of making a gift of real estate is that any appreciation on the gift following the date of transfer will avoid gift and estate taxation. In most QPRT planning situations, the gift consummated to the QPRT is planned so that no current gift taxation on the transfer should occur. This is accomplished by making a gift which would be covered by your remaining exclusion ($1 million in 2002–2003, increasing thereafter).

From a gift tax perspective, upon setting up a QPRT, you have transferred the ultimate ownership of your house to your children (or other family members), even if the children (or other heirs) must wait to actually obtain possession. Thus, you have made a gift that is currently subject to gift tax. However, as a result of the fact that the children do not benefit from the transfer for 10 years (or any other period of years)—until the trust terminates, the value of the gift isn't the current value of the house, but rather the current value reduced to reflect the waiting period.

If you give your house to a QPRT, the tax basis of the house in the hands of the trust and the remainder beneficiaries is what you paid for the house (plus improvements), the carryover basis of the property. Thus, a downside to the QPRT is that your heirs won't receive a step-up in the tax basis of the property after your death.

CONCLUSION

There are numerous trusts that can be useful in planning for your real estate. Proper trust planning can save taxes, minimize liability risks, provide for succession of management, and help meet other important objectives.

23 TRUSTS FOR PENSIONS AND EMPLOYEE BENEFITS

Pension assets represent a major asset for millions of taxpayers. This chapter highlights some of the many ways trust planning can be used in conjunction with planning for your pension assets. Because of the complexity of pension assets, be certain to review income tax issues with your accountant, and pension issues with your pension or employee benefit adviser. Many pension (profit sharing, money purchase, and the like) and employee benefit trusts (such as VEBAs) are not discussed in this book.

RABBI TRUSTS

Many closely held and other businesses provide pension or other retirement benefits. These qualified plans, however, must generally benefit a substantial portion of the employees. In order to benefit selected employees, nonqualified plans are often used. When funds are set aside for such a plan, they must still remain nothing more than an unsecured promise of the employer to pay. If the money is protected for the employee, the employee could risk facing current income tax on the money. The trade-off is the risk that the employer will not remain financially sound until the nonqualified benefits are paid, or face current income tax cost to secure those benefits. Even if the employer appears financially secure, future creditor claims, a takeover by another entity, and other developments could all jeopardize these benefits.

There is a compromise. A special trust can be used that will provide some greater measure of comfort to the employee than a mere promise of the employer to pay the benefit, but a level of protection that is not so great as to cause the employee to be taxed currently. This special trust is called a *rabbi trust* because the first case in which the IRS approved it was for a synagogue seeking to provide benefits for its rabbi.

A rabbi trust is a trust to which the employer makes contributions on account of the deferred, but nonqualified, compensation arrangement with the employee. Because the trust is a grantor trust, creditors of the employer can reach trust assets. This risk is sufficient that the IRS will not tax the employee on the money contributed. However, the terms of the trust also prohibit the employer from making use of the money contributed to the trust. This restriction gives the employee greater security and protection than simply having the employer's promise to pay.

Since a rabbi trust is planned to qualify as a grantor trust, the employer, as grantor, is taxable on any income earned by the trust. Also, because the trust is a grantor trust, when payments are made to the employee from the trust at some future date, the employer is deemed to have made the payments and thus could be entitled to a tax deduction for the compensation so paid.

The use of rabbi trusts has become so common that the IRS has issued a model form. The form is obtainable from the IRS.

Pension Subtrusts

Pension plans are a common asset. Also, for many people, pensions are a major portion of their estates. As a result of the large balances in pension plans, many insurance agents have promoted the purchase of life insurance by qualified retirement plans. The intended purpose is to use pretax dollars for the purchase of insurance. This can be a substantial tax advantage. However, there is a cost to this type of arrangement. If improperly handled, this can result in the inclusion of the insurance proceeds in the insured's estate. The use of a pension subtrust to prevent the inclusion of insurance proceeds in your estate is a possible option to address this problem.

The pension subtrust is a concept similar to the insurance trust discussed in Chapter 19 that is adapted for use inside a pension plan to own insurance. It can be used to avoid inclusion in your estate of any insurance owned by your pension plan. The technique is called a *sub*trust because a trust is used that is subsidiary to, and incorporated under, the primary pension trust in order to hold the life insurance. Since a special trustee of the insurance subtrust under the pension plan, and not you as the insured (nor the trustees of the pension plan itself where you control the corporation and hence the trustees of the pension plan), controls the insurance policies, and where the subtrust is properly structured so that no incidences of ownership are attributable to you, the insurance in the pension can arguably avoid estate tax inclusion.

Requirements for Subtrusts

The subtrust should meet the following criteria:

- An independent trustee, and successors, are named.
- It is irrevocable.
- Powers of the subtrust special trustee are structured:
  — With consideration to the plan requirements.
  — In a manner to assure the special trustees control over the insurance policies held in the subtrust.

- It proscribes any control by the special trustee of plan assets in the plan but outside of the subtrust (generally anything other than the insurance).
- It permits the special trustee to designate the beneficiaries under the insurance plan.
- It permits the sale of the insurance policy to the insured for its fair market value in the event that the policy for any reason cannot continue to be held in the subtrust.
- It prohibits any distribution, as part of the participant/insured's plan benefits or otherwise, of the insurance policy, an annuity, and so on to the insured.
- The insurance policy cannot be converted to an annuity for the benefit of the participant/insured.
- On the death of the insured, it pays the policy proceeds to the beneficiary designated.

Problems, Risks, and Considerations

Provision for a safety-valve QTIP or marital trust can be provided for in the subtrust plan documentation. In the event that the subtrust concept is not approved by the IRS (which would mean that the entire subtrust insurance proceeds would be taxable on your death), or if the policies are transferred into the subtrust less than three years prior to your death, a tax could be due. Where a marital trust default provision is provided, similar to the savings provision included in many first-to-die trusts, then the argument would be made that the insurance would pass to the surviving spouse in a qualified martial deduction trust and no tax would be due on the first death. This approach raises two issues. First, it is not clear that a decision by the special trustee of the pension subtrust would meet the requirements necessary to qualify for a marital deduction. (Do the proceeds pass from the deceased to the spouse?)

The manner in which the subtrust language/agreement is added to the pension plan warrants consideration and verification of conformity with any plan or ERISA requirements.

If the plan (exclusive of the subtrust) has inadequate assets to pay the required retirement benefit to the participant/insured, the cash value of the insurance plan may have to be utilized.

USING PENSION ASSETS TO FUND MARITAL (QTIP) AND CREDIT SHELTER TRUSTS

Individual Retirement Accounts (IRAs) and qualified pension and other plans are a major asset for many people. Often, these assets need to be used to fund a credit shelter trust (to protect the unified credit of the first spouse to die) because there are inadequate other assets. You may wish to have pension assets paid into a marital QTIP trust on death in order to protect the assets for children from a prior marriage, or for other reasons (see Chapter 14). When planning to achieve either of these goals, the complex tax rules discussed in Chapters 10 and 14 are compounded by the even more complex tax rules that apply to IRAs, pension plans, and other qualified plans. You can use pension assets with many of the trusts discussed in this book to best achieve your personal goals and minimize estate taxes.

CONCLUSION

Pensions and employee benefits are a major asset for many people and should not be ignored in trust planning. To properly plan for the use of credit shelter and QTIP trusts with pension assets, some basic pension tax and distribution concepts must be considered. If your employer has a human resources department, begin your investigation and inquiries there. They may have dealt with the same issues you face many times and thus be in a position to offer guidance. After that initial inquiry, coordinate pension and employee benefit planning with your estate planner, accountant, and pension adviser.

Part Five

TERMINATION OF
YOUR TRUST

24 TRUST TERMINATION

Trusts, except for perpetual (dynasty) trusts, must come to an end, whether as a result of the provisions of the trust agreement, actions of the trustee, or as required by law. It is important to understand how, when, and why a trust can or should be terminated. Even a perpetual trust may end if it runs out of money, if it becomes uneconomical to continue, its purpose no longer exists, or for other reasons. These considerations should affect how your trust agreement is written. Whether you are a trustee or beneficiary, there are also important tax and legal considerations involved in the termination of a trust. You need to know your responsibility and rights to properly protect your interests and fulfill your responsibilities. This chapter reviews several of these considerations. Tax considerations are also discussed in Chapter 12.

WHEN CAN A TRUST BE MODIFIED OR TERMINATED?

The most common situation for a trust to end is where the trust has achieved its purposes so that its life naturally closes.

EXAMPLE: You set up a trust for your children. Your objective is to provide for management of money that you've set aside for your children's benefit, and to assure, to the extent possible, that the monies remain insulated from your creditors. To provide flexibility for your trustees to provide funds to the child most in need, you've set up a single trust for all three children. When the youngest child reaches age 25, you're confident that the children will all have completed (or nearly completed) their college and postgraduate educations and should have the maturity to handle financial matters. Thus, your trust provides when your youngest child reaches age 25, the trust should terminate and the trustee should distribute all remaining income and principal equally among your children. Thus, on your youngest child's 25th birthday, the trustee begins making final distributions and starts to wind up the trust. Your trust will terminate soon thereafter.

Your trust may be modified or terminated in specified (often limited because of tax reasons) circumstances, which may include the following:

- You, as the grantor of the trust, may have reserved the right to revoke your trust where you set up a revocable trust. You could have had a provision included in your trust specifically reserving the right to modify or revoke the trust. Be aware, however, that this right has consequences. Trust income may be taxed to you, and there may be no protection of trust assets from your creditors.

SAMPLE CLAUSE: The Grantor declares that any trust formed under this Trust Agreement, and the Trust Estate created hereby, are revocable. The Grantor, during Grantor's life, may revoke change, amend, or modify, in any manner and to any extent, the provisions of this Trust Agreement. The Grantor has retained every right and power to do so.

Where your trust is not specifically revocable by you, court approval would probably be necessary to revoke or modify the trust.

- An irrevocable trust may be terminated where all of the beneficiaries, and anyone else with a material interest in the trust, consents and no material purpose of the trust is defeated. Where a trust has, for example, a spendthrift provision (prevents creditors from attacking the trust assets and prohibits beneficiaries from assigning their trust interests), then the termination of the trust by agreement of the beneficiaries may defeat a material trust purpose. However, if the grantor also consents in such a situation, the trust may still qualify for termination. Court approval is often necessary. The determination of who has an interest in the trust and must therefore consent to an early termination (or other modification) of the trust is not a simple task. Not only must the provisions of the trust be carefully analyzed, but applicable state law should be considered. State law could require that the grantor, and all persons beneficially interested in the trust, approve the termination. This approval must also comply with formal requirements.

What if the beneficiaries are alive, but are minor children, or are disabled and thus unable to make legal decisions for themselves? Clearly the consent of these children or disabled beneficiaries is required, but they themselves cannot legally provide the consent. If a court will accept the decision of a guardian of these individuals, then the trust can be revoked or amended. If the court will not accept a guardian's signature, then such a trust may not be amended or revoked. The court's decision as to whether to accept the guardian's consent may depend on whether the changes or termination of the trust would be in the best interests of those minor or disabled beneficiaries. A court may appoint its own guardian to represent the interests of the minor(s). You should discuss the concept of a virtual representation clause in the trust, as may be provided under local law, with your attorney. This might enable a parent to decide on behalf of minors claiming under him, without the need for court intervention.

- Your trust could be rescinded or reformed if there was fraud, duress, undue influence, or mistake when the trust was set up. These situations, however, are unusual.

- A trust can be terminated in accordance with the terms of the trust agreement. This can be accomplished by a provision that establishes a specified period for the trust, where the trust agreement grants the power to another to terminate the trust. Under broad distribution provisions, the trustee could over time distribute all of the income and assets in the trust, if the distribution is in accordance with the purposes of the trust and complies with the standard established by the trust. Sometimes these rights may be given to a trust protector, rather than the trustee.

There are other ways in which your trust can terminate, if you have provided the appropriate flexibility in your trust agreement.

EXAMPLE: You establish a trust for the benefit of your only daughter. The trust is to terminate when your daughter reaches age 35 and all income and principal is to be distributed. However, as a result of large distributions to help your child acquire her first home, and a few years later to start her own business, the trust only has $12,565 when your daughter is age 31. It is uneconomical to continue the trust since the trustee fees, accounting fees, and administrative costs are unusually large for such a trust. If you provided your trustee with the right to terminate the trust where its operations are uneconomical, then your trustee could terminate the trust at this earlier date and distribute the proceeds to your daughter.

Where a trust for a child is involved, the trustee can be given a limited right to defer termination of the trust and distribution of the assets in the trust where the child is disabled. In some cases, the power is broad enough for the trustee to defer the distribution and termination of the trust where, in the trustee's discretion, it would be inappropriate to distribute the property. (See Chapter 8.)

- Subsequent impracticability, impossibility, or illegality of the trust may result in the termination of the trust, where such conditions did not exist when the trust was formed.
- A trust can terminate upon merger. This is a legal doctrine which provides that where the trustee and the beneficiary are the same person there can be no trust.
- A trust can be terminated or modified by operation of law. There are several possibilities when state law may require the termination of a trust. Many states, for example, still have laws that require that a trust not continue beyond some specified time. These laws are known as the *rule against perpetuities*. A typical such statute would require that the trust be terminated within 21 years of the death of the last person living when the trust was formed. The persons used as measuring sticks for this test are generally current beneficiaries of the trust. The common approach for dealing with this rule is for every trust to contain a provision providing that if the trust has not already terminated, it will terminate at the date prior to violating the rule against perpetuities.

ACTUAL FINAL TERMINATION OF A TRUST OCCURS AFTER WINDUP PERIOD

Where a trust has terminated under any of the situations described in the previous section, the trust itself may continue to exist for an additional period during which the trustee is allowed to wind up the affairs of the trust. During this period, the trust will continue to exist as a separate taxable entity (assuming it was previously a taxable entity distinct from the grantor). Also, the title to some of the trust property may remain with the trustee, who has the duty of making a full accounting and then distributing the trust property subject to any claim for trustee's compensation or reimbursement for expenses. However, the trustee is obligated to distribute amounts held within a reasonable amount of time.

For example, if a trust for a minor child terminates when the child reaches age 21, the trust does not automatically terminate on the child's 21st birthday.

EXAMPLE: A trust is set up for the life of your spouse. On your spouse's death, the trust is to terminate and the income is to be distributed to a designated charity. On the death of your spouse, the trust would not immediately terminate. Time is necessary for the trustee to complete the administration of the trust, including preparation of an accounting, filling out tax returns, and distributing assets.

Once all trust assets have been distributed, the wind-up phase should include the preparation of a final accounting by the trustee. This accounting should then be submitted to all of the beneficiaries for their approval. Generally, the trustee will require the beneficiaries to approve the accounting in writing and sign a release to the trustee absolving the trustee of any further liability. Once the trustee has received the release, all of the remaining assets will then be distributed to the beneficiaries. A final tax return will then be filed.

TAX CONSEQUENCES OF TERMINATING A TRUST

A trust does not automatically terminate for tax purposes when an event occurs by which the duration of the trust is measured. A trust is recognized as a taxable entity until all trust property has been distributed to successors, plus a reasonable time after this event necessary for the trustee to complete the administration of the trust. A trust is considered terminated when all of its assets have been distributed except for a reasonable amount set aside in good faith to pay unascertained or contingent liabilities and expenses (other than a claim by a beneficiary in his capacity as such). However, where the final distribution of the trust principal is unreasonably delayed, the trust may be considered to have terminated at an earlier date.

Where a trust is considered terminated for tax purposes, the gross income, credits, and deductions of the trust subsequent to termination are considered to be the gross income, credits, and deductions of the beneficiaries who succeed to the property.

Although trusts are entitled to an exemption ($300 for a complex trust, $100 for a simple one), if a final distribution of assets is completed during the tax year, all income of the trust must be reported as distributed to the beneficiaries, without reduction for the exemption amount. A trust cannot be characterized as simple if it distributes principal. Therefore, no trust can be characterized as simple in its final year, although this will not make it lose its $300 exemption.

Other special rules apply in the final year of a trust. Where there is a net operating loss, deductions in excess of gross income, or a capital loss carry-over, these tax attributes become available to the beneficiary succeeding to the property in distribution. Thus, deductions in excess of trust income in the final trust year are all passed to the beneficiaries. This is an exception to the general rule that applies to a trust during all tax years except its last. In other years, tax losses generally are not be passed through to the trust's beneficiaries. Thus, in the final tax year of the trust, any losses the trust realized in prior years on the sale of capital assets which could include stock, bonds, real estate, and other assets that did not offset capital gains in those years, will be passed through to the beneficiaries.

All capital gains realized in the year a trust terminates are included in the trust's calculation of distributable net income (DNI). If the distribution is postponed until the year following the sale, the gain may still be taxable to the trust.

After a trust terminates, questions can arise concerning what income is required to be paid out currently, and which is not. Where income was earned before the terminating event, that income should be treated in the same manner, even though it was actually paid out to the beneficiaries after the event resulting in the termination of the trust. Income and capital gains that are earned after the termination of the trust will be treated as being required to be distributed currently if the trust agreement or state law require this treatment. This income will then be taxed to the beneficiaries and not the trust. In many situations, the trustee will not be able to distribute income currently because of the need to retain some monies pending determination of expenses or the exact amount distributable to each beneficiary. This temporary withholding of funds by the trustee should not affect the tax treatment of this money as being taxable to the beneficiaries and not the trust.

WHY DISTINCTIONS BETWEEN TRUST ACCOUNTING AND TAX ACCOUNTING ARE IMPORTANT

It is important to understand the distinction between trust accounting and tax accounting. The tax accounting rules, as described in detail in Chapter 12, are used to determine the tax costs to the trust and the beneficiary. Accounting rules used by the trustee (called "fiduciary accounting") are used in determining the calculations of income and principal distributed to the various beneficiaries. These fiduciary accounting rules will be reflected in the accounting rendered to the beneficiaries by the trustee.

What Is Fiduciary Accounting?

A trustee of a trust will often provide some type of accounting when the trust terminates. This is done as part of the trustee's request for the beneficiaries to sign a release to the trustee in advance of the receipt of the final distribution from the trust. Where a new person assumes the responsibility of being a trustee, or an existing trustee resigns, it can be advisable to have some form of accounting completed in order to establish the status of the trust at such time.

If you are an incoming successor or replacement trustee, insist on a detailed accounting to cut off any liability that you may have for matters which occurred prior to your becoming a trustee.

Trusts often, however, contain general provisions absolving the trustee of any responsibility to provide any accounting unless required by law. Where any accounting is provided, the trust agreement may provide that the accounting should be conclusive and binding on the beneficiaries.

The trustee must adhere to the provisions of the trust agreement and applicable law for purposes of trust accounting and reporting.

Unfortunately, there is no common meaning of *fiduciary accounting*. The accounting principles can be governed by state law, the trust agreement, or local custom.

Distinction between Accounting and Tax Concepts

Examples of the differences between trust accounting and tax reporting rules include:

- The trustee may choose a tax year based on the date the trust was established. However, most trusts must use the calendar year for tax reporting.
- The trustee may have to distinguish between principal and income deductions. For income tax purposes, the distinction is not relevant.

NOTE: Grantor is divorced and remarries Spouse 2. Grantor establishes a trust for the benefit of Spouse 2 and the only child of the prior marriage. Income is to be paid to Spouse 2 for life, and on Spouse 2's death, the remaining investment (the principal or corpus) is distributed to the child. Deductions incurred by the trust must be categorized as to those relating to income and those relating to principal. This is critically important since it will affect the actual amounts to which Spouse 2 and child will be entitled.

What Is a Final Trust Accounting?

The cover page of a trust accounting should disclose basic background information such as the name of the trust, the date the trust was established, the names of the trustees, the date of the accounting, and the period covered by the accounting.

An accounting should include some type of summary that indicates the level of detail the report provides, and separate totals for assets at the beginning of the accounting, transactions during the period, and assets at the end of the accounting period. The summary should be followed by detailed schedules that analyze each of the components of the summary. For example, the balance of the trust at the beginning should show all of the assets originally transferred to the trust when the trust was formed. This can often be accomplished quite readily by attaching a listing that was attached to the original trust agreement, or that was included in the estate of the person under whose will the trust was created. For assets transferred to the trust under a will, the fair value of the assets at the date of death could be disclosed.

The transactions during the period of trust operations being reported on could indicate the total dividends and interest received, in aggregate, on each security owned. A separate section should detail capital gains and losses on the sale of any trust assets. (For certain transactions, however, items should be listed individually and not grouped.) Items that deserve this detailed disclosure could include: penalty and interest charges incurred on tax returns and extraordinary appraisal costs. Where stock dividends, stock splits, dividend reinvestment, and similar transactions occur, the details should be disclosed in the report since they will be necessary to analyze the results of the trust.

Trustee's commissions and fees must be disclosed. Distributions to the beneficiaries should be disclosed with sufficient detail to identify specific bequests, distributions of income, and distributions of principal. Details as to payments of expenses and, if applicable, payment of creditors and funeral and other administrative expenses should all be disclosed. This detail is necessary so that it can be determined that income, principal, and deductions have been properly allocated among the beneficiaries.

As a guideline to determine which disclosures are necessary, consider what information is necessary to determine trustee commissions and fees. Where trustee fees are based on income or asset values, then the appropriate details will have to be disclosed.

For assets purchased by the trustee during the term of the trust, the cost of the assets should be disclosed. Where assets are received during the administration of the trust, such as from the grantor, the fair value of the assets on the date of their receipt may be the appropriate figure to disclose. Where assets are received and sold, it is important to disclose the method of accounting used to determine the gain or loss.

EXAMPLE: A trust is formed with 1,000 shares of XYZ Corp. common stock which were valued at $10 per share on the date the grantor formed the trust and transferred the shares. Years later, the grantor dies and under the grantor's will an additional 1,000 shares of XYZ Corp. common stock are transferred to the trust. The value of the shares is $1,000 per share. Three years later, the trustee sells 500 shares of XYZ Corp. stock for $1,150 per share. If the trustee calculates the gain on the basis of average cost the gain will be far different than if it is calculated on the assumption of first-in, first-out (FIFO). Under the average cost method, each share cost $505 [[(1,000 × $10) + (1,000 × $1,000)]/2,000 total shares]. The gain is thus $645 per share [$1,150 − $505]. On the FIFO method, the cost of each share sold is the $10 initial value of the first shares received. The gain under the FIFO method is $1,140 per share [$1,150 − $10]. If the trustee commissions are based on income, the consequences can be substantial.

Generally, the value of assets first reported should be used consistently throughout the reporting done by the trustee. One exception, however, is where assets received from the grantor's estate are subject to an IRS audit and the values finally determined by the IRS differ from those reported initially. In some states, a new (successor) trustee may disclose an adjustment to the initial asset values in order to disclose the value of the assets at the date the trustee began to serve.

To make any report meaningful, the current fair value of each asset could be disclosed along with the carrying value determined as described in the preceding paragraphs. The extent of the effort to obtain current value estimates may depend on state law, or the use of the asset. For example, marketable securities can readily be listed at their fair value based on published stock listings. Real estate would have to be appraised to provide a determination of value. The cost of an appraisal will make this uneconomical in many situations. For example, where the real estate is a house being used as a personal residence with no reasonable expectation of being sold for the foreseeable future, an appraisal is obviously less necessary or appropriate.

If the accounting is to be filed with a court, it will be notarized and signed under oath. In addition, any particular requirements of the court where it will be filed will have to be followed. For example, where there is a charitable beneficiary, the filing requirements may be more onerous, to allow the state to protect the interests of the charity.

WHAT TO CONSIDER WHEN REVIEWING A FINAL TRUST ACCOUNTING

When you receive a trust accounting, whether as an incoming successor trustee, or as a beneficiary, what should you look for? Consider the following:

- What is the total of trustee commissions and fees paid? How were they calculated?
- Is the basis on which the trustee commissions and fees calculated correct? Does it comply with the provisions of the trust agreement and local law?
- If there is more than one trustee does state law, or the trust agreement, provide for a maximum fee for all trustees in the aggregate? If so, has it been complied with?

- Verify that the math in the report is accurate and that the numbers on all of the detail schedules agree to the summary.
- Review any losses reported for unusual items. Was the trustee responsible for the losses incurred?
- Review administrative expenses. Are the amounts and nature of the expenses reasonable?

CONCLUSION

The termination of a trust can have important legal and tax implications. When and how a trust can be terminated also presents several important issues. Both the trust agreement and the requirements of local law must always be considered.

INDEX